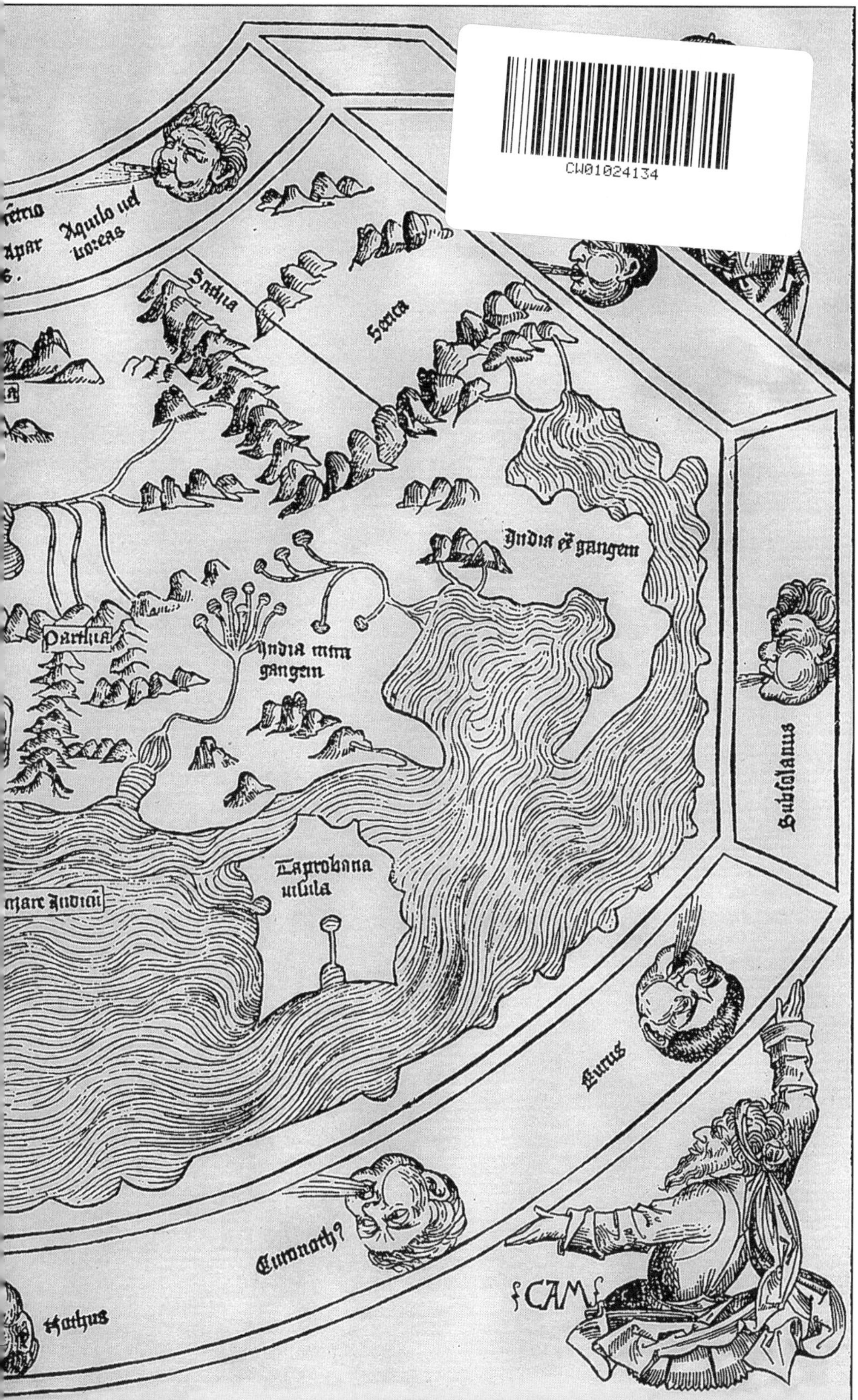

Aquilo uel boreas
Scithia
Serica
India ex gangem
Parthia
India intra gangem
Taprobana insula
mare Indicum
Subsolanus
Eurus
Euronoth?
Nothus
CAM

The Book of *Abramelin*

Title page from the Worms synagogue *Mahsor* (prayer book). As the Rabbi Jacob ben Moses ha Levi Möllin, better known as the MaHaRIL, Abraham would have held this book in his hands. The original 13th-century book is in Jerusalem, an exact copy is in the city archives of Worms, Germany.

The Book of *Abramelin*

A New Translation

Abraham von Worms

Compiled and edited by Georg Dehn

Translated by Steven Guth

Foreword by Lon Milo DuQuette

Ibis Press
An Imprint of Nicolas-Hays, Inc.
Lake Worth, Florida

First published in 2006 by
Ibis Press, an imprint of
Nicolas-Hays, Inc.
P. O. Box 540206
Lake Worth, FL 33454-0206
www.nicolashays.com

Distributed to the trade by
Red Wheel/Weiser, LLC
65 Parker St. Ste. 7
Newburyport, MA 01950-4600
www.redwheelweiser.com

Note to Readers: The folk remedies in Book Two are for informational purposes only. Readers should first contact a medical professional whenever they have health concerns and before attempting any procedure that may affect his or her health. Neither the publisher nor the author are responsible for the results readers may experience from using these methods.

Library of Congress Cataloging-in-Publication Data available on request.
ISBN 978-0-89254-127-0
MV
Cover design by Phillip Augusta. Cover art is adapted from Emblem 23 of Michael Maier's *Atalanta Fugiens*.
Typeset in Adobe Caslon; display type, Archive Copperplate
Printed in the United States of America

12 11 10 09 08 07 06
7 6 5 4 3 2 1

The paper used in this publication meets the minimum requirements of the American National Standard for Information Sciences—Permanence of Paper for Printed Library Materials Z39.48–1992 (R1997).

Contents

List of Illustrations .... *ix*
Acknowledgments .... *xii*
Foreword .... *xiii*
Translator's Note .... *xx*
Introduction .... *xxii*
Opening Hymn .... *xxix*

THE TEXT **1**

BOOK ONE **3**

Chapter One. The Reason for This Inheritance 5
Chapter Two. How I Learned from Others 7
Chapter Three. Countries and Lands I Visited 11
Chapter Four. I Find Abramelin 13
Chapter Five. Other Masters I Have Found 19
Chapter Six. The Beginning of Wisdom 22
Chapter Seven. God Returned Me to My People 27
Chapter Eight. Magical Things I Have Done 29
Chapter Nine. Be Careful in Everything You Do 33
Chapter Ten. What Our Fathers Have Been Given 35
Chapter Eleven. Helping Other People 37
Chapter Twelve. Be Careful about These Two Things 39

BOOK TWO **43**

Chapter One. For Serious Diseases 45
Chapter Two. About Antagonisms and War 49
Chapter Three. For Friendship, Marriage, and Love Affairs 53
Chapter Four. For Birthing 58
Chapter Five. Against Water, Fire,
Tempest, Ghosts, the Devil 60
Chapter Six. To Burst Open Cliffs and Walls 63

Chapter Seven. Protecting Houses and Buildings from Earthquake and Thunder 65
Chapter Eight. Addressing Courts and Potentates 66
Chapter Nine. In Times of Hunger and Starvation 67
Chapter Ten. To Make Oneself Invisible to One's Enemies 68

The End of the Second Book *69*

Book Three 75

Foreword *75*

Chapter One. [The Types of Magic...] 77
Chapter Two. What One Should Consider before Beginning 80
Chapter Three. The Age and the Qualities that You Need 82
Chapter Four. Most So-Called Magic Books Are Fraudulent 83
Chapter Five. [No Special Days for the Sacred Magic] 86
Chapter Six. The Planetary Hours and How Most Astrologers Are in Error 87
Chapter Seven. What One Should Do in the First Six Months When Learning This Art 90
Chapter Eight. What Should Be Done in the Second Half Year 94
Chapter Nine. How to Behave in the Third and Final Half Year 95
Chapter Ten. The Arts a Person Can Study, Practice, and Do, Which Will not Hinder the Work 97
Chapter Eleven. How to Choose the Location to Call All the Spirits. How to Prepare the Accessories 98
Chapter Twelve. How the Person or Magus Should Consecrate Himself, the Prayer Room, and Its Accessories 101
Chapter Thirteen. How the Good Spirits Should Be Called 105
Chapter Fourteen. How the Unredeemed Spirits Can Be Called and Overcome 108
Chapter Fifteen. What to Request from the Spirits 111
Chapter Sixteen. How to Retire the Spirits 115
Chapter Seventeen. How to Answer Questions and How to Deal with Requests 115

Chapter Eighteen. Other Things One Should Do
Regarding the Spirits 115
Chapter Nineteen. The Names of Spirits You Can Call 119
Chapter Twenty. How to Carry Out the Work 124

Progress toward Book Four *129*

Book Four 143

Chapter One. How You Can Discover
All Past and Future Things 145
Chapter Two. To Have Reports about
All Sorts of Doubtful Things 147
Chapter Three. To Make Every Spirit Appear 148
Chapter Four. To Create Visions 148
Chapter Five. To Obtain Servant Spirits—either Free or Sealed—
and How to Send Them Away 149
Chapter Six. For Working Mines 151
Chapter Seven. To Have the Spirits Make Alchemy Work 152
Chapter Eight. To Make and Prevent Storms 152
Chapter Nine. To Make People into Animals—
and Animals into People 153
Chapter Ten. To Prevent and Remove All Other Magic 154
Chapter Eleven. To Obtain Lost Books,
Hidden Manuscripts, and Such 155
Chapter Twelve. To Research and Hear from People the Hidden
Plans and Plots of a Person 157
Chapter Thirteen. To Make a Dead
Person Walk for Seven Years 158
Chapter Fourteen. For Invisibility 159
Chapter Fifteen. That the Spirits Bring All Sorts
of Things to Eat and Drink 160
Chapter Sixteen. To Recover Treasures 163
Chapter Seventeen. Traveling in the Air 165
Chapter Eighteen. Healing Sickness 168
Chapter Nineteen. To Achieve All Sorts of Friendships 170

Chapter Twenty. For All Types of Animosity 173
Chapter Twenty-one. To Take on Different Appearances.......... 175
ChapterTwenty-two. To Make Sickness in People..................... 176
Chapter Twenty-three. To Collapse Walls and Houses.............. 177
Chapter Twenty-four. For the Return of Things........................ 178
Chapter Twenty-five. To Stay and Move around under Water for as Long as You Want.. 179
Chapter Twenty-six. To Spring Open All Sorts of Closed Things and to Relock Them without a Key. 179
Chapter Twenty-seven. To Make All Kinds of Things Appear... 180
Chapter Twenty-eight. In Times of Trouble, to Have as Many Coins as You Need.................................. 184
Chapter Twenty-nine. To Make All Sorts of People and Armor Appear.. 185
Chapter Thirty. To Have the Spirits Perform All Kinds of Music, Singing, and Juggling.. 187

APPENDICES ....

A. The Editor's Quest.. *191*
B. The MaHaRIL and Abraham from Worms: A Historical Analysis.. *221*
C. Where Was Abramelin's Hermitage?................................ *229*
D. Lamech—A Kabbalistic Investigation. *234*
E. The Word Squares *236*
F. Spirit Names—Comparisons between Sources.................. *243*
G. Abraham's Links to Modern Jewish Scholarship............... *261*

Bibliography... *265*
About Georg Dehn and Steven Guth.................................... *269*

Illustrations

The four corners of the world.
Fifteenth-century woodcut.................................*front endleaf*
Title page from the Worms synagogue Mahsor...................... *ii*

Fig. 1. Title page of MS 2 in the Dresden library........................2
Fig. 2. Another page from the Worms synagogue *Mahsor*...........4
Fig. 3. Worms with dragon symbol..5
Fig. 4. Mainz 6
Fig. 5 Rhine River...8
Fig. 6. 17th-century copper etching
of the Jewish section of Worms....................................... 10
Fig. 7. Map of the Nile River and location of hermitages 12
Fig. 8 Map of the Nile River, north of Luxor............................ 14
Fig. 9. Remains of a bathhouse in Araki 15
Fig. 10. Oil painting of emperor Sigismund 30
Unnumbered figures.
Count Frederick, Pope John XXIII, Pope Martin V,
Count Ludwig, from *Schedelsche Weltchronik*................... 31
Fig. 11. Title page of MS 1 in the Dresden library..................... 42
Fig. 12. Jewish couple from medieval times 55
Fig. 13. A page from the MS in the Wolfenbüttel library........... 72
Fig. 14. Directions for decoding the other MS in
the Wolfenbüttel library.. 74
Fig. 15. Abraham's astrology lesson... 89
Fig. 16. Recipe for oil and incense from
Peter Hammer's edition 100
Fig. 17. A page from the encoded MS in the Wolfenbüttel
library, containing the recipes for oil and incense......... 102
Fig. 18. Another page from the encoded Wolfenbüttel MS,
containing the spirit names 114
Fig. 19. Spirit names from Peter Hammer's edition.................. 120
Fig. 20. Copy from microfilm of Dresden MS 2....................... 122
Fig. 21. Title page to Book Four from Dresden MS 2............. 142

Fig. 22. Copy from microfilm of Dresden MS 1, of the first square from chapter one ... 144
Fig. 23. Dresden MS 1, second and third squares from chapter one ... 146
Fig. 24. Chapter eleven squares from Dresden MS 2 ... 156
Fig. 25. Squares corresponding to chapter fifteen from Dresden MS 2 ... 161
Fig. 26. Text for chapter fifteen squares, from Peter Hammer's edition ... 162
Fig. 27. Squares corresponding to nos. 2–6 from Dresden MS 2 ... 166
Fig. 28. Text for chapter seventeen squares, from Peter Hammer's edition ... 167
Fig. 29. Squares corresponding to chapter eighteen, Dresden MS 2 ... 169
Fig. 30. Squares from Dresden MS 2. In square number 10, the word SALOM is found ... 172
Fig. 31. From Dresden MS 2, chapter twenty-eight, squares 1–3 ... 186
Fig. 32. From the Hebrew manuscript at the Oxford University library ... 188
Fig. 33. An old Arab map from Abou' l-Hasan 'Al ibn Said, dated 1286 ... 193
Fig. 34. The Nile Delta detail from "Karte von Africa," by Marin de Sanudo ... 194
Fig. 35. Title page of *The Sixth and Seventh Books of Moses* ... 198
Fig. 36. Oven used for baking holy bread in a Coptic monastery near Araki ... 200
Fig. 37. A wadi (valley) in the desert, south of Araki and west of Luxor ... 202
Fig. 38. Searching, in 1986, on a rented East German MZ motorcycle ... 203
Fig. 39. The two sisters in the shape of Anubis and Horis ... 204
Fig. 40. Letter found inside a book, *Feriae Aestivales* ... 206
Fig. 41. Title page from the first edition of *The Egyptian Great Revelation* ... 207
Fig. 42. Canopen figures ... 209
Fig. 43. The two sisters. In the middle stands the magician ... 211

Fig. 44. Luxor 212
Fig. 45. Collapsed cave 214
Fig. 46. Marker stones above the cave 215
Fig. 47. Official *Regesten* of Sigismund for the year 1426 217
Fig. 48. The MaHaRIL's gravestone 221
Fig. 49. Jewish Holy Sands cemetery 222
Fig. 50. Washing well, the *Mikwe*, next to the Worms synagogue 223
Fig. 51. Traveler's check from the 13th or 14th century 227
Fig. 52. Map of the monasteries and Pharaonic temples in upper Egypt 230
Fig. 53. Map showing the probable location of Abramelin's hermitage 231
Fig. 54. Rough map of the major international trade route through Egypt 232
Fig. 55. Demons 254

Europe. Venice is to the south, Constantinople is in the east, Iceland is to the north, and Paris is in the west. The map shows the importance of rivers at the time. Fifteenth-century woodcut from the Worms city archive .... back endleaf

Acknowledgments

I thank my friend Steven Guth for his help and generosity. He helped me analyze, interpret, and translate the text. Steven has been involved with the material for many years and tells me he has enjoyed and benefited from the experience. The final period that we spent working together on the manuscript in Canberra has been a useful spiritual experience for both of us.

I thank the Rabbi of the State of Saxony, Dr. Salomon Siegl in Leipzig, who served me so kindly with his scholarship and presented me so much of his patience and rare time.

Thanks also to Sabine von Below, who organized the book's first printing in German; to professor Hans Biedermann, who was the first to encourage me to publish the book; to Fernand Debono, who showed me the records of Napoleon's expedition to Egypt that contained Araki and clarified my family history; to Lucien Dehen, the shopkeeper in Alexandria who placed me on the path to Araki; to Sergius Golowin, who told me about the historical importance of the witch's story in Book One and encouraged me to work toward publication; to John Guth for critiquing and correcting the manuscript; to Gabi Gloeckner, Stephen Mace, Peter Pistivsek, Barbara Roca, and Tamara Zakrajsek for critical questions, patience, and their friendship. I am grateful to Joseph Peterson for the impulse to keep working on the English translation, and to Robert Brautigam for some historical research.

I also thank the Curators of the Bodleian Library Oxford, Herzog August Bibliothek Wolfenbüttel, Sächsische Staatsbibliothek Dresden, Egyptian Institute and Universitätsbibliothek Leipzig, Bibliothèque de l'Arsenal Paris, Universitätsbibliothek Hamburg, Institut Français Kairo, Stadtarchiv und Stadtbibliothek Worms.

Foreword

> *The unredeemed Spirits and their followers, their works, and all their doings—be their unrelenting enemy and try throughout your life to command them and never to serve them.*
>
> —Abraham of Worms to his son, Lamech
> Book Three, p. 149

As a young student of the Western mysteries, I was thoroughly enchanted by stories of the celebrated magicians of the Hermetic Order of the Golden Dawn. The *dramatis personae* of this modern myth could not have been more colorful: the dashing young Irish poet William Butler Yeats; the beautiful actress Florence Farr; the fabulously wealthy tea heiress Anne Horniman; the brilliant magus MacGregor Mathers; and let's not forget the devilishly naughty Aleister Crowley. As backdrop to this tale, what more romantic milieu could we ask than the Holmes-and-Watkins-esque world of late Victorian London? Here, in the fog-shrouded capital of the empire upon which the sun never set, at a moment in time when the industrial revolution, Darwin, and Marx were eroding the tired soil of two thousand years of human history and hurling the world forward into uncertainty, these modern Merlins were occupying their free evenings plunging backward into the distant mythological past on a quest for illumination and magical power.

An important cast member of this drama, however, was not a person, but a book—an ancient book of magic, penned in German between 1387 and 1427 by a German Jew known as Abraham of Worms. Originally titled *Buch Abramelin*, a 1750 French translation of the text rested virtually undisturbed in the Bibliothèque de l'Arsenal in Paris until 1893, when it was translated into English by Samuel L. (MacGregor) Mathers, who subsequently published his translation in England as *The Book of the Sacred Magic of Abramelin the Mage as Delivered by Abraham the Jew unto His Son Lamech: A Grimoire of the Fifteenth Century.* This book would have a profound impact on the world of Western occultism and elevate the oft-denigrated art of spirit evocation to a status equal to the sacred spiritual sciences of the East.

The feature that sets *The Sacred Magic* apart from contemporary grimoires (some of which oblige would-be magicians to embark upon scavenger hunts for bat blood and body parts of exotic amphibia) is a doctrine that states (please allow me to paraphrase) that in order to wield god-like magical power, the magician must actually be possessed of god-like virtues of character.

This is not to argue that it is impossible for reprobate magicians, by memorizing and following certain recipes of formulaic magic, to temporarily bamboozle the unredeemed spirits to obedience. But it is a tenuous ability at best. First of all, unenlightened magi are not possessed of sufficient clarity of vision to determine whether or not their desires and actions are in harmony with their own best interests. Second, the spirits (who apparently have eternal season tickets to every performance of *Faust* and *Don Giovanni*) inevitably ferret out the chinks in the moral armor of the magician and amplify and exploit these weaknesses in order to extricate themselves from the magician's control. On the other hand, the magician who has gained a significant level of spiritual illumination and self-realization is qualified (by virtue of who he or she *is*) to safely summon and wisely command the spirits and put their potentially dangerous powers to use toward more noble ends.

While portions of Abraham's book are concerned with classic formulae, recipes, and magic squares, he makes it clear that these devices are tools to be used only after the magician has undergone a profound and personal spiritual transfiguration. The centerpiece of the book deals with this transcendent experience, outlining in exacting detail a step-by-step procedure whereby the magician, after months of purifications, fasting, and intense prayer, attains communion with a transcendent spiritual being referred to as the "Holy Guardian Angel."

The exact nature of the Holy Guardian Angel defies proper definition. The book makes it clear, however, it is a divine entity uniquely linked to each individual—in essence the magician's personal spiritual soul mate. Another way of looking at this relationship would be for us to consider the magician as being a spiritually incomplete *human* unit until united with the Holy Guardian Angel—and to consider the Holy Guardian Angel as being a spiritually incomplete *angelic* unit until it has become one with the magician.

The concept of a personal guardian spirit or angel who must be acknowledged or placated before one begins to operate is nothing new to the traditions of Western magic. The concept of the Holy Guardian Angel as presented in the Abramelin operation, however, goes far beyond an obligatory toast to the good angels or a quick prayer for God's blessing before conjuring demons. The lengthy (and increasingly intense) preparation ceremony is a serious and arduous regimen that ruthlessly pushes the magician month-by-month toward a single-pointed passion for the Angel. The operation is crowned by a supreme invocation and ecstatic consummation of the divine marriage.

Students of Eastern mysticism will at once recognize this part of the ceremony as being very similar to that of the Bhakti yogi who achieves ecstatic union with his or her deity by means of focused love and devotion. The Abramelin operation, however, does not stop here. In order for the magician's consciousness to be a worthy eidolon of the divine it must thoroughly reflect not only the highest heavens but also the lowest hells.

For three days after the supreme invocation, the magician remains locked in blissful intimacy with the Angel as his consciousness melds with that of the Angel and his metamorphoses become complete. Then, and only then, guided by the omniscient wisdom of the Angel, the magician systematically conjures to visible appearance each and every "unredeemed" spirit of the infernal regions. One-by-one, in order of their rank in the hierarchy of hell, the magician compels the unredeemed spirits to confess their subservience and swear complete and unconditional obedience. Only after all this has occurred is the magician ready to safely use the magic squares in the back of the book.

The systematic, almost scientific, approach of the Abramelin method appealed instantly to the late-19th-century esotericists. The few volumes of the first edition of the Mathers translation were immediately snatched up by members of the Golden Dawn and other interested parties, many of whom were naturally more interested in the theoretical aspects of the work than actually performing the operation. Still, its reputation as a bona fide "magic book" (rather than merely a book about magic) soon spread, and with it the dark notion that because the book revealed the secrets of how to conquer the world's evil spirits, then the evil spirits would do anything to keep this knowledge from the world. Rumors spread that *The Sacred Magic of Abramelin the Mage* was a sorcerer's handbook—that it was dangerous to even have a copy in one's home. Sadly, from almost the moment of its publication, the bright glories of this marvelous and unique document were eclipsed by the most ridiculous fears and superstitions.

I confess. In 1976, when I first ran across a copy in a used bookstore in Hollywood, my hand actually shook as I pulled it from its place on the dusty shelf. Fearing demonic attack, I very cautiously drove home and tucked it away in a black borrowed slipcase and kept it apart from my other books. Not wishing to take responsibility for the unspeakable evils that might befall them, I refused to loan it or even show it to curious friends.

Today I feel pretty silly about the whole thing, especially considering the fact that the book that caused me to quake in my boots and lose friends—the book that established Mathers's reputation and caused such a supernatural uproar over a hundred years ago—was itself so incomplete and dissimilar to the original German texts as to be almost worthless as an accurate rendering of the content and intent of the original documents.

This is not to say that Mathers's *Sacred Magic* is not a valuable contribution to the library of Western magical literature or to suggest that he did a poor job of translating the 1750 French manuscript into proper English. On the contrary, experts tell us Mathers did a wonderful job. The problem rests with the woefully incomplete and "doubtful French text" from which he worked.

Even though I was at the time completely unaware of this fact, I was delighted when a few years ago I discovered that Mr. Dehn had compiled and edited a new German edition of *Buch Abramelin* from material gleaned from the earliest surviving manuscripts of the text. Naturally, I lamented the fact that I could not read a word of German, but was soon cheered by news there would soon be an English translation. I contacted the publisher to offer my assistance and was sent the partially edited manuscript. The moment I set it side-by-side with Mathers' translation I realized that nearly everything I thought I knew about the magic of Abramelin was going to change.

The first and most obvious difference between the two texts is the style of the writing itself. I was delighted how easily and naturally Mr. Guth's translation flowed compared to the formality of Mathers's King James style. This I more or less expected. What I didn't expect was how the text itself differed in content. First of all, the original book was comprised of four "books" instead of only three that are found in the Mathers edition. Second, we learn that the heroic six-month preparation program that is outlined in Mathers is actually a much more complex ceremony lasting *eighteen* months.

These are in-and-of themselves exciting and significant differences, but as I read on I discovered more numerous and profound dissimilarities, so many in fact that I soon abandoned any thoughts of itemizing them for this Foreword. For those readers who are familiar with the Mathers edition, these will become abundantly obvious the moment you open the book. I feel I must, however, point out something in particular that is likely to be quite unsettling for all those who have held in particular reverence the section of *The Sacred Magic* that concerns itself with the magic squares.

The fourth book of *The Book of Abramelin* (Book Three in the Mathers translation) is comprised of thirty short chapters that present us with a series of magic squares containing letters arranged upon a grid of smaller squares. The magic squares for each chapter are numbered. They are also preceded by a numbered index outlining each square's particular virtue and power. Justified or not, in the minds of many practicing magicians, this section of the book is magically the most important.

Once the magician has successfully gained knowledge and conversation of the Angel, he or she is instructed how to use the magic squares to affect all manner of wonders. As one might expect, this part of the book has always been alluring to dilettantes and would-be-wizards who turn straight to this section and find themselves devilishly tempted to use the squares without first going to all the trouble of invoking their Holy Guardian Angel. Many a fabled misfortune (real or imagined) suffered by Golden Dawn-era magi has been blamed on the premature use of these squares. Crowley himself treated them with particular respect and carefully hand copied a complete set and bound them in an expensive folio. He warned students to be especially careful to not leave them laying about, cautioning that they have a tendency to escape the magician's control and do their mischief on the world.

Grady McMurtry (a young U.S. Army lieutenant stationed in England during World War II and a student of Aleister Crowley) told me of the day Crowley (upon returning from the kitchen with a fresh pot of tea) caught McMurtry thumbing through his book of Abramelin squares. Frail as Crowley was he managed to scare the young man nearly out of his skin by shouting, "Don't touch that! You don't know what forces you could unleash!"

Such was the mystique the squares of Abramelin held on the magical imagination of Golden Dawn-era magicians. One can only imagine what they might have thought if they knew that virtually none of the information concerning the magic squares in the Mathers translation agrees with that found in the original German manuscripts.

For instance, there are 242 squares in the Mathers edition, 160 of them (over two-thirds) are only partially filled in with letters. The German edition, on the other hand, itemizes material for 251 squares, all of them completely filled in. Furthermore, there is dramatic (almost universal) disparity in how the magic words that would fill the squares are spelled; how the squares are distributed within the chapters; and how the squares are indexed and identified.

It almost breaks one's heart to think of the countless hours Mathers consumed writing his commentaries on the squares as he heroically labored to justify qabalistically the possible meanings to *misspelled words* that fill *incomplete squares* that are *out of order*, *incorrectly distributed*, and *misidentified*.

I realize it may appear that I'm being unduly hard on poor Mathers. That is certainly not my intention. I have the highest regard for this great magical genius whose work continues to enlighten and inspire new generations of serious students of the Western mysteries. We owe him an immeasurable debt. Our focus should be not on what his translation was *not*; rather, we should celebrate what the new Dehn-Guth translation *is*; an elegant and accurate exposition of an ancient and artful technique for self-realization and self-initiation. I for one welcome this important and highly readable edition of the book that is once again destined to make a profound impact on the world of Western occultism.

Lon Milo DuQuette

Translator's Note

Georg and I did all our translations by working through spoken language; he read the German aloud as I translated into English. We sensed the Spiritual world participating with our work.

I tried to retain in the English text the spiritual insights often alluded to, rather than stated, in the German original. My background in several spiritual traditions has helped me enormously in this respect.

Abraham's surviving manuscripts are all written in German, without useful paragraphs or punctuation. We have added these.

Book One is relatively easy to understand and I have taken the liberty of retaining much of its original tone: that of a letter from a Jewish father to his son. The other books have been translated straightforwardly, with modern word usage to improve their readability.

We puzzled over the best translation of several German words, which were often archaic. Two worth mentioning are *Herr* and *böse Geister*. The usual English translation of *Herr,* in this context, is "Lord." We felt that this translation creates spiritual, social, and political connotations in the mind of the English reader that are not what Abraham intended. We settled on "Adonai" as having the closest tone to the original. This issue is expanded upon in the Introduction.

We noticed—by observing the context—that when Abraham wrote *böse Geister*, he meant what Anthroposophical literature would call "unredeemed spirits": trapped or lost spirits, rather than directly destructive or manifestly evil entities. The more literal translation of *böse* into the English "evil" would, we felt, create a feeling in modern Christain readers that Abraham, a Jew from the Middle Ages, would not have shared. So we have used "unredeemed spirits" which suggests that Abraham's art is indeed, as he says, proper and correct.

Steven Guth

Introduction

I began working on this book in the summer of 1980. Since then, I have been involved in many wonderful experiences. I take this to be a confirmation that this book has recieved the blessings of the higher worlds.

From a historical perspective, Abraham's work contains perhaps the world's first example of a technique for self-development and self-initiation.

In the last hundred years, since the first translation of this work into English, the text has received a reputation as a sorcerer's handbook. It has been my endeavor to remove this stigma from the material and to present it in a form as close as possible to Abraham's original intentions.The most significant questions one can ask about a text from the Middle Ages are: Who wrote the material? Who edited it? What was added to it during its transcriptions?

The Book of Abramelin was written during the 14th and 15th centuries, the period after the European plague. In 1349, Europe was ravaged by the Great Plague, which was blamed on the Jews. The parents of Abraham were among the few who survived the plague and the subsequent pogrom against the Jews. The Jewish population in the huge Holy Roman Empire was reduced to thousands. In a few large towns there remained only a handful of Jews, and we know that in the three towns in which this story unfolds—Speyer, Worms, and Mainz—the entire Jewish population was driven away and only allowed to return in 1356.

The name "Abraham of Worms" can be found in only one offical record of the period. In the *Regesten* of Kaiser Sigismund there is mention of a Jew Abraham, who had helped him and Duke Frederic of Saxony many times (see fig. 47, p. 217). A translation of the entry reads: "Sigismund, in appreciation of his former services to himself and the Duke Frederic of Saxony, places Abraham the Jew, inhabitant of the city of Leipzig into the position of his 'special Jew and private servant' and grants escort and protection in the whole empire for himself and his family." This confirms Abraham's biography as he set it out in Book One.

We have records of only a small number of important Jewish intellectuals in the Renaissance. There is a historical person who was born in a similar time period as "Abraham from Worms," who was known to have had the same education, similar positions, and matching periods in life. This was the well-known scholar Rabbi Jacob ben Moses ha Levi Möllin, more commonly known as the MaHaRIL. This is fully discussed in Appendix B, where details establish that Abraham of Worms was a historical person.

This issue of historicity has many fascinating details. One is the question of Abraham's teacher, Abramelin. Was Abramelin a literary tool or a real person? In an attempt to settle the question by archaeological evidence, I have on three occasions searched in the area of the hermitage described in Book One. The exact location of the hermitage still needs to be confirmed, but the probability that Abramelin existed seems high. These journeys of discovery are discussed in Appendix A, "The Editor's Quest."

Manuscript sources used in this edition

Two manuscripts—one encoded and the other a clear copy, both dated 1608—are from the Library of Duke August in the town of Wolfenbüttel, near Hannover, Germany. This manuscript is mentioned by the Rosicrucians and is considered by them to be a work that anticipated important thoughts of the Rosicrucian movement and alchemical philosophy (see 1997 exhibition catalog, *Cimelia Rodosthaurotica,* Wolfenbüttel.) Catalog number for the manuscripts are Codex Guelfibus 10.1 and 47.13.

In the Dresden library, manuscript no. 1 is obviously the younger one of the two and appears to have a different origin than the Wolfenbüttel manuscripts. It is badly written in Latin script and we used it to verify occasional words only when the older German script style proved mystifying. Circa 1700, SLUB MS N 111.

Dresden manuscript no. 2 is a very attractive and precisely-written manuscript, possibly from the library of a Saxon duke. Circa 1750, SLUB MS N 161.

An edition by Peter Hammer, publisher in Cologne. A very rare book, evidently known by the members of Fraternitas Saturni, the German branch of the Ordo Templi Orientis. Wilhelm Quintscher, one of Aleister Crowley's German friends, had a copy. Neither Quintscher nor Crowley recognized the differences between this edition and the Mathers translation (see below). Dated 1725. Reprint, by Scheible, in Stuttgart, ca. 1850.

Anonymous French manuscript from Bibliothèque de l'Arsenal, Paris. Written in the Latin script of the time, this manuscript is easy to read. The French translator had considerable difficulties with the German text. Problems arose from the baroque German script and the unique way in which some of the German letters of the time were shaped. Abbreviations are confusing. The coding in Wolfenbüttel appears to have been a problem for the translator. Circa 1750.

Samuel Mathers's edition as an English translation of the French translation. Mathers translated the doubtful French text with great care, rendering it into the style of English that is used in the King James version of the Bible. Completed in 1893, the translation was first published later. Reprint, New York: Dover, 1974.

Oxford manuscript, Bodleian Library, Hebrew, anonymous. According to respected Kabbalist Gershom Scholem, this manuscript is translated from German.[1] Rabbi Salomon Siegl translated back into German at my request. The Hebrew text shows scholarship and is interesting. It may come from another yet unknown manuscript. The compiler uses a language that interprets the German words for students with kabbalistic knowledge. This manuscript was first discovered by Moritz Steinschneider and mentioned in his bibliography of Hebrew manuscripts.[2] Circa 1740. MS.OPP.594.

During my research, the elementary works of importance reduced themselves to the encoded Wolfenbüttel library MS, Dresden library MS no. 2, Peter Hammer's edition, and the Hebrew Oxford MS. From the texts it is clear that Abraham wrote in German. The author lived in southwestern Germany, in an area were Jews have been integrated since Roman times.

Worms is a Jewish holy city and has been called "Little Jerusalem." The German language of the Worms district was the *lingua franca* of the regional Jewish communities and in time spread to Eastern Europe.

Another reason for the use of vernacular German was that Abraham seemed to have no contact with his son Lamech, who was to inherit the books. He mentions many times throughout the text that he does not know if Lamech will become a learned Jew or an "ordinary person." Only the learned Jews could read Hebrew.

---

1 Gershom Scholem, *Kabbalah: A Definitive History of the Evolution, Ideas, Leading Figures and Extraordinary Influence of Jewish Mysticism* (New York: Meridian, 1978), p. 186.

2 Moritz Steinschneider, *Catalogus librorum Hebraeorum in bibliotheca Bodleiana*, 3 volumes (Berlin: Friedlander, 1852–1860).

The Creation of the Four Books

Book One was written last, shortly before Abraham's death in 1427. It is autobiographical and personal. I have verified much of the material in it from existing historical records. My Egyptian travels have also confirmed Abraham's story. The text contains geographical information that could never have been known to a European compiler.

Book Two contains material from the mixed Kabbalah. The recipes were probably collected during Abraham's student days before 1400. They consist of a extensive collection of folk traditions that might have been otherwise lost in the years following the plague.

A further collection of traditions and customs—known as the Minhagim material—was written under Abraham's proper name of Jacob Möllin (the MaHaRIL). This is the larger and theologically more important part of Jewish folk traditions. Similar to Jacob Möllin's work is the Minhagim material collected by his teacher, Abraham Klausner. The dynamic Isaac Tyrnau and Jacob Möllin's pupil Salman von St. Goarshausen were all part of the creative impulse that lead to the development of the material in Book Three and Four.

Abraham mentions songs that are useful in some of the magical arts. This is what the MaHaRIL collected as a part of the Jewish folk traditions and set to musical scores. The MaHaRIL material is still used in synagogues.

During the early Renaissance, the Jewish culture's emphasis on self-development as illustrated in the *Abramelin,* engendered the perception that every Jew was potentially a wizard. This is in contrast to the Christians of the time who were under the control of a hierarchical organization that was easy to influence for political ends.

We can see an effect of this Christian culture in Mathers's choice of vocabulary for his translation of the *Abramelin.* When referring to God, the German *Abramelin* text uses, as did Martin Luther a hundred years later, the word *Herr*. Even today, Germans call their God "Mister." Mathers used the King James Bible's choice of word for God, and King James named his God "Lord," after his nobility.

For these reasons we could not use "Lord," the usual English biblical equivalent of *Herr*. The word "Mister" was also unacceptable, so we settled on the Hebrew word "Adonai."

The recipes in Book Two were easy to translate into modern English. Yet, while working with these translations, we developed the feeling that we may have missed subtle connections that could make the recipes work more effectively. For example, hidden inside the 160 recipes are some fascinating numerological suggestions:

The number 1 appears five times. The number 2 appears seven times. The number 3 appears eighteen times. The number 4 appears once. The number 5 never appears. The number 6 appears three times. The number 7 appears one hundred and twenty nine times. The number 8 appears three times. The number 9 never appears. The next number to appear is 24 which is seen once and the last number to be seen is 49 which appears once.

We have translated 36 representative examples from each of the ten chapters of Book Two.

The prayers that go with each recipe, with a few exceptions, are from the Old Testament. We have left Abraham's text and translated it into English from his vernacular 14th-century German. In brackets, below our translations of the prayers, we have placed (when we could find them) identical biblical quotations from the Authorized King James Version.

Book Three contains the material for self-development and self-initiation. It contains the mature development of the "Magic Art" that was given by Abramelin, and was written after 1409. It alludes to many fascinating esoteric concepts that are not explored in the material. The spirit names listed in Book Three have held the interest of esotericists for hundreds of years.

Book Four consists of word squares and Abraham requires that they be read only after Book Three has been studied and understood. The direct visual impact and mathematical complexity of the word squares undoubtedly contribute to the continuing fascination that they hold for people. For example, in Book Four, chapter 17, Abraham gives a four-letter word square for "traveling in the air on a cloud" containing the letters NASA—coincidence or convergence?

All four manuscripts used as sources for the material in Book Four have the spirit names written in line form, as we have presented them in this edition. Into this we placed a few examples from the Dresden manuscripts to show the completed word squares.

The spirit names are written in alphabetic script. While working with the word squares, it becomes clear that they were directly derived from Hebrew names, with the German alphabetic pronunciations.

The word squares offer many interesting routes to interpretations. Their construction borders on the mathematically magical. The word squares, their background, and some possible methods of interpretation are discussed in Appendix E.

The appendices contain some of the material that I have collected in the more than 20 years that I have worked on the *Abramelin* text. When, and if, important new material becomes available, I will place it on my German publishing company's web site, *www.araki.de*. The site has a link to my email address. I would appreciate your comments and correspondence.

Opening Hymn

I

There was a conjunction of Neptune and Pluto in Gemini from 1398 to 1404. These two slow planets rarely meet—roughly every 500 years. The conflict within the sign of Gemini lies in its hesitancy and tendency to drift into a kind of helplessness. If the occult powers of these outer planets are cultivated in personal discipline, they are useful for developing consciousness, research, discovery in all kinds of fields, new theories, visionary recognition for collective transformation. Around the same time, between 1398 and 1399, Saturn and Uranus formed a conjunction in Sagittarius. This indicates a rational (or spiritual) period of alertness, communication, and innovations. Power issues should be set aside in such a climate, or else divorce (like the schism of the Catholic church) will ensue. If spirituality is subordinated to claims of power, abuse is sure to follow.

Abraham von Worms lived in one of the darkest chapters of Jewish history in Germany. The year of the plague and subsequent pogrom of 1349 was only a few years before his birth. The period was marked by the bad situation of the rural population (The Peasant's Rebellion in Worms, in 1431) on one hand, and the flowering of the cities, trades, and crafts on the other.

In the second half of the 14th century, humanism was founded in Italy. At the beginning of 15th century, the Renaissance started. The 1380s and 1390s saw the foundation of the universities of Heidelberg, Cologne, and Erfurt. The Western Schism of the Church created antipopes as well as different Reformers like John Wycliffe (1330–1384) and Jan Huss (1371–1415). Germany was ruled by the Luxembourgs.

Abraham's story is a mirror of that time. As an emancipated Jew, he is a consultant to church principals and politicians. A man of his time, involved in its development, he lives in two worlds. Jewishness, its mentality, and way of life is not as assimilated with the population as it will be in the 18th to 20th centuries. Abraham anticipated the progress of social learning and the emancipation. It is self-evident for him to write in German, the common language for the Jewish. Books One and Three show no hint of translation from Hebrew. Book Four, as the occult part of his inheritance, shows evidently Hebrew roots, but not exclusively. Book Two contains customs that have been handed down in all parts—including Christian—of society.

I investigated Abraham's time primarily for biographical reasons, and while doing so I discovered a contemporary, whose picture of life, or biography, was very parallel to Abraham's. I realized then that they were one and the same person. Against the backdrop of those times it is easy to see how someone of that function and education (or skill) could have led two different lives and built up two different identities. This man, who used the name Abraham von Worms as a pseudonym, was Rabbi Jacob ben Moses ha Levi Möllin, the MaHaRIL.

In the following it may be possible to show symbolically which karmic consequences our Jewish scholar survived. Never mind whether it was conscious or unconsciously.

II

It is the time of the Hundred Years' War in France. Upon the stage of world history appears the Virgin, who turns into the tool of Archangels, Principalities, and Powers (the three celestial hierarchies); despite that, blind humankind makes her a martyr. Gilles de Rais, Joan of Arc's captain, was born in 1404. His father died in 1415. Two important data show synchronicity with Abraham's data. Additionally, two contemporaries without any obvious connection except a shared interest in Abraham's story also encountered de Rais's: Joris Carl Huysman and Aleister Crowley.

Gilles de Rais is accused of performing magical rituals. He confesses, embellishes them, shows details and atrocious delusions. The doors of hell seem to be opened in an epoch during which they couldn't be closed, because it has never been regarded as a period of transformation. Things of the spiritual planes that are symbolically put in a demonology of the underworld of the soul—which exist visually and are designed like in the Tibetan or Egyptian Book of the Dead, in the Book of Dead Names (the Necronomicon), in the paintings of Hieronymus Bosch, the devils of Abramelin, or the aberrations of the priesthood—have torn into physical reality; the hell as an element of reality was left to the carnal world. Because of that, humankind was deprived of its maturing and initiating process for centuries; whole societies were nailed in traumata and the rigidity of fear. We see the light of the Renaissance opposing the darkness of the Inquisition, but few people nowadays comprehend how we can build the bridge over oblivion.

Crowley, ever the cynic, exposed the unconscious mechanics in a shattering lecture about Gilles de Rais: anger and bitterness speak out of it. However, new witches' actions are encouraging when they, for example, let Catholic priests say Mass for burnt women.

That era slid into a world war (what else can one call the Thirty Years' War?). Today at least we can say what should never happen again. We retained some of the old wisdom and discovered new wisdom in an Aeon that doesn't overvalue itself. And so we can realize a chance for simple living and being in harmony.

It is irresponsible to mistreat history. History is full of tragic figures and not everybody who thinks beyond the templates of his time succeeds like Crowley in stirring his environment with sincere opposition. Superstition is not vanquished by any means, whether it be the still-unbroken might of allopathic medicine, which evokes demons like AIDS, or the inquisition of political power that murdered somebody like Wilhelm Reich. Jimmy Hendrix, Janis Joplin, and Kurt Cobain ultimately died of modern Western society's failure to embody and respect the reality of the inner realm.

Gilles de Rais was not a magician. He was the anima of the Virgin of Orleans, whose courage horrified the reigning powers. Abraham von Worms, the true magician, who fought his battles in the deserts of Egypt and Mount Sinai—real sites and metaphors of the unexplored inside the lonely (perhaps cosmic) spaces of the soul—carried home invisible trophies: the Secret and the Wisdom. He withdrew himself from the grasp of history, hid his legacy as a secret inheritance in an ordinary wooden chest, where it could rest for a time, to be discovered again in a later time of transformation. This might reveal Abraham's existences in between, perhaps as a Reformer, or as an author of the age of Illumination.

It would thrill me to prove Pico della Mirandola's identity in our century with a wealth of indications. He could have invented the motto "live fast, die young." No one since Jim Morrison has studied the classical poets, the alchemists, and the mythical heroes with the same enthusiasm. Our time is full of heroes from the Renaissance. And of course such an age has its dawn again.

This book is dedicated to the Divine in us all, to the Light and Wisdom that we possess solely by the fact that we are human.

Abramelin

The book of the true practice of magical wisdom

BY

Abraham the son of Simon, son of Juda the son of Simon

Four Books

1. A record for my son Lamech . . .
   Author's biography
2. Useful workings from the blended secret Kabbalah . . . A formulary for altering situations
3. Accessing the gifts of Adonai . . .
   Abramelin's method of self-initiation
4. The fruit of the preceding three books . . .
   An index for accessing and working with spirits

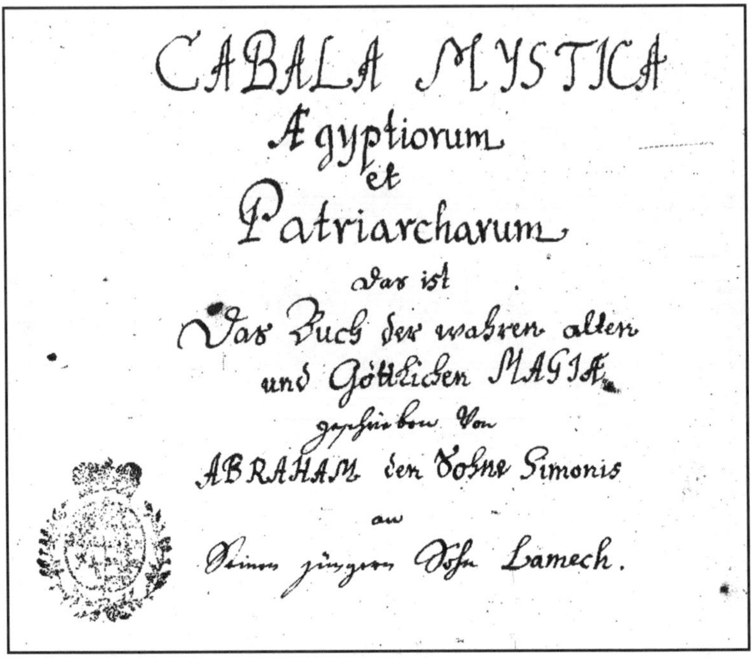

CABALA MYSTICA
Ægyptiorum
et
Patriarcharum
das ist
Das Buch der wahren alten
und Göttlichen MAGIA
geschrieben von
ABRAHAM dem Sohne Simonis
an
seinen jüngern Sohn Lamech.

Fig. 1. Title page of MS 2 in the Dresden library. A possible source of the French translation, which entered the English language through S. L. MacGregor Mathers's *Book of the Sacred Magic of Abra-Melin.* The paper and script style suggest a transcription date of about 1720. The French MS is on a similar paper and uses a similar script of the time. Library records show that no one had viewed the manuscript for 200 years. Dresden, State and University Library of Saxony.

Book One

This is the book of the true practice of Magical Wisdom. It has been passed to me—Abraham, the son of Simon, son of Juda, the son of Simon—by oral tradition.

Some parts of this book have been given to me by my father and other wise, studied, and practicing people. The other parts of this book contain things that I have learned, discovered, and tested by making great events occur.

I have written this manuscript and placed it in a chest so that my youngest son, Lamech, will have a special treasure as his inheritance. My firstborn son Joseph received the holy tradition and Kabbalah from me. From this book, my second son, Lamech, will be able to see, recognize, and use the wonders of God.[1]

---

1 The Preface text from the 1608 MS.

Fig. 2. Another page from the Worms synagogue *Mahsor*. Thirteenth century, Jerusalem; facsimile in Worms's city archives.

Chapter One

The reason for this inheritance.

This chapter deals with the reason for this special inheritance. I shall not repeat here what will be obvious in the third book.

In this book I avoid all unnecessary words—the truth does not need any long and complicated explanations. The truth is simple and straightforward—what is true is true.

Fig. 3. Worms. The city's famous dragon symbol is in the foreground. The German word for "dragon" is *worm*. The illustration was made by a Jewish artist. 15th-century drawing in Worms archive.

Only follow what I tell you in this book. Stay simple, remain religious, and be considerate. In this way you will experience more good things than I can tell you about.

The Holy Ghost does not give everyone the honor and duty to be able to learn and experience the important secrets of the Kabbalah, the Law, and the Talmud, so you should do and enjoy what has been given to you by Adonai. You should stay with the situation into which you have been placed by the will of God. Otherwise, if you try to fly too high you, in your pride, could—and will—be led into the situation that was experienced by Lucifer and his angry associates. Adonai may send you a strong wind to throw you to the ground and break your

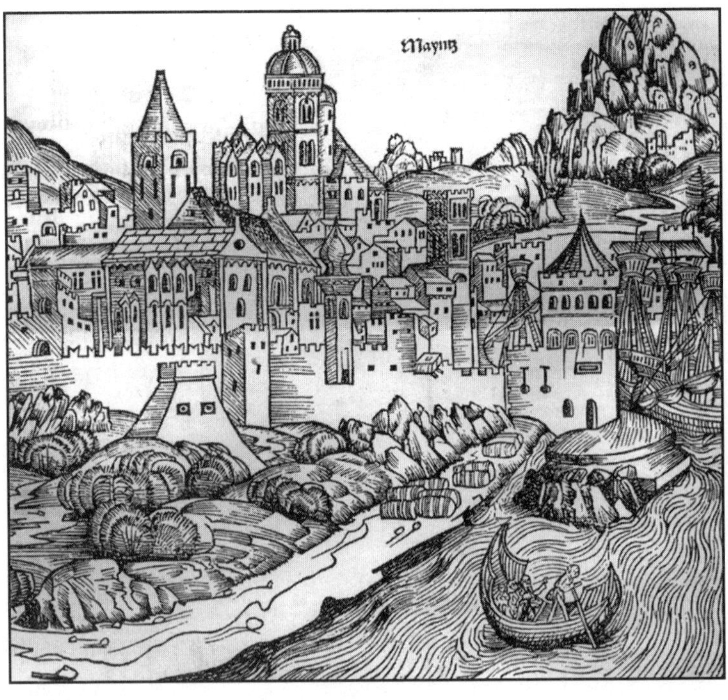

Fig. 4. Mainz (also "Mayntz" or "Mentz"). Print from 1493 as it appeared in *Schedelsche Weltchronik,* one of the first books to be printed in Germany.

wings, so that in the future you would be frightened, fearful, and unable to fly.

So remain clever and wise and correctly understand what I am telling you.

Remember, because you are too young, that in this book I am spooning pabulum into your mouth. How to cook and use the pabulum you will learn—step by step—as you grow older from good cooks, the wise masters, and yes, also the good holy angels of God.

Nobody is born as a master—everyone needs to learn and to become a master—this is what happened to me and to everyone else. Engage yourself deeply in this study and you will be rewarded with experiences; the most shameful and disgusting title is "ignorant."

Chapter Two

How I learned from others.

You should also know how I learned from others to become a master. What happened is that my father Simon—shortly before he joined his fathers—gave me, by word of mouth, signs and advice about the holy secrets. He taught me as much as was correct.

But he—who knows all—also knows that he gave me the mercy to fully understand enough of the holy mysteries. My father did not strive correctly toward the holy mysteries, so I did not learn the correct way to work toward the mysteries.

I was an immature 20 years old when my father died. I had happiness and joy from the mysteries of Adonai—but, alone, I could not find the correct path.

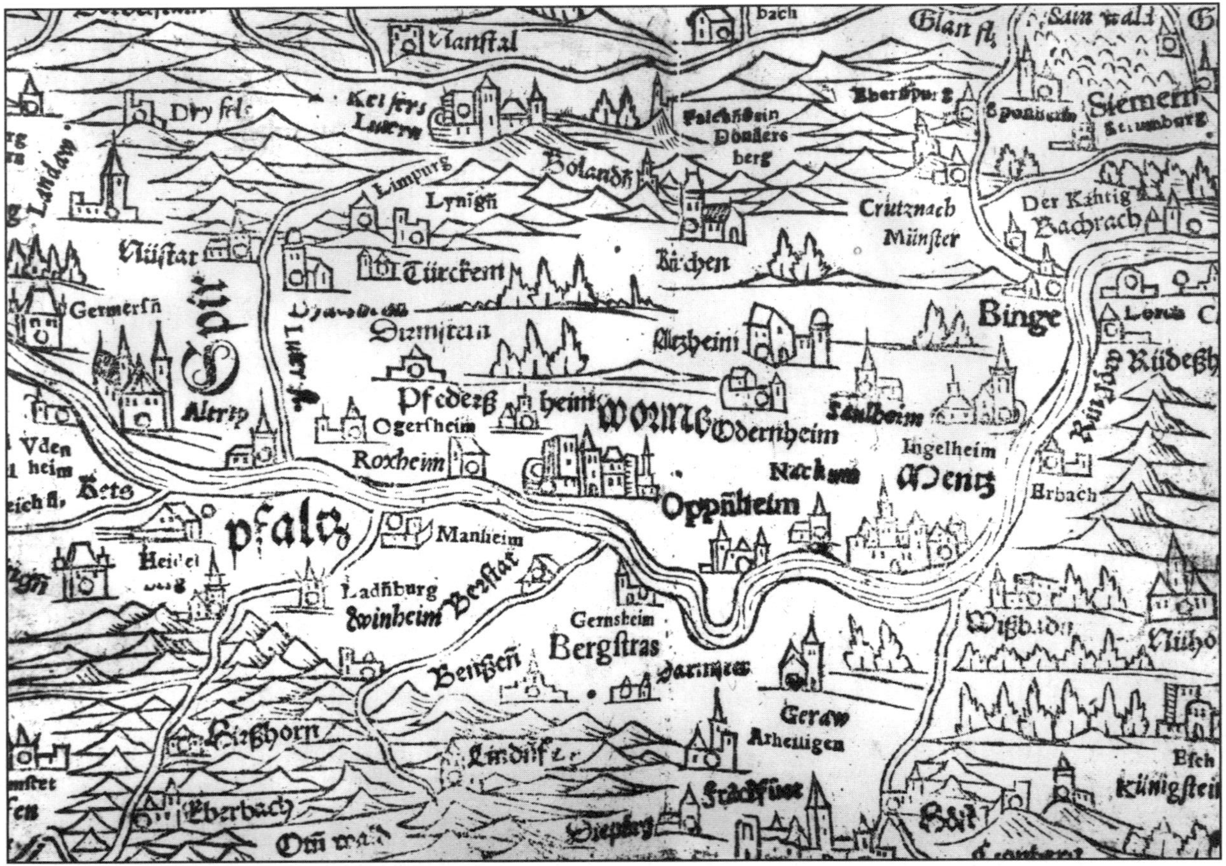

Fig. 5. Rhine River. Worms is in the middle. Other towns mentioned by Abraham are Speyer (shown as "Spir" on this map), Mainz (Mentz), and Ladenburg. Print, 16th century, Worms archive.

Gossip told of a wise rabbi in Mainz who was full of godly wisdom and magical knowledge. I gave myself to him to learn and become wise. The rabbi had not received the full gift of mercy from Adonai. He helped me understand some of the high secrets. What he taught was not complete or satisfactory. In his magical system he followed the ideas of people who were atheists or agnostics.

He used pictures from the Egyptians, herbs from the Medes and Persians, stars and constellations from the Arabs. He took from all people and nations—even from Christians—diabolical crafts. Spirits created false mirror images to blind him, so he believed his efforts to be true magic. As a result he made no further efforts to search for the real holy magic.

I also believed that I had achieved the right knowledge until ten years later when I met Abramelin, the old wise father in Egypt. He showed me the right way, which I will tell you about later.

The highest mercy was given to me from the Father of Kindness, the active great God, who again and again gave enlightenment to my mind. He opened my eyes so that I could see the holy secrets.

In time, I have become able to recognize the holy angels and the good spirits. I now share their friendship and have discussions with them. They have explained to me the basis of true magic and how unredeemed spirits need to be—and must be—controlled.

To finish, I need to say that I learned the holy secrets through Abramelin's teachings from God himself; and I learned to do the true, not false, magic from the holy angels.

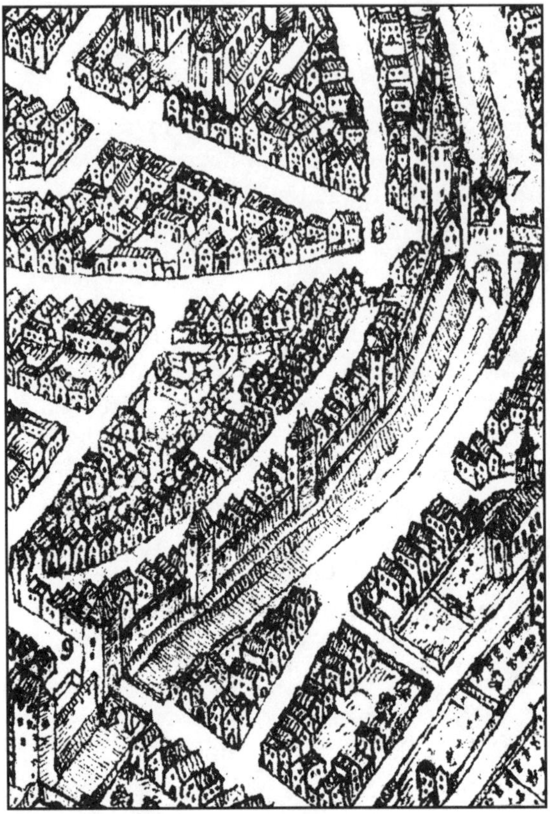

Fig. 6. Accurate 17th-century copper etching of the Jewish section of Worms. Worms would have been very similar in Abraham's time. The Jewish ghetto runs from the Mainz gate and bridge, on the right edge of the illustration, along the inside of the wall with its four watchtowers. Judengasse is the curved road inside the wall and you can see one entrance to the ghetto at top end of this street. Outside the wall is the moat. The curved road that runs down to the left from the Mainz gate is the Friedrichstrasse. At the other end of Judengasse at Baerengasse is the other ghetto entrance. The synagogue is right in the center, along Judengasse and Hintere Judengasse. The Jewish school, called Raschi House, and the *Mikwe* (the well for ritual washing) are between them. Sporergasse and Sterngasse border the ghetto on the left. In 1689 the French burned down the town. Today the streets remain the same as they were in Roman times, but the houses are larger. Illustration by Peter Hamann.

CHAPTER THREE

Countries and lands I visited.

In the last chapter I told you how, after my father's death, I searched for the truth and the secrets of Adonai. Now I shall tell you about the towns and countries I traveled through for the purposes of study.

I do this to give you a rule and some examples so that you can organize your youth properly rather than spoil and waste it uselessly, the way little girls who sit around the kitchen fire do. There is nothing more needy of criticism and worthless than general disinterest. He who does not journey does not return. He who does not have foreign experiences does not know how to organize his time and energies at home. The stay-at-home is like an archer painted on the wall: shooting continuously but never hitting anything.

After my father's death on the sixth day of the month of Thebith in 1379, I stayed for four years with our friends, brothers, and sisters. During this time I tried to correctly understand and properly use what my father had passed on to me.

When I realized that I could not do the necessary things by myself—and for myself—I organized the most important of my affairs and businesses. I said farewell to all friends and moved to Mainz to be with old Rabbi Moses.

Gossip had given me the hope that I would find in Mainz what I was seeking. But there was no foundation for spiritual wisdom within Rabbi Moses. I worked four years with him. I intended to return home believing I had learned what I needed.

Then I met Samuel from Bohemia, a young man of our religion. His demeanor and behavior showed me that he traveled on the path of Adonai. I befriended him and he confided in me that he intended to travel to Constantinople to meet his father's brother, and from there travel on to the blessed land where our fathers lived. I had an extremely strong desire to travel with him and had no peace until we made an agreement, promised and swore to travel on together.

On the 13th day of Tiar, 1387, we made our way through Germany, Bohemia, Austria, and eventually Hungary toward Constantinople. I stayed there for two years and would have remained there if Samuel had not caught a severe illness and died.

So was God's will. In my heart I constantly wanted to keep moving and traveled on from town to town until I came to Egypt. I was there for four years, journeying back and forth. The more I saw and experienced the less I liked the magic that I had learned from Rabbi Moses.

From Egypt I returned to our beloved fatherland where I encountered only grief, misery, and distress for a year. Then

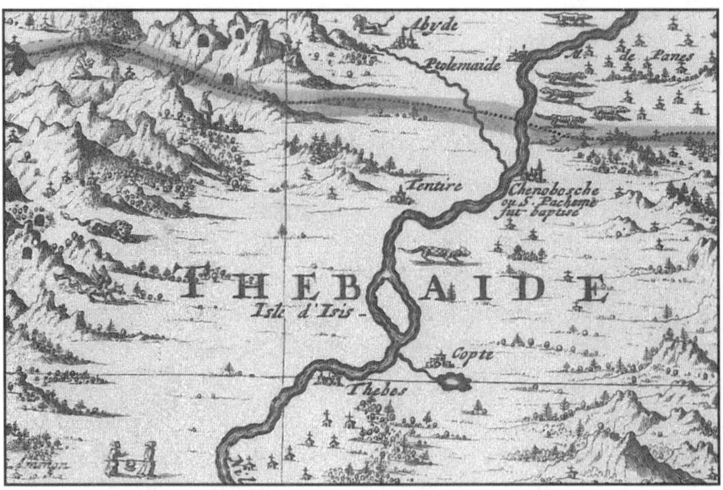

Fig. 7. Map of the Nile River, showing hermitages. Thebes—modern Luxor—is in the center. The map is inaccurate, but it does show the large number of Christian saints and hermitages that are ascribed to the area. Detail from a larger map printed in 1690. Bibliothèque Nationale de France, Paris.

I met a fellow traveler who, although Christian, searched for the same as I. We agreed to move to the wilderness of Arabia because we had been told of the many holy hermits who lived in the area. They lived here so that they would be undisturbed in their search for the skills of their art.

We searched for five years but could find nothing that suited what we sought. Then a wonderful but difficult thought entered my head: I should discontinue my journey and return home so that I would find what I was searching for. I told my companion Christopher about this but he wanted to continue his search through Arabia. We parted company, he went further into the desert, and I retraced my steps toward home.

Chapter Four

I find Abramelin.

After traveling around for a time at great expense, I became depressed and decided to return home. I moved again from the Arabian desert, to Palestine, to Egypt, and remained there for almost a year. I came to Araki, a small place near the Nile, and again met Aaron, a very old man of our origin. Half a year before, on a previous visit, I had stayed with him. He asked me about the success of my journey and if I had found what I was searching for. I replied, with a sorrowful heart, "No," and told him about the experiences on my journey with so much emotion that my eyes overflowed from my frustration and pain. This touched the old man's heart and he comforted me. He told me that while I was away he had heard of an unusually wise man who was close to Araki. He advised me to visit Abramelin because it appeared that the good God had been touched by the desires in my heart.

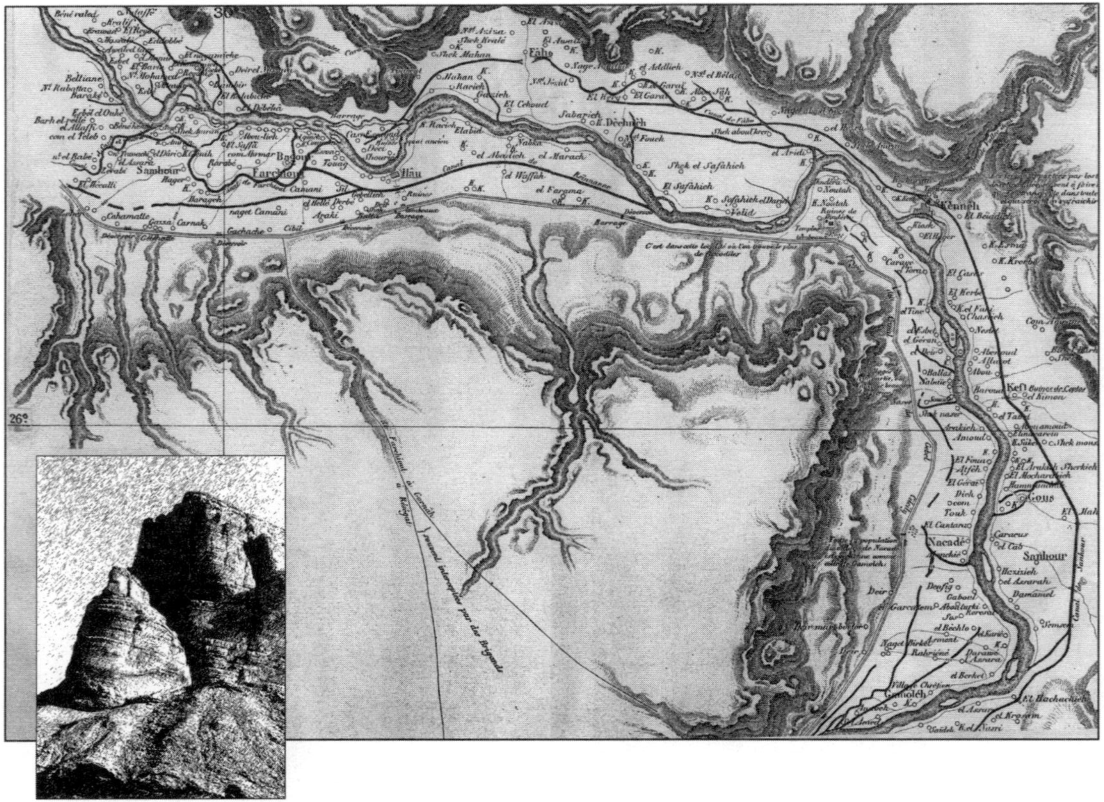

Fig. 8. Map of the Nile River, north of Luxor, which is a bit off the map to the south. The map shows the complex of modern irrigation channels that branch out from the Nile. Araki is near the top left of the map, at the lower point of a small triangle with Farchout and Hau (Hiw). Kenneh (Quena) the largest town on the map is on the bend in the Nile. The map is accurate within the flood plain of the Nile but the wadis (valleys) that run south into the barren tableland in the bottom left quadrant are not accurate. One caravan road is marked as running up a wadi from near Araki. Perhaps this was the route that Abraham took from Araki to Abramelin's hermitage. The journey, he says, took one and half days. Map, 1860. Institute Français Kairo.

I considered that I had heard heavenly rather than human advice and was cheerful and happy. I was restless until good old Aaron found me a man who knew his way around the district. I journeyed with this man for one and a half days over an uninhabited, stony plain until we came to a little hill on which grew bushes and trees. Here, my guide informed me, I would connect with my man. I asked my guide to go on, but he refused, turned around with his mule—on which was carried food and drink—and for some unknown reason immediately left me.

I knew of no other way of getting help and advice than to submit to the ultimate help and cried out his high name. He quickly heard me, because as I lifted my eyes, I saw an old man approaching. His friendly greeting was in the Chaldaic language, he asked me to follow him. I did this with happiness and thanks: In this event I recognized the high foresight of God.

Very politely he lead me into the place where he lived. There I learned his name—Abramelin—and in time also the foundation and structure of wisdom.

Fig. 9. Remains of a bathhouse in Araki. The only remaining medieval building in the town. Editor's photograph, 1989.

For days without end he spoke about the fear of God. He warned me that I needed to live an ordered life. From time to time he told me of mistakes that are easy to make because of human weakness. Later he made it clear to me that he rejected the gaining of wealth and possessions—a thing we ceaselessly do in our towns because of nastiness and greed—things forced on us by our neighbors.

I solemnly swore to him to alter my way of living and not to embrace the false beliefs of our society but to live on the path and according to the rules of Adonai. I never broke this oath. This has made me appear to my friends, relatives, and other Jews as a bad and crazy person. I say to myself, let the will of God happen, and no matter what other people think, I must follow the right path.

Abramelin, knowing my strong desire to learn, gave me two scripts. These very secret manuscripts were similar to this one which I bequeath to you. Abramelin impressed on me the need to copy them with great care. I did this and copied both books with sincerity.

Abramelin asked if I had any money. I answered, "Yes." He asked me for 10 gold guilders which he—as an obligation to Adonai—was required to distribute as alms to 72 people. The recipients were required to pray certain psalms.

After the Sabbath he made his way to Araki. He had asked me to swear that I would fast for three days—Wednesday, Thursday, and Friday—and to satisfy myself with one meal a day, which should contain no blood or anything dead. He requested that I do this with exactness and not to make any mistakes. He said that to work well it is important to start well. He advised me to repeat the seven psalms[1] every day during these three days and not to do any hard work.

On the appointed day, he went off with the money that I had given him. I did everything that he had asked me to do. He returned 15 days later. On the following Tuesday he

1 The psalms of repentance, Psalm 6, 32, 38, 51, 102, 130, 143.

impressed on me the need before sunrise to make, with great sincerity, a general confession to Adonai of my whole life. I needed to make a firm and true promise to serve and fear Adonai as I had never done before, and to wish to live and die within his holy law and to be obedient to him.

I carried out my confession with great attention and exactness. It took until sunset. On the next day, I presented myself to Abramelin, who with a smiling face said, "I like you like that." He led me into his room where I took the two manuscripts I had copied and asked me if I truly and fearlessly searched for the holy wisdom and correct magic. I answered him that this was the reason and motive for my long and tiresome journey; I hoped to receive the mercy of Adonai.

"Because of my heartfelt confidence in the mercy of God," said Abramelin, "I grant and give you the holy wisdom that you must discover in the way it is written in these two small manuscript books. Do not leave out the smallest imaginable part of their contents. Make no marginal notes or location marks on what is written. Realize that the creative artist who completed this work is the same God who made everything out of nothing.

"You must never use the holy wisdom to insult the high God or to do bad things against those next to you. You should tell it to no living person who you do not thoroughly know through long experience and conversation. Examine thoroughly if the person really wants to work for God or the devil. Those who you give it over to need to be carefully and exactly watched—as I have done with you. If you do differently, the recipient will have no fruits to harvest.

"Avoid, as you would a snake, selling and making a business of this knowledge. The mercy of God is given free to us, without charge, and we must not in any way sell it. This true knowledge must stay within yourself and in your care for 72 years—it will not stay longer in our sect. Do not let your curiosity make you seek to understand this, but imagine we are so good that our sect becomes unbearable for the whole human race—yes, even for God, himself!"

On receiving these two small books, I wanted to throw myself on my knees, but Abramelin prevented me, saying, "We should kneel only before the face of God."

I assure you that I have written these two books so exactly that when—after my death—you see them, you will understand my regard and respect for you.

Before I continued on my journey, I sincerely and carefully read the books. When I had difficulties or problems with the text I would discuss them with Abramelin, who explained things to me with patience and kindness. I stayed with Abramelin for a year until I properly connected, understood, and experienced the truth.

I intended to return home and put my art and what I had leaned to good use. With Abramelin's fatherly blessing (a sign not only of the Christians, it was also a habit of our forefathers), I joyfully went on my way.

I followed the route to Constantinople. There it pleased Adonai in his divine wisdom to test my patience with a long, tiring sickness. For one and a half years I lay sick in bed until Adonai gave thought to my sadness and by his mercy freed me from fate.

Fresh and happy, within six weeks I met a Christian German who wanted to sail from Constantinople to Venice. With many words and much money I attached myself to him and got myself onto the boat. Happily I came across.

I went to the brothers who after a while recognized me through validating signs; they showed me much good will and friendship. They told me that in France and Italy there were some well-known and very wise people of the art. I wanted, before I went home and gave myself to stillness, to visit these wise people and observe their art.

From Venice I traveled through Italy's most famous towns. I traveled over the sea to France, most of which I went through. Traveling overland I journeyed to the Rhine in Germany where on the 12th of Elul, 1404, I returned to my father's house in Worms. I arrived because I was under protective cover and in the company of the Holy Guardian Angel of Adonai.

Chapter Five

Other masters I have found.

It is not enough that one wanders over many lands like a dog in a kitchen. It is necessary to understand more afterwards than before. Everyone should be able to describe properly what he has seen and learned. A clear description of what has been seen gives listeners the opportunity to judge whether a traveler's boasts are true.

So as to give you examples in this chapter I will tell you about people who call themselves masters of the art and I will tell you about how they manage their art. In the sixth chapter, I intend to explain to you what I have seen and learned. And I will also tell you whether, on reflection, I found their doings true or not.

The very first master I visited was Rabbi Moses from Mainz. Religious, but incompetent in holy secrets and magic knowledge, he was superstitious, with his art patched together from a collection of atheist and agnostic systems. Because of this, he received no response or help from the holy angels and good spirits. The unredeemed spirits joked with him, sometimes for their own pleasure, they helped him with childish things, and so were better able to trick and hinder him. He did not continue searching for the right basis or correct system.

In Strasbourg I met Jacob, a Christian, regarded as a marvelous Master. But it was all tricks and cheating: in the correct art he could do less than nothing.

In Bohemian Prague I found 25-year-old Anthony, a confused young man who showed me exceptional supernatural things. But God protect me, you, and everyone that anyone should sink so low! The fool told me that he had sold his body and soul to the devil—totally rejecting the highest creator and all his associated beings. In return, the devil Leviathan promised Anthony that for 40 years he would do whatever he requested. He quickly tried to persuade me to become trapped into the same situation. I moved from him and finally fled from him and his arts. His pitiful end, two years later, is known to every child; a song about it is still sung in the streets. Oh, forbid, my faithful God! Let this be an example and a warning to you: flee far from such young fools.

In Austria I found many people but all were bad or crazy; some were caught in the same pitiful situation as the Bohemian I have just told you about. But it is not worth the trouble to write about simple, unskilled, and crazy people.

In Greece I found fine, skilled elders who were mostly unbelievers. Three were special, all lived in the wilderness, and they showed me exceptional things. They made unexpected thunder storms, snow, hail, sunshine at night and night in the afternoon; they made running water stand still. For all their work they sang special songs and rhymes in their own language; they used these together with gestures and ceremonies.

In Hungary, I found people who served neither god nor devil and were worse than the beasts of the field.

In Epiphus, close to Constantinople, lived a person who instead of song wrote special formulas on the ground. With these he made incredibly unusual visions and discoveries—but all them were useless. They appeared for the wrong reasons and worked slowly; and when things did not succeed, he had a thousand excuses.

In Constantinople I found two of our house, Simon Moses and Rabbi Abraham. Both had learned the same magic as Rabbi Moses from Mainz, but Abraham knew more about the

Kabbalah. Both apologized for not having searched further into the magic.

In Egypt the first time, I found five men honored as clever men. Of these, three—Horay, Alkoran, and Selikh—worked through astrology from books; satanic oaths; monotonous, long, godless prayers; and powerful ceremonies. The other two—Halimeus and Abimelech—honored the devil to whom they offered licenses, and figures that they made to talk and move.

Similarly, in Arabia they did magic by taking into account the times and configurations of the heavens. Where the Egyptians used pictures and similar things, the Arabians used herbs, and precious and ordinary stones. These and other similar people I found in the Arabian wilderness. They called themselves masters of magic but they were hopeless; most could do little or nothing.

Finally, guided by the mercy of God, through the Holy Angel, I was led to Abramelin. He was the first and only person who showed me the source of all the holy secrets and the true old magic—as it was used by our forefathers; he unlocked and opened these for me and showed me how to use them.

Later in Paris, I found the learned master Joseph who had turned from our belief and holy law to become a Christian. He was like Abramelin in his magic but not in its entirety because the righteous God never gives the right and true treasure to those who deny him. Otherwise he is the friendliest upon whosoever the sun may shine.

In Italy, and later in Germany, I found and recognized several masters, especially Master Albrecht. I recognized them from their person and from their writings. But all their doings had neither hand nor feet and they were like Rabbi Moses from Mainz in their doings. Some were even worse; there is no sense in even talking about those who hope, with false stories and lies from books, to try to understand and become wise. They become crazy, lose their humanity, and become donkeys; I shall tell you about this later.

Chapter Six

The beginning of wisdom.

The beginning of wisdom is the fear of God, as is mentioned in Sirach chapter 1, verse 14.[2] He who does not fear Adonai and yet pursues the Wisdom either becomes crazy or falls into the webs of Satan and Lucifer or Leviathan. This is because he builds on sand without a foundation on which his house can stand.

The first master, Rabbi Moses, imagined he was a prominent artist in the magical wisdom when with unintelligible words and unusual statues he made all the church bells in the town ring. Or, when with spells he made the image of a thief appear in a glass. His greatest and most reliable piece of art (because the others often failed him) was with water, which he had secretly prepared with long, ungodly spells; he transformed himself from an old man into a young man, but this transformation never lasted for more than two hours.

Dear son, all these things are but a mixture of simple jokes and devil's doings in which there is no use—just the opportunity for great suffering and dangers to the soul. That is why I cast them out of my mind when I discovered the right truth and the godly magic. All that cheats God and insults others I have removed from my heart.

The second master, Jacob from Strasbourg, was only a cheat and trickster. Whenever I asked, he could show me ghosts in a mirror—sometimes an animal, sometimes a rider, sometimes a child, sometimes a girl, and so on. These gave no answer and made no movement; it was as if they were frozen or made out

---

2 Sirach is the lost book of the Bible, supposedly lost for a thousand years. Rediscovered in 1898.

of something solid. Finally, I saw that they were small pictures that he repeatedly and secretly stuck on the wall. His trick was to hold a curved glass in front of my face in which the picture appeared and seemed alive. At night he showed tiny pictures in devil's clothes that sprang and danced about. Later, in the company of two honest people, I confronted Jacob and we made him admit that they were pulled by hidden threads, made from horse or lady's hair.

With the help of his friends, the godless Bohemian from Prague showed me wonderful things. In my presence he made himself invisible. For half an hour, I saw him fly two ells[3] high over the ground. He went out and came in through keyholes and properly locked doors. He told me things that only God, and no other creature in creation, could have known. He was in pact with the devil. His art was to scorn God and damage others. Finally, his body was rendered into uncountable pieces and thrown onto a garbage heap. His head, without tongue and eyes was found in a small, unused room.

Fourthly, the masters in Austria. Here I found countless people like the Bohemian. They could only kill animals, cripple people, change the weather, and make hail. They could destroy marriages, weaken nature, make witches' knots in willow trees, stop the flow of mother's breast milk, and similar things; altogether bad doings executed with simple words and rituals. All these people had previously given themselves to the devil, rejecting the creator and all religious people.

All had more or less a pact for two, three, four, or five years after which they had a fate similar to what befell the Bohemian. From this you can see, my son, how blind is the world and into what idiocies curiosity drives people.

Among the others I met in Austria was a woman in Linz, the daughter of a Christian, whose mother and father had

---

3 An ell is an English linear measure equal to 45 inches, formerly used in measuring cloth.

recently died. She offered to take me to a town that I wanted to visit. She told me that there was no danger or risk and I agreed to go. She persuaded me to go to the house where she lived alone—I went there at 3:00 in the night.

She gave me an ointment, which she rubbed onto the arteries of my hands and feet. It felt like I was journeying to the town which I in my heart had wished to visit and which I had not told her about. I told her nothing about what I had seen. Awaking from a deep sleep, it seemed as if I had been far away; in my head I had a melancholic confusion or depression, but no pain. When I came to, I saw her sitting next to me; we both described what we had seen. Our experiences were very different.

I was in great wonder and surprise because I thought that I had traveled away in my body and had personally experienced everything. I thought about this for a few days, then I asked her to travel by herself to a town that I named. I asked her to bring news from a good friend who I knew was at least 100 miles away. She promised to do this within the hour; she then thoroughly rubbed herself with ointment and lay down next to me.

I was fearful when she lay there as if dead for four hours. Finally she breathed again, turned, and moved in her sleep. She sprang up, ran happily toward me and began to tell me about the town she had visited, the meeting she had with my friend, and what he was doing. I know that all this could not all be true, and that it was all quite simply a dream. The ointment was nothing other than a good and fantastic sleeping ointment that made all imaginations appear as realities. The natural masters believe in such ointments, but it is unnecessary to write about them here.

I have investigated the Greek art many times and I have come to the conclusion that it is a devil's mixture kept going by unbelievers who wish to remain in blindness. A Greek, Pilovior, on a sunny clear afternoon, created for me a dark night with lightening, a thunder storm and rain. I sweated in fright. It snowed, even though it was summer, to a height of half a wade. This carried on until the old man took me by the hand and walked me six paces out of the snow; then, when I turned around, everything had disappeared and the sky was sunny and clear.

Pilovior achieved all this with an old Greek song that he sang four times in a very loud voice. He wrote it out for me. He had called on neither god nor the devil. I think that good people have become so startled and confused by the devil that they do not recognize the devil's might. This confirms my opinion that nothing useful is achieved by the Greeks who say that their art does not help either themselves or their friends even though they have books full of old Greek and Latin songs from fortune-telling old sibyls and also the pagan poet Virgil and other similar authors.

One art is called white and black, another one is like the angelic Teatim. An old symbol writer, Philip of Epiphus, gave me invocations that achieved only bad things. He showed me and gave me songs to take with me, he showed me how they worked. With numbers he made things happen. All the numbers were different; they were crooked and threefold. As proof, he destroyed his apple tree in half an hour—leaves and fruit fell and rotted. He explained a great secret in numbers that cause good and bad, friendship, riches, and marriages. He had used these often but never got them to work. Abramelin later taught me that these work out of the divine secret of the Kabbalah and hang together with it; without this understanding, nothing can be understood. The songs and superstitious hymns, some 40 pieces I burned in Abramelin's house and scattered the ashes into the wind; I did this because these harm us and hindered us from the finding the right wisdom of God.

The most important of the Egyptian masters, the fiddler Halimeg, was sincere when he showed me his art. He forced a spirit into a piece of a timber; it moved itself three paces and answered clearly in my language, easy to understand but confusing, so that you could also think that the spirit was a singing bird. Later, when Halimeg showed me how to control the spirits, I realized that his was not the way of the true magic because the picture had to be carved at an exact astrological time. The praying, the bathing, the oiling, and the fanciful smearing all had to be done at special times. He never prayed to Adonai, he only called for the devil in cooked-up Chaldaic words.

Similar were the works of other Arabs. These forced their spirits into stones—ordinary and precious—and flowers and herbs. Alkyky, a young Arabian priest, conjured up a flower and threw it in front of an old woman passing by. She smelled it and changed into a goose; six hours later, she returned to her old shape—I saw this for myself.

I was shown these, and many similar arts, which were given to me with goodwill; I burned all of them in Abramelin's house. I did this because all these things were against God, his holy law, and neighborly love—they changed people from being children and servants of God to being children and servants of the devil.

From this you can see how easy it is for people to fall if not protected and led by the angel of Adonai. I also would have come into such blindness and harm if I had not come to the truly wise Abramelin. He, before I could even ask, took me as his student, fulfilled my desires, and knew and answered everything even before I opened my mouth. He told me of my father's death. He told me everything I have done and said. In flowery and prophetic words—which I only later understood—he told me about my future and especially about my serious sickness in Constantinople.

Importantly, he uncovered for me the source of the holy revelation and wisdom of the Kabbalah, which, according to the way of our forefathers, I have given to your elder brother Joseph as his inheritance. He also showed me the source of the true art and magic that our beloved forefathers Noah, Abraham, Jacob, Moses, Samuel, David, Solomon, and uncountable others used so much. Later, in a clear and fatherly way, I will describe this art and magic to you. This is so that if God, the owner of my soul, should ask me for it before you reach the age of manhood and inheritance, you will have trustworthy protection and schooling from this book.

Many of the arts you find described in the fourth book I have seen with my own eyes at Abramelin's and have done them for myself. I have never met anyone like Abramelin again.

Although Joseph from Paris was on the same path, God did not show him complete mercy—he did not lay before Joseph all the divine law and ceremonies because (and this is certain) a born pagan, Christian, Jew, unbeliever, or anybody can become a complete master of these things—but not a renouncing Jew who has left Adonai's law and has whored with other strange religions' obligations.

Chapter Seven

God returned me to my people.

After faithful God returned me healthy and rested to my family I repaid my financial vows and thanked him for all the fortunate things that he had done for me—especially for what he had let me see and learn from Abramelin.

The very first thing I planned to do was to start the work—exactly as I later write about. Many things prevented this from happening—also partly because of your mother Melcha (even though she did much to help me). Only in the third year and after we were married in Worms did the opportunity occur. The town itself was a difficulty; the people, the running around, working, and so on. I even thought of going to the Black Forest, into isolation for the specified time. But this would have been impossible without damaging and ruining my household.

So I followed Abramelin's advice for such a situation and divided my household into two parts. I also rented another house in town; it was here that I put my relatives and business. I gave it over to my mother's brother so that he could carry on the household and business for two years—he paid me a considerable yearly rental for my necessities and expenses. I, your mother, one servant and a maid—married together—stayed in this house where we have continued to enjoy the mercy of God; and so also you and your brother will enjoy the same mercy if you follow the way of Adonai.

In this correct and withdrawn way of life, I started by avoiding all unnecessary talk and company. This was not easy for me because of my melancholic mood. I did this until the time of Passah, which I celebrated with all the relatives of the household in the usual way and according to habit. On the next morning I started with the work, creating the order that I write about below, in the name of and to honor Yehovah, creator of heaven and earth and of all creations. Until the eighteenth month I pursued this end; in between, early in the eleventh month, your mother presented me with her firstborn son Joseph. After eighteen months—while I was carrying out my final services to Adonai in my upper prayer room, right next to the summer veranda—he presented me with his holy angels to my great joy and happiness: It is impossible to tell of this, and it is not correct to do so.

I experienced this vision in humility and bliss for three continuous days. I was addressed lovingly and with friendship by my guardian angel. He explained the godly wisdom and Kabbalah and later completely explained the complete truth about this magic. He told me also about the effects of what I had received from Abramelin and showed the way I can form and do similar things. He also gave me clear advice, teachings, and knowledge about how, over the next three days, I could deal with the unredeemed spirits and make them listen to me. I did this and let them all appear on the veranda where I, protected by the mercy of God and his holy angels—indeed, and with much help from them—forced the spirits to remain for the hour; in recognition and submission, they stayed.

The mercy of Adonai and the protection of his holy angels never move from me, Abraham, and my two sons Joseph and Lamech and my whole house. So that we in our misery, sorrow and imprisonment can find no other way to be than in the way of the law of Adonai. Amen.

CHAPTER EIGHT

Magical things I have done.

So you can see how a person needs the gifts of God and how these are to be used to honor God and help one's neighbors, I shall now tell you about things I did with the help of the highest and my art. I write not to boast or to seek acclaim or out of idle pride—this would be a great sin against God, because he is the one who does everything. I tell of these things so that his mercy and wisdom can be further praised and so that you also can recognize how plentiful are the treasures of Adonai. You have to thank him that he gives you mercy and lets me—without any effort or work on your part—tell you about things I have done.

Here are some things—after my death, you will find more set out in my register. I started to practice my art in 1409 and now, with God's help, I have reached an honorable 79 years. I have helped about 40 people who were enchanted in different ways—men and women, Jews and Christians. I made them healthy and dissolved their enchantments.

A. Kaiser Sigismund, our most gracious Lord. I helped him with a very friendly duke—a familiar spirit of the second hierarchy—whom he had requested from me; he used this spirit with intelligence. I also helped Sigismund with his marriage.

Fig. 10. Oil painting of Sigismund, emperor and king of Germany, Poland, and Hungary, who made Abraham a member of his court. He died in 1437.

He wanted to have the secret of the whole operation but Adonai cautioned me and so he was satisfied with what he was allowed as a private person rather than as a lord. With my arts I helped him overcome the great difficulties that were in the way of his marriage.

hertzog Friderich

B. Count Frederick, I freed from the hands of Duke Leopold with the help of 1,000 magically created knights. I describe this in chapter 29. He was captured and would also have lost his reign.

C. To the bishop of our town I showed the betrayal of his official at Ladenburg half a year before it happened. I'll say no more about this because as a priest he remains silent about the things I later did for him.

Johannes der .xxiij.

D. Who helped your cousin out of the jail in Speyer?

E. The duke of Warwick was freed from the English jail the night before his [scheduled] decapitation.

F. I helped the duke and Pope John to flee from the Council of Constance, otherwise they would have fallen into the hands of the kaiser. John could also confirm my prophecy about his question: which—John XXIII or Martin V—was to win the Papacy?

Martinus der fünft

G. In Regensburg it happened as I predicted. Because of important matters, I was staying with the duke of Bavaria. There the door to my room was broken open and jewelry, money, and account books to the value of 3,000 guilders were stolen. When I returned I forced the thief, a bishop, to personally return everything and to confess to me why, for heaven's sake, he did such a thing.

Ludwig hertzog zu bayrn

H. Both of the popes mentioned above have often, and in secret, asked for my advice and opinion on future events. They never found it untrue.

I. If the Greek emperor had believed the letter that I sent him half a year ago, then things would not be going so badly for him now. Or, as I worry, they are likely to do in the next few years. I explained to him the poor condition of his kingdom, which is at the edge of ruin, if he does not extinguish the rage of God. As I do not have much time left in my life, I leave it to the future to confirm this prophecy.

J. The operation in Book Four, chapter 13, I have done twice: Once in the house of Saxony and another time in Magdeburg. I was the reason that the heritage has passed on to the children.

Now, once access to the holy magic has been achieved, it is permitted to demand from the Angel a sum of coined money proportional to birth, status, and authority. This will be granted without difficulty; the money is taken from the secret treasures. It is important to note that God permits us to take a fifth of all treasures.

K. My own special treasure was given to me in Wurzburg, where I performed the operation of Book Four, chapter 6. It was in no way ancient or guarded; it was raw gold that I had spirits smithy and make into guilders—it took a few hours.

L. My own inheritance was small and worthless. I was so poor that I had to use my art to marry someone with a big dowry. I used the 3rd and 4th signs in Book Four, chapter 19, and married my cousin with a dowry of 40,000 gold guilders, which was enough for my happiness.

M. All signs in chapter 18 I used so many times that I have lost count.

N. With Book Four, chapters 2 and 8, I have made large and wonderful experiments. The first sign, in the first chapter, is the best.

It is necessary to be clever and consciously precise in these matters. Because in doing God's things, we can make larger mistakes than Salomo. I have never failed to complete matters, the spirits have always listened to me. Everything succeeded because I followed the will of God. Point for point, I followed the advice and suggestions of my Angel. Also, I followed the teachings of Abramelin, which is exactly what is in these books.

The advice that I received, even when in unclear words and hieroglyphs, have made it possible for me to achieve my goal and never to have made a mistake, or to let me fall into pagan ways or superstitious idolatry. I have always remained on the path of Adonai, who is the only true and infallible way to succeed with the holy magic.

Chapter Nine

Be careful in everything you do.

A blasphemer never lacks the opportunity, and jealous Belial with his associates likes nothing more than to suppress and reduce God's wisdom. This lets him blind people and enables him to lead people around by their noses so that they continue to live in stupidity and error and do not have the opportunity to find the path of true wisdom. True wisdom damages Belial's kingdom and changes him from lord of humanity to a servant. So he needs all his arts, cleverness, work, and patience to completely root out the true wisdom; he does this so that humanity cannot sense his intentions.

He brings much false and imagined magic into the world, as I described in chapters 4, 5, and 6. So, I beg you, my son, be careful in your doings and do not leave the way of the wisdom of Adonai. Do not let the devil and his associates lead you astray—he is a liar from eternity. You can be sure and certain that if you follow the written law you will not only receive everything you wish for, but that you will also receive the mercy of Adonai, and experience the assistance of the holy angels who are happy that you faithfully search for their advice and follow the will of God. The art of wisdom has its foundations in the secrets of the highest and in the holy Kabbalah, which belongs to your elder brother Joseph and not to you.

And so, as with our forefathers who always gave the first-born the Kabbalah and gave to the youngest the wisdom—this was the reason for the argument and swap between Jacob and Esau:[3] It was about the first's birthright and came about because the Kabbalah is more valuable than the magic.

Lamech, for you the secret of the wisdom cannot be achieved through the Kabbalah. Similarly a woman's son is not led to the Kabbalah—not until today—and also not a son from outside a marriage; only legitimate children, as was the case between Isaac and Ismael.[4]

As you see below, the way of achieving wisdom can give you a true sign. Be satisfied with this book and do not investigate further than is your right. This is so that you don't anger the highest God with your disbelief or give the devil a hand to lead you from the right road to a false path that would be the start of your miseries and ruin.

The old snake, from the time of the discovery of this book, will try to confuse and falsify it with his poison; or attempt to suppress it; or at least create gossip against it. As your trustworthy father, I suggest that you do not discard or disbelieve this book; call God as your witness and trust him. Remember, even if you do not have a teacher to show you the secret of the wisdom and its preparation, after eighteen months your angel will reveal to you everything that is necessary.

---

3 See Gen. 25:27–34.

4 Gen. 21:10.

The secret of God and the wisdom of Adonai require that all the signs of Book Four are written in the letters of the fourth main monarchy. The puzzling words containing the secrets have their beginnings in Hebrew, Latin, Greek, Chaldaic, Persian, and Arabic. Through all the world's tongues and languages flow special secrets of the wisest practical master who cares for all things and underlay this art. Not the wisdom but the secret is opened in this way. Study and consider the wise sayings of the holy prophet Daniel and you will be greatly inspired by your Guardian Angel.

Chapter Ten

What our fathers have been given.

We have to deal with a large and powerful enemy in our work, whom even with all our human cleverness and power we cannot resist without the help of the holy angels and spirits. So keep God and his holy word in front of your eyes so as not to anger him. Do not insult or annoy the angels and the spirits who stand by you, or you will chase them away.

On the other hand, do not in any way listen to Belial, Satan, Lucifer, and their whole snake of followers. Do not make sacrifices, do not obey or in any way listen to them; they want you to be a hypocrite. To listen to them means your ruin and the destruction of your soul. This is what happened to the heirs of Noah, Lot, Ishmael, Esau, and others who lived in the promised land before our fathers. They passed on the true wisdom from generation to generation but little by little they listened to the wily enemy and so let demonic sorcery and godlessness creep into their magic (they did not have the Kabbalah). So God punished them, removing them like weeds and chasing them out of the fatherland. Our fathers were appointed in their place.

In my opinion, the reason for our misery and imprisonment comes from our forefathers who, in their doings and dealings, ignored God's mercy and followed the lies of the devil. So, Lamech, take care—don't support the devil in thoughts, words, or doings. Remember that he can catch you through your curiosity like a bird in a net. He will in some way touch you, cheat, threaten, or frighten you. He will discuss and promise to bring you things through other people that appear to be holy and godly but are inwardly supported by poison's pus and devil's works. Take the example of the Bohemian—mistrust those who magically produce angels or worlds, for they have no substance.

At the beginning of the operation, a man appears of majestic appearance, who with great friendliness promises wonderful things. Without God's permission he can give nothing—he promises things to destroy; he damages those who trust and believe him.

This is what happened to Pharaoh and his people in the book Schemoth when they did not listen to Moses' and Aaron's true wisdom. They let the devil bridle them and let him place so much wisdom in front of them that they became completely blinkered and fully constipated; this is how they were tormented and punished by God. Finally, they were drowned in the Red Sea.

So hold to your God and his holy angels, listen and be obedient to them. Then the devil, his associates and the unredeemed spirits will listen, follow and be obedient to you: He must follow and be obedient to you, not you to him.

Chapter Eleven

Helping other people.

So know, my son, I studied this art because of my love for the wisdom of Adonai and to serve my neighbor, not out of curiosity or amusement. I have never used this art to satisfy curiosity, or for unimportant or degrading things, let alone unnecessary, bad, or harmful things. I always tried to honor the God of our fathers and to help with my whole will and with good heart all God's creatures—animal and people; friend and enemy; young and old; relatives and strangers; believers and unbelievers—one like the other, as I have shown above.

Because God does not show anyone his art or wisdom to keep for themselves, it is to be used to give blessings to others who need examples, to be of use, and to help. So follow my example; I wrote this book for this very reason. If you do not give to others, you will cast your own spell on yourself and the hands that will deliver your blood will be your own. I have told you this so that I can now excuse myself in front of God and the world.

If you want to be a bee and collect honey, you will find a surplus with me. But if you want to be a troublesome spider, you can find poison even in a rock. God does not give or tell his blessings to make evil, even if it seems that some chapters are harmful and bad, rather than of use to your neighbors. Realize that both good and bad can be done with this art. So be very careful to avoid the bad and do the good. The faithful angels will help you until your last day if you do good. If you do bad, the angels will leave you, and you will stay in the claws of the wily enemy from whom it will be hard to escape.

My son, keep the holy laws of God before your eyes; they should reflect your situation and your life. Through the first tablet, God showed us the holy secret and the Kabbalah; with the other tablet, he gave us the holy wisdom and magic that is in these writings. So practice and do the following things; make them into an unbreakable guideline.

As soon as you see that a person is using any kind of magical arts for bad ends, evil, or damaging things, flee from him and his doings. Such a person is no mage but a devil's magician as is described in the Tora and especially the fifth book of Moses, where such people are definitely condemned by God.

When a person wants an operation, not for himself but for a child or a relative who does not deserve a treasure, then the person who requests the operation becomes responsible for great misery—he loses the mercy and wisdom of Adonai and also his heirs will lose this forever.

Avoid the business and company of people who in searching for this wisdom do and say things that lead to the bad; such people can become the devil's magicians. Here, I have to warn fully—and even exaggerate—because once an operation has been done correctly, it cannot be undone—that is certain. Take into consideration the story of Bileam, and see how he was strangled by the angel of Adonai just because he rode with people who wanted to use his art for evil and against people. This happened even though he planned to use his art only in the way suggested by God. Now, think of the strength of God. What will happen to people who plan consciously and maliciously to sin and use this art for evil?

On the other hand, if—after an exact examination and investigation—a person is tranquil and honest, you must help them to come to the wisdom. Because God, who helped you, wants you also to help them. This is why he made you his assistant and gave the holy wisdom to your hand—he trusted you to teach it in his place.

Do not let your own body or bad company lead you astray or harm your neighbor for the sake of love. On the other hand, seek freedom in friendship and in freedom expect its continuation.

Attempt to reduce evil and increase good; if you follow this path you will have God, angels, and people as friends, while the devil and bad spirits will remain prisoners and lowly servants.

With good conscience, you can live and end your life with honor, peace, and happiness with your family and all religious people. Please keep this book as a reverent treasure, don't tip it to the pigs, like empty husks. I present this treasure to you, keep it for yourself. Share parts of it with whoever you can. Do this and it will grow richer for you.

In this land we are captured and dishonored servants; so serve your lords as much and as well as you can. But keep this treasure a secret so that your children, and not the godless, will be the owners of these riches.

Chapter Twelve

Be careful about these two things.

This first book should not have become so long, but fatherly concern and the importance of the matter—also the foolishness of your adolescence—has made this book so long. I should have written more, but I am confident that in these four books I have covered everything that can happen. The first book, even if it seems unnecessary, has in every line my carefully considered teaching and advice—this is important!

With parental concern, I remind you not to start the work until after you have spent half a year in the daily study of this book. You must read through the first and the third parts and consider and weigh every word. If you do this I am sure that no problems will occur that you cannot, by yourself, destroy; and I am sure that from day to day you will awaken more will, laughter, and pleasure in yourself.

There are other arts connected to the holy secrets in addition to this one—these also need the holy secrets to be taught; I shall talk about these later. The holy secrets I call the Kabbalah. The holy wisdom I call the magic. Surely, you will discover all imaginable effects by yourself, if you do not behave like an arrogant fool.

To give you a good beginning to the godly wisdom and arts, I am giving you the next book. In the second book there is a considerable collection of the effects that I have discovered from the holy secrets. In it are mixed other arts which I have tried and found effective—I leave these for you. But pay attention to two things:

Only use, or wish to use, any of the arts in the second book when there is the greatest need. Remind yourself that on the first tablet of the law of the holy Kabbalah, the very first commandment is not to use the name of Adonai for unnecessary things that can be ignored or forgotten, and this is what you would be doing if you used one of the pieces without a real need. If you were to do this, the Kabbalah would work against you and the work would produce no results; and you would also lose God's mercy, so when you next have trouble, he will not help you again.

Secondly, every woman and man, every belief and practice can achieve the results of the pieces on themselves and others if for seven full moons (seven has a special mystical strength in the Kabbalah) they have no doings against the second tablet of the law (which belongs to the Godly wisdom or magic) with murder, burglary, and adultery. People who know they are guilty should not do anything or evil will come to them. This I say with great weight so that open shame and public scorn do not occur to harm the secret, the wisdom, and the honor of God. So I want to end and close the first book with praise to the high and mighty name Adonai—the same who shines his light over us and allows us his freedom.[5] Amen.

5 The Blessing of Aaron. See Num. 6:24–26.

MAGIA ABRA
Hami.

oder

Unterricht Von der Heiligen Cabala!
wie solche beschaffen, zu suchen und zu
erlangen, auch heilig zu gebrauchen sey,
welche dieser obgedachte Rabbi seinem Soh=
ne Lamech zum Testament hinterlassen
mit vorhergehender beschreibung seiner Reise,
und was ihm währenter Suchung solches
Mysterii zu handen gestoßen, benebst
treüer Warnung vor der falschen
Magia

Fig. 11. Title page of MS 1 in the Dresden Library. This MS is in an easy-to-read and attractive handscript. It is incomplete and may well be a copy of MS 2. The monogram is an important clue as who commissioned the transcription.

Book Two

The other book of Abraham the Jew

This considers holy things that I, Abraham, have learned in addition to what was taught by Abramelin. The material comes from the five books of Moses and other holy books and things that I have found out for myself and with and without the use of the Kabbalah. I have tried and used everything in this book.

Chapter One

For serious diseases.

I. [Against plague]

When there is a serious plague in the land, in the morning, before sunrise, collect seven kinds of wood from seven different parts of the land, bring them together into the center of the land.

Write the words: *Adonai Zebaoth have mercy on us.* on pure wax. Sprinkle incense powder[1] over the wax plaque to totally cover the wax. Lay this on top of the wood, and, under an open sky, burn it to ash. Leave it untouched until after sunset. Then take it and throw it toward the seven places from which the wood came, saying continuously:

> *Adonai, we have sinned and your hand is too heavy, but it is better to fall in the hand of Adonai, because his grace is very powerful.*
>
> [I have sinned greatly in that I have done. Let us fall now into the hand of the Lord; for his mercies are great . . . (2 Sam. 24:10, 14).]

II. For cancer and other open injuries

Take a very clean glass, consecrate it with incense before sunrise seven times in seven different directions. With honey, write on the glass and then take good, ordinary healing oint-

---

1 Incense powder recipe can be found in Book Three, chapter eleven.

ment and using it, wipe away the writing and remix the ointment. Besmoke the glass continually in the usual way. You will see that the word of God will improve your health at least half the time. The words:

> *Adonai makes accidents and bandages, he destroys and his hand heals.*
>
> [For he maketh sore and bindeth up: he woundeth and his hands make whole (Job 5:18).]

III. To reduce all kinds of diseases

At all meals, write with honey or butter onto bread (if the patient is eating), and on the glass that the patient uses to drink, the words below. Besmoke the glass after each meal. Do this for seven days and you will see a reduction of the disease.

> *Thus speaks Adonai, I want again to search for the lost and bring back the erring and bandage the wounded and wait for the weak. What is solid and strong I will watch and care for properly.*
>
> [I will seek that which was lost, and bring again that which was driven away, and will bind up that which was broken, and will strengthen that which was sick (Ezek. 34:16).]

IV. A general blessing for all sicknesses and occasions

He who wears the following words—written on gold or silver or pure wax—on his bare body all day long on the Sabbath, is secure from sickness, sorceries, and other evil if he does not violate the commandments of God:

Adonai reign and watch over you, Adonai let his face shine on you, he blesses you and gives you his grace. Adonai looks with his face upon you and grants you peace.

[The Lord bless thee, and keep thee: The Lord make his face shine upon thee, and be graceous unto thee: The Lord lift up his countenance upon thee, and give thee peace (Num. 6:24–26).]

V. For all sorts of sick days and diseases

Take seven clean glass bowls and, before sunrise, write with honey the following words:

I shall not die but live and proclaim the works of Adonai.

[I shall not die, but live, and declare the works of the Lord (Ps. 118:17).]

Also, take seven small breads or biscuits, eat each with seven bites, write on them too. Always put one bread in a bowl, besmoke it, and say:

Thank Adonai, because he is friendly and his mercy is eternal, because he, Adonai raises you to health, but does not give you death.

[O give thanks unto the Lord; for he is good: because his mercy endureth forever. The Lord hath chastened me sore: but he hath not given me over unto death (Ps. 118:1, 18).]

Keep the bread and glass bowls clean, so no dust can fall on them, and each day give the sick person a bowl to drink from and bread to eat. Every day it should be his first food; do not leave out other foods and medicines.

VI. For dangerous occurrences in secret places

Take a seven-sided sheet of copper and, before sunrise, prick into it:

> *Send again the ark of the god of Israel to the right place, so that he does not destroy us.*

Besmoke it for seven days, and after every incensing wash the copper with running water in which you have measured camphor and salt. With this water, wash the secret place and say:

> *Holy Adonai, protect us from the plague of Dagon and the damage of Gath, because God's hand lays heavily on us.*[2]

VII. For heartache and depression

Before sunup, write with honey in a glass bowl, besmoke it, tip mead or strong wine over it, sprinkle over it some smoke incense in the sign of Mars, and give as a drink in the evening. Do this for 7 days. The words:

---

[2] See I Samuel 5. The Philistines took the Ark of the Covenant and placed it in the house of Dagon, a pagan god. As a sign that this was wrong, God gave them "emerods." The same happened when they took the ark to Gath. Here, "dangerous occurrences in secret places" seems to refer to colorectal ailments. Camphor is a powerful medicine and should only be used under professional medical supervision.

The eyes of Adonai see you, so is it in life, he makes for a contented heart and a happy face, he protects from sickness, problems, and unhappiness.

VIII. For impaired ears and eyes

Besmoke a clean sheet of tin or copper and write on it the words below. They must be written in mother's milk—from a women who gave birth to a son seven days before. Allow the milk to dry, then wipe it off with almond oil. Smear this onto the eyelids or drop it into the buzzing ear. Do this ointment for seven consecutive days.

An ear that hears, and an eye that sees, were both made by Adonai.

[The hearing ear, and the seeing eye, the Lord hath made even both of them (Prov. 20:12).]

Chapter Two

About antagonisms and war.

I. So that your friend can conquer his enemy

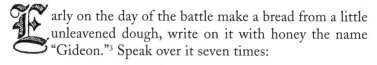

Early on the day of the battle make a bread from a little unleavened dough, write on it with honey the name "Gideon."[3] Speak over it seven times:

[3] Judges 6–8. Gideon fought the cult of Baal and the ruling Midianites and was a judge for forty years.

> *Remember the contract with your servant and let my friend* [name] *go with your might so that that he can rescue his life from his enemy.*

Saying nothing, carry the bread to your friend. When you see him, say three times:

> *Adonai is with you, you true hero.*
> *Adonai blesses you.*

Then ask your friend to eat all of the bread.

II. To conquer your enemy in a battle

With almond oil, write the prayer on the top of your crest or flag. Then wash it away with running water and sprinkle it over your whole army. Then attack with trust in the name of Adonai, your God. You should not be unsuccessful. The prayer:

> *When Adonai sharpens his sword and stretches out his hand to punish, he will take revenge against his enemies and will repay his clan. He will soak his arrows in blood and give our swords flesh to eat, plus the blood of those strangled in their jail, and let them lose their helmets.*

> [If I whet my glittering sword, and mine hand take hold on judgment; I will render vengeance to mine enemies, and will reward them that hate me. I will make mine arrows drunk with blood, and my sword shall devour flesh; and that with the blood of the slain and of the captives, from the beginning of revenges upon the enemy (Deut. 32:41–42).]

III. To make your enemies unlucky

After sunset write on an iron plate with lead the words...

> *Bad luck will fall on your head and spite cover your head.*
>
> [His mischief shall return upon his own head, and his violent dealings shall come down upon his own pate (Ps. 7:16).]

Then, besmoke the plate and repeat seven times the prayer:

> *Stand up, Adonai, in your rage, and raise yourself in anger upon my enemies.*
>
> [Arise, Oh Lord, in thine anger, lift up thyself because of the rage of mine enemies: and awake for me to the judgment that thou hast commanded (Ps.7:6).]

IV. To make your enemy unlucky

On pure wax write the words below:

> *Adonai, banish him away like you banish the smoke away—and as the wax dissolves in water, so should all the godless stand before God.*
>
> [As smoke is driven away so drive them away: as wax melteth before the fire, so let the wicked perish at the presence of God (Ps. 68:2).]

Then, place the wax on seven glowing coals—let it melt, dissolve, burn. Meanwhile, say seven times:

> *Oh my God, stand up and let your enemies be destroyed and let those that hate me fly from you.*
>
> [Rise up, Lord, and let thine enemies be scattered; and let them that hate thee flee before thee (Num. 10:35).]

V. To revive exhausted troops

Take as much bread as you need in large loaves. Write on each loaf, in molten beeswax, the prayer below.

On a glass bowl containing some water, write with the same wax; fill up the bowl with vinegar; pour the vinegar out of the bowl into a barrel of wine, beer, or water, so that all the troops can have a drink. When you cut the bread, throw the crusts into the barrel, and say as you put each crust into the barrel:

> *Adonai, you strong and mighty God, give energy to the tired, and sufficient strength to the weak, so that they can fly like the wings of an eagle.*
>
> [He giveth power to the faint; and to them that have no might he increaseth strength . . . But they that wait upon the Lord shall renew their strength; they shall mount up as with wings as eagles . . . (Isa. 40:29, 31).]

Then give everyone a piece of bread and a drink. You will wonder at the strength of Adonai arising in them.

> *Adonai, the everlasting God who has created the matter of the earth and organized its end, you grow neither tired nor sleepy, your higher wisdom is unknowable.*

[Hast thou not . . . heard, that the everlasting God, the Lord, the creator of the ends of the earth, fainteth not, neither is weary? There is no searching of his understanding (Isa. 40:28).]

Chapter Three

For friendship, marriage, and love affairs.

I. To make an unbreakable friendship between two people

Before sunrise, bake a cake from honey, spices, and flour. Write onto it the names of the two people. Leave it under the open sky for seven nights. Every morning before sunrise, take the cake and say the following prayer over it:

> *Oh, Adonai, you God Zebaoth, please accept this work and intention of your servant, and send your might into the hearts of* [Name] *and* [Name] *these they will connect with each other faithfully and lovingly as did the hearts of Jonathan and David. And so that each will love themselves as truly as they do their own heart.*

> [. . . the Soul of Jonathan was knit with the soul of David, and Jonathan loved him as his own soul (1 Sam. 18:1).]

Then give the cake to the two people to eat.

II. To make undying friendship between husband and wife

After sunset on the day of the marriage, before you consummate the marriage, take two turtle doves—male and female—and write with their combined blood on pure beeswax and new paper. Place it under the pillow of the marriage bed. At the same time, write with honey on a glass bowl, pour wine on it, and drink half. Give the other half to your spouse. You will have a friendly and happy marriage for the rest of your life. The words:

> *Your God is my God, and my people are your people, where you go I want to follow, if you die I will want to die with you and be buried with you. Adonai, let this happen, let only death separate us.*
>
> [. . . For whither thou goest, I will go; and where thou lodgest, I will lodge: thy people shall be my people, and thy God my God: Where thou diest, will I die, and there will I be buried: the Lord do so to me, and more also, if ought but death part thee and me (Ruth 1:16, 17).]

III. For Marriage

If you want a marriage—which may be difficult—to go and end well, get up before sunrise and speak over water that has not been touched by the rays of the sun:

> *Adonai, God of Abraham, grant me today what I ask and give as proof your blessing to me and my father's house.*

[Now therefore, I pray you, swear unto me by the Lord, since I have shewed you kindness, that ye will also shew kindness unto my father's house, and give me a true token (Josh. 2:12).]

Wash your face with the water, and then quickly go and pour the water on the doorstep of the house where the daughter lives and say seven times:

Remember me, my God Adonai. You, the God of our father Abraham.

Fig. 12. Jewish couple from medieval times. They have the Jewish mark on their cloaks. To make identification more certain, the man is holding a bunch of garlic and a money bag, while the woman clutches a goose. From city of Worms archive.

IV. For fertility

Over a glass of almond milk throw a little fine incense. Read over the glass Psalm 113 seven times and give it to the woman to drink. Do this for seven mornings before breakfast. Also on the first day hang a gold, silver or pure beeswax tablet on her. The tablet is besmoked and on one side is written:

> *Praised is the name of Adonai, from now to eternity.*
>
> [Blessed be the name of the Lord, from this time forth and for evermore]

And on the other side:

> *He who lets the unfertile live in the house and become the one who gives joy to children—hallelujah.*
>
> [He maketh the barren woman to keep house, and to be a joyful mother of children. Praise ye the Lord (Ps. 113:2, 9).]

V. That a man will love his wife

Before sunrise, the wife should take a new incense burner and place in it seven newly-lit coals. Place it under a fruiting apple tree. Spread incense on it. Go to running water and wash your hands and face. Write the words below with a gold or copper stylus on pure beeswax. Then throw it on the coals. When it has burned away, pick the nicest apple that has been well-smoked and give it to the man to eat. The words:

> *Like an apple tree between wild trees, so is my friend among the young men.*

[As the apple tree among the trees of the wood, so is my beloved among the sons. I sat down under his shadow with great delight, and his fruit was sweet to my taste (Song of Sol. 2:3).]

If the apples are not ready, do the same with flowers or with the apples blossoms, and give it to the man to smell.

VI. That a wife will love a man

The man does similarly [as the wife in section V] under a rose bush. Pick off three roses and give them to the wife to smell. On the wax he should write:

As the rose is among the thorns, so is my friend among the daughters.

[As the lily among thorns, so is my love among the daughters (Song of Sol. 2:3).]

VII. To confirm peace among two enemies

Write the words below with clarified honey seven times in a beautiful glass bowl, pour good white wine over it, and let both [people] drink—but give it with your left hand. It should also be taken with the left hand.

Peace be between you, peace be between your associates; then your God will help you.

[. . . peace be unto thee, and peace be to thine helpers; for thy God helpeth thee (1 Chron. 12:18).]

VIII. For a woman to excite a man

Before sunrise, pick a wine grape leaf and write on it, with a mixture of honey and myrrh, the words below. Add your name and his name. Besmoke the leaf. Pick a newly-opened rose in the morning, before it has been touched by the sun's rays. Pulverize it. Sprinkle it over the besmoked leaf . . . Let him smell [it]—this will awaken affection in his heart before the end of the day.

> *My beloved is mine and I am his, he grazes under the roses until the day cools and the shadows lengthen.*
>
> [My beloved is mine, and I am his: he feedeth among the lilies. Until the day break, and the shadows flee away (Song of Sol. 2:16–17).]

Chapter Four

For Birthing.

I. For [help with] a dangerous birth

On a belt or strip of white-wool lamb's skin, write the words below. Besmoke it and tie it around the stomach—directly onto the skin. She will deliver within seven hours.

Look Adonai, the children are ready for birth and there is not enough strength for the delivery—if you, Zebaoth, do not help.

[This day is a day of trouble, and of rebuke, and blasphemy: for the children are come to the birth, and there is not strength to bring forth (2 Kings 19:3; Isa 37:3).]

II. For an easy birth

Write the words below, with olive oil, on a silver spoon. Besmoke, wipe off the writing with the forefingers of your left hand. Rub the oil into her navel.

I was birthed from the body of your mother, you are my God from the body of my mother, do not be distant from me, because fear is near and I have no helper except you alone, God Zebaoth.

[I was cast upon thee from the womb: thou art my God from my mother's belly. Be not far from me; for trouble is near: for there is none to help (Ps. 22:10–11).]

Chapter Five

Against water, fire, tempest, ghosts, the devil.

I. Against tempests, ghosts, and visions prepared by evil people

Take flowing water, throw in some grains of salt. Then, with the blood of a wether or steer—into which has been mixed sulphur and gall—write the words below. Wash this off with the salt water. Sprinkle this water at the tempest or against the vision.

> *Adonai Zebaoth, threaten them, so that they will fly away. Haunt them like the wind puts dust upon the hills, and like the tempest comes before the whirlwind.*
>
> [. . . But God shall rebuke them, and they shall flee far off, and shall be chased as the chaff of the mountains before the wind, and like a rolling thing before the whirlwind (Isa. 17:13).]

II. Against bad weather and continual rain

Fast three days and nights without eating and drinking—do this with deep devotion. Take some beeswax and make seven tablets. Write on them the words below and besmoke them.

Light charcoal—under the open sky—and on each fire place a tablet and let it burn. The fires should be put out by the rain. You will see how the creatures willingly obey their creator.

> *Adonai our ruin gives you no pleasure, because after the tempest you let the sun shine and you pour over us joy after the sorrow.*

III. That evil people and magic cannot damage your house

Write on seven tablets of pure beeswax. Bury them in seven locations around your boundaries, or place them under the edges of the roof of your house. The house will be secure, evil will not be able to approach. The words:

> *The godless have pleasure from doing harm, but the seed of the righteous will bear fruit.*

IV. So that a drought does no harm

Take clay or brick tiles—as many as you have fields—wash them before sunrise with running water. Take an olive or almond twig, and dip it in good almond or olive oil and write on the tiles. Besmoke them, and shortly before sunrise, bury them in the middle of each field. Even if rain does not come immediately, the night dew will bring the blessing of Adonai.

Do this exactly with the following words, bury the tablets immediately after sunset:

> *The benediction of Adonai—the proof of your faithfulness is in the blessing which is like a morning cloud full of dew, and like the dew that*

spreads itself in the morning. Or better yet, comes as a red morning sky followed by rain, just like the evening rain that dampens the land.

[Then shall we know, if we follow on to know the Lord: his going forth is prepared as the morning; and he shall come unto us as the rain, as the latter and former rain unto the earth. . . . for your goodness is as a morning cloud, and as the early dew it goeth away (Hosea 6:3, 4).]

V. Against bewitchment

The day before the Sabbath, take running water that has not been exposed to the sun. Speak the words below seven times and throw incense into the water. Add seven drops of olive oil. Let stand until night and then wash your feet with it. This makes the wizard's bewitchment fall on his own head.

An embittered person tries to damage, but a fierce angel will overcome him.

[An evil man seeketh only rebellion: therefore a cruel messenger shall be sent against him (Prov. 17:11).]

VI. To put out fires started by evil people and spirits

Stretch out your right hand towards the fire and speak:

See Leviathan: my God—whom I honor—can easily rescue me from your fire and from your hand.

Then spit seven times toward the fire. It will disappear immediately.

Chapter Six

To burst open cliffs and walls.

I. To burst cliffs and stone in time of need

If you are chased by an enemy and you cannot proceed because a steep cliff, call three times to Heaven:

Adonai, Adonai, Adonai.

With outstretched hands, hit the cliff while saying:

The mountains melt like wax in front of Adonai—the ruler of the whole earth.

[The hills melted like wax at the presence of the Lord, at the presence of the Lord of the whole earth (Ps. 97:5).]

Then, with amazement, you will see the mighty wonders of God. Take care to follow the second commandment of God.

II. If you are locked between iron doors by an enemy

The greater the danger, the greater the wonder and help of Adonai. Hold the highest wonders in great respect and use them carefully. What follows is true, I have tried it on your cousin Esau.

If you are caught and in danger of injury and death, fall on your knees and call fervently to Adonai that he will hear you and help you in your need. Then go to the gateway and say seven times in different ways:

> *Adonai we want to thank you for the grace and wonders that you show to humankind.*
>
> [Oh that men would praise the Lord for his goodness, and for his wonderful works to the children of men! (Ps. 107:15)]

Then write or scratch the words below on the door; if this is not possible, then write with spit using your right index finger:

> *Remember David and his promise*

Under this write *Yah*, and below this write:

> *He breaks armored doors and removes rivets from iron.*
>
> [For he hath broken the gates of brass, and cut the bars of iron in sunder (Ps. 107:16).]

Strike against the door seven times. As soon as you see the door open, say before leaving:

We who are released by Adonai, and those who have been saved from their need should say, "Praise Adonai because he is merciful and his grace lasts for eternity.'"

[O give thanks unto the Lord, for he is good: for his mercy endureth for ever (Ps. 107:1).]

CHAPTER SEVEN

Protecting houses and buildings from earthquake and thunder.

I. THAT A HOUSE BE SAFELY PROTECTED FROM MISFORTUNE

Take a clean, seven-sided building block that has never been wet. Wash it before sunrise with running water and scratch into it, with a new gold or silver stylus, the words:

Blessed be the one who fears God and finds pleasing his commandments. He will have surplus and abundance and his righteousness will be carried forever in his seed.

[Blessed is the man that feareth the Lord, that delighteth greatly in his commandments. His seed shall be might upon earth: the generation of the upright shall be blessed. Wealth and riches shall be in his house: and his righteous endureth for ever (Ps. 112:1–3).]

Besmoke it seven times, the last time after sunset. Then bury it one ell deep under the same house. Mark the place. With each new moon, after sunset, burn incense at the same place. Do this for three months.

Chapter Eight

Addressing courts and potentates.

I. To get a favor from an important person

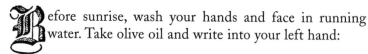

Before sunrise, wash your hands and face in running water. Take olive oil and write into your left hand:

> *Oh, Adonai, let your ears listen to my prayer and give me mercy from your heart.*

Hold the hand over incense and say:

> *Hear, my God in heaven—you great and awesome God—who keeps his promises and gives mercy to those that love you and keep your commandments. Let your ears listen to the pleas of your servant and let me experience grace today. Generate mercy in the eyes of Lord* [Name].
>
> [O Lord, I beseech thee, let now thine ear be attentive to the prayer of thy servant, and to the prayer of thy servants, who desire to fear thy name: and prosper, I pray thee, thy servant this day, and grant him mercy in the sight of this man (Neh. 1:11).]

Then wash the hands in a basin with running water, sprinkle this onto your face, body and clothes. You achieve everything that you can use.

VI. To go before court

Bake an unleavened bread before sunrise. Write on it, with honey, the words below. Eat it, wash your face seven times with water that has not been exposed to the sun. Go confidently to the judge. Your mouth will speak to his ear, but the word of Adonai will go to his heart.

> *You do not judge people for humans but for Adonai—the same Adonai that is with you in the court.*

Chapter Nine

In times of hunger and starvation.

I.

This superb and true secret I used during the last big famine with amazement—and found true. This effect—with its secret—is the one the prophet Elijah (in I Kings) and Elisha (in II Kings) worked. It is also found in the stories of the Christian prophet who fed many people with a little bread. The reason why it works can be found in the holy secrets and in three elements of the blended Kabbalah.

This is how it is done: Pray evening and morning for seven consecutive days. Pray seriously and with concentration to Adonai. After the morning prayer of the last day, take a leaf from an eatable plant or tree—which ever is convenient. Write on it with honey, dew, or rain water the words below. Besmoke it and give it to someone to eat. It will nourish him for seven days without hunger. In this way a person can survive 49 days without food or eating anything else—but not longer. This was the famous bread that was shown to the prophets in the desert; it was brought to them by the angel.

Write on one side,

Behold. Bread I want you to rain from heaven.

And on the other side write,

Manna.

[Behold, I will rain bread from heaven for you (Exod. 16:4).]

Chapter Ten

To make oneself invisible to one's enemies.

I. To disappear from the sight of an enemy

During your flight remove your left shoe. Circle it seven times around your face and head. Then face your enemy and—in the air—strike out against him seven times while speaking:

> *Adonai punishes the wise in their duties, and destroys the advice of the hypocrite that they walk in darkness during the day and reach out at mid-day as if it were night.*

You will see great wonders. The blindness of your enemies will be to your benefit.

The end of the second book of Abraham the Jew

So, my dear son Lamech, you have a great treasure, the most useful workings that have come out of the blended secret or Kabbalah.

Although all came out of the Kabbalah, there are none which have added to the Kabbalah. All have bits of the Kabbalah mixed in, all depend on it—some more and some less so—as I have said in my big work on the Kabbalah and also explained to your older brother Joseph when I told him about the usefulness of the Kabbalah. In the twelve families of magic or wisdom, all are dependent—to a greater or lesser extent—on the Kabbalah. Without the Kabbalah, none could stand alone, so by necessity, all needed to be blended with the Kabbalah.

Our correct wisdom, as I shall discuss in Book Three and Four, has nothing to do with this material. It is independent and stands by itself as a true wisdom that is effective without any additions.

I want to tell you again, do not to use the art without thought or for the wrong reasons. If you do, you will awaken the punishment of God and have bad luck strung around your neck.

If you want God to help, you need to start correctly. First, you need to trust God completely and never doubt his mercy. Second, you need to fear God and obey his commandments. Third, you need to behave correctly and be a pious man.

If you do this, you will have everything you wish; ignore it and you will lose mercy, help, and hope—altogether. You can see from the above examples that such recipes have to be done with the fear of God (but not for evil reasons) because they are grounded in, and done with, the word of God.

Note, that when you use one of the recipes, or give another person a recipe for practice or use (which you can do for pious people, but certainly not for evil people) always give it in the person's own language. Let him practice and use it in his mother tongue; it is no use in another language. How can a person ask for mercy from Adonai, how can Adonai come and help if you, yourself, do not know what you say or ask for? This would be a big mistake—a mistake that many people make.

It is true that our holy language is the most comfortable and strongest before God. But how few are there who know it and speak it? Who knows if you can manage it? Therefore I have written this whole book in simple, everyday language—keep to this. It is better and safer to do this than to take a risk, because those who like danger will die by it.

If you become a learned Jew, then write and use the holy words in holy language. If you are a common person, then use the language that you understand. If you are a Greek or foreigner, then write in Greek, Egyptian, German, or other language. Always understand what you ask for and write.

When using incense—which in our holy law is frequently used instead of offerings and prayer—avoid strange and unnatural incense that would be a cruelty rather than an offering to Adonai. So use the incense that I describe in Book Three, this is pleasing to Adonai: He mentions it in his law. If you do this, you will avoid the experience of evil that befell Aaron's sons when they brought foreign incense and fire. Because what the almighty God requests should be done properly—to the smallest detail. To do otherwise is neither merciful nor helpful but rather brings an unforgivable, terrible, and serious punishment—like mentioned above to Nadab and Abihu—and many other examples in the Bible.

I have said enough of the recipes that I have mostly tested for myself. These were given to me by inspiration and the works of the highest. Everything else I have learned—or has been given to me—by my father Abramelin and other wise men.

All else belongs to the Kabbalah or holy secret, in part or in whole. Everything else is uncountable in a detailed description of the usefulness of the holy secret or, even, in the other book containing the fruit of the Talmud; one without the other is all too high and difficult for you.

Enjoy and be satisfied with this. Thank Adonai and his hierarchy that has told us—and given to us—so much.

Fig. 13. From the MS in the Wolfenbüttel library. The oldest known MS, it is dated 1608. It is encoded, there are no paragraphs, and only very occasional punctuation. The script is small and hard to read. Each page is divided into vertical thirds. If you hold the page at a sharp angle you will see two straight lines running up the page. This gives each page three divisions.

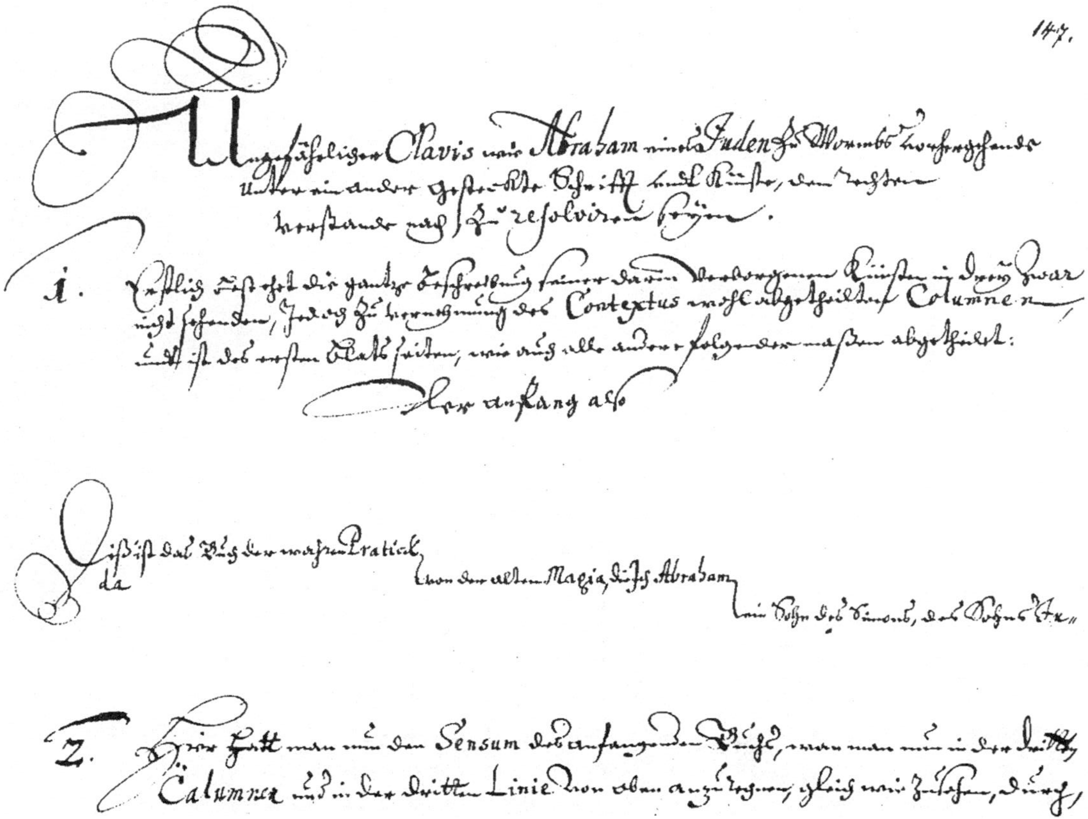

Fig. 14. Directions for decoding the other MS in the Wolfenbüttel library. Dated 1608, it is probably a clear copy of the encoded MS. At each division the line drops down one line (even in the middle of a word). The script is German, not the more easily-read Latin. This makes it difficult for someone who reads only Latin, English, or French script to understand. The MS also uses many abbreviations and this makes the use of the old German capitals particularly confusing.

Book Three

Foreword.

Like a bottomless well, the wisdom of Adonai is inexhaustible. Remove what you want, it always remains full, it never diminishes. No human has yet been born who has ever seen all the sources of the wisdom of Adonai.

All the holy fathers—the ancestors, the prophets and the wise men—have drunk from this well and all have been fully satisfied.

Nobody has been able to know or understand the principles and origins of the wisdom of Adonai; the creator of all things, who is a zealous god, has retained this for himself. He wishes that we humans enjoy the fruits but asks we neither touch the stem nor dig out the roots.

So, dear Lamech, we do not want to change the ways of our dear parents. And so in this book we do not try to understand how God works, reigns, or manifests things. This would be an intrusion into the mind of God.

It is sufficient for us to know what huge benefits God can give us—what huge gifts he grants and how he lifts us humans above earthly and celestial things. He gives us power over these things.

It should also satisfy us to use these things correctly and to leave behind our curiosity about such things.

I will make a real effort to be as brief as possible and describe only what is necessary, because too many words will destroy the work and darken the teachings.

In its own time, everything will reveal itself to you. Follow the instructions properly and diligently. Any lack of understanding—brought about by your weakness of mind—will be made good to you by the loyalty of your Guardian Angel.

Follow the work exactly—this is most important. Make a good start and half the work is already done.

No great skill, effort, or intelligence are necessary. It is sufficient to have a true fear of God, an unblemished life, a true sincerity, and a clear intention to learn the wisdom. Those who commence the work in this way and work properly and correctly can be assured of achieving the desired result.

And so in this third book—in the name of God Zebaoth—we want to start with the number of wisdoms and kinds of magic. Then we can see what sort of special magic is described and taught in this book.

Chapter One

[The Types of Magic.]

This chapter deals with the number and types of magic, and what is genuine. I will teach you about this in this book.

So numerous are the arts and effects that today are described as magical wisdom that it would be foolish to try to describe them all—as foolish as trying to scoop out the ocean. Nowadays, every juggler's jump and every monkey's dance is called magic; I will describe a few of them for you.

Sorcery, idols, and tricky illusions are seductions of the devil and the work of charlatans. This is true of both natural and supernatural things, and applies to everything that the blind mob cannot touch with their hands. All this has been given the name of sacred wisdom, or magic.

The physician, the astrologer, the poet, the sorcerer, the witch, the idol worshipper, the atheist, the blasphemer, even the devil himself want to be regarded as magicians and wise men.

One has his knowledge from the moon, the other from the sun, another from the stars, the fourth from an angry ghost, the fifth from a loose woman, the sixth from a stupid animal, the seventh from a steer, the eighth from a pig, the ninth from a piece of wood, the tenth from a stone, the eleventh from herbs, the twelfth from words—and from so many other incredible things that heaven itself wonders about what is happening.

They foretell the future from the earth, from the air, from fire, and from water. From pictures, from faces, from hands, from glass, from mirrors, swords, wine, bread, from birds, animals, and their intestines. The wisdom of God is abused and diminished even to the point of being found in dirt and shit—all this has been believed to be wisdom and magic.

Oh, poor daughter, tender pure virgin, how badly you have become smeared and slandered. Lift your face out of the dirt and dust, show who you are! Cover the mouth of liars! Make it impossible for the sons of bitches to go into your father's house and to sit at his table. Chase them away, yell out loudly, "I am the true Wisdom, the daughter of the living God and the treasure of his heart. Go from my sight, you daughters of impurity."

Live on my sister, you unknowable secret of Adonai, we share the same heart. Let us stand against our accusers. Let us further our honor and sweep away the accusers. Then the world will recognize that we are both still alive and well, and that we have only slept. Let us save our creator's honor and reputation.

My son, who do you think are those two sisters? Do you know them, too? Have you heard of them? No, you are too young. They have not been discussed for a long time. But so that you know, now listen carefully: these two sisters are God's Secret and God's Wisdom—the Kabbalah and magic.

Their father and creator is the great God. Both of them have been thought dead and lost for a long time, but now they wake up. Wisdom is the younger; she secretly calls for help against those who falsely use her name, those who called themselves magicians but are charlatans. It needs no further description.

Look at her carefully. You will recognize her by her colors. You have not heard her name; she is called "God's Wisdom." Her mantle has two colors. The first is the fear of God, the other is righteousness.

Take her as your master, clothe yourself in her colors and wear them. To wear them is to make her power yours. Be fearful of God and behave righteously, so as to become her servant.

If you want to know more—who and where she comes from—read the Holy Scripture, especially the book written by wise King Solomon about her wisdom. In this way you will get the information you need.

This is the old, godly Wisdom, which our forefathers have used for years since the beginning of the Earth. This Wisdom was given by Noah to his son Japhet, Abraham to Ishmael, Isaac to Esau. This is the Wisdom that Abraham, Esau, and Jacob all used; the Wisdom that Lot used to escape from Sodom; the Wisdom that Moses received from the burning bush and later taught to his brother Aaron.

This magical Wisdom and the secret of the Kabbalah belonged to Joshua, Samuel, David, Salomon, Elias, and all prophets and all saints of God.

Jesus of Nazareth—whom the Christians regard as God—with his apostles used some of this Wisdom. The best apostle was St. John, his book Prophecy is excellent and still available.

So, Wisdom, the beloved daughter of Adonai, has passed down to the present day, even though she was completely hidden from the unseeing, sleeping world.

In addition you also should know that this magic is independent and not connected to anybody. The magic is similar to—but weaker than—the Kabbalah. It can bring about the same results without the use of the Kabbalah. It requires no outside help.

There are other magical arts that appear to be like wisdom and magic but are different. These have become intermingled with the holy secrets; from these has come the blended Kabbalah.

There are twelve of these magical arts:

One that with dreams and visions works.

Four, that in odd numbers 3, 5, 7 (in the blended Kabbalah, 7 is the most important as can be seen in Book Two and as it has been proved in the fruit of the Talmud) plus the even number 6.

Two that deal with stars and the movement of the heavens—called astronomy. Three that deal with metals, and two that deal with herbs.

All these, when they are sufficiently mixed together with the sacred Kabbalah—which is what Josua and Daniel did—share a common beginning in the sacred wisdom.

Those that use these arts separately, or mix them with things that have no connection with the Kabbalah, come to grief or get tricked by the devil when they attempt to do magical acts. Things done in this way can only have natural results. They have no strength or value in spiritual or supernatural things. If spiritual or supernatural results should occur these are the result of sabotage by the Devil, who can give power to a swindler. This is not Magic or Wisdom but sorcery.

Finally, the three foremost honorable arts that can come out of the divine secrets are: the true Kabbalah, the blended Kabbalah, and the true magic. (Mixed magic is not included because it can be both sorcery and devilish.)

The true Kabbalah is not connected to any of this. The blended Kabbala is written about in Book Two. In this book, and in Book Four, I shall, with clear and simple writing, describe the true, divine wisdom and magic.

Chapter Two

What one should consider before beginning.

I am sure that you can understand the sort of magic that I will teach you. Not the natural, devilish, or human arts, but the old, true, sacred magic that—as an inherited treasure—our forefathers bestowed on the following generations, as I am doing.

Realize before you take this treasure how great is the present that you are receiving. Honor it, keep it, and use it with respect for its value. This seems a difficult step, but if you begin at the right place it is easy. Remember the two colors and start from there: the fear of God and righteousness. These two are the foundation of the two tablets—the Kabbalah and magic. And this is your direction.

So think like this: "To come to the true magic, I need to fear God and follow the first tablet," with a true heart and with all your soul. Here I need to say that righteousness begins by guarding against what is forbidden in the second tablet. When you take care in this way you are on the right path. Soon your Guardian Angel will secretly stand by your side and place suggestions in your heart on how you should organize your life and how to follow everything that is written in this book.

Your Guardian Angel will remind you that you should not undertake this work for the following reasons: for entertainment; to show off; esteem; curiosity; and even less so for excitement; for immoral reasons; or to cause damage to others.

Your Guardian Angel will ask you to start so that in doing so you will praise and honor God the highest, the holy Adonai, the mighty and powerful Zebaoth and his name. Also, in this way, to praise and honor your enemies and friends. Also, so as to praise and honor the whole earth with all God's creatures—to bring them advantage by giving them inner harmony and help in their welfare.

There are other lesser circumstances to be considered: Is your position and personality adequate to carry such a heavy load? Remember, that you are not dealing with people but with Adonai himself, his Holy Angel, and all the good and bad spirits.

Do not show off or be a hypocrite, but be an honorable and pious person. You are dealing with a master who sees into your heart and does more than just watch your hands. It will go easily if you have started properly with a solid foundation.

People often change; they start well and end badly and remain unsettled. Reflect before you start, are you like this? Because to start in such circumstances would be to make fun of Adonai. You will be severely punished if you start well and finish badly.

Furthermore, you should think about your business and profession, whether they can withstand the work. Your position should give you time and a place. The people around you, your servants, children, and wife should not hinder you. Weigh all this carefully and do not forget to consider your health.

If you are weak and easily get sick, then impatience may destroy your ability to complete the work. If this is the case it is better to wait than continue.

Take care to find a location for the work where the enemy is not too powerful or can drive you away before the end of the work, because you need to finish the work at the place where you started.

Of all the important items in this chapter, the first is the most important. Fear God, then the right answers will present themselves. Because God helps everyone who has confidence in his wisdom and has the desire to live a proper life and tries to live honestly in this deceitful world.

You will detest the deceitful world and its viewpoint—these will mean nothing to you when you have perfected your practice of the sacred magic.

Chapter Three

The age and the qualities that you need.

To make it better and easier to do the right things, I shall give a rough explanation of the qualifications that are required. I shall also make some suggestions about possible obstacles.

First, one should live a religious life; be educated in good manners; neither be loose, careless, or arrogant. One should love solitude and not surrender himself to the enemies—stinginess and usury.

It is good if one is born from good, honest parents, but this is unnecessary for the study of the sacred magic, whereas no illegitimate person is allowed to study the secret Kabbalah.

One's age should not be over 50 or below 25. One should be free of inherited diseases, leprosy, or epilepsy; one should have a healthy body without a disfiguring injury. It does not matter whether one is married.

If one can start the work in the first year of marriage like I did, it is good and promises well. This is because the first year has the blessing of Adonai. Otherwise, it is better to be single and complete the work before marriage.

There are fewer obstacles if you are free and independent. Take care, if you are a servant, that this work and your duties don't hinder each other. An indentured laborer will probably never finish the work because duty can call day and night, and so he would be unable to wait for things to manifest.

In regard to women, virgins are the fittest. Others should avoid the work because of their impurity. Generally, my advice—for many reasons—is that women should stay away from the work.

Chapter Four

Most so-called magic books are fraudulent.

I cannot wonder enough at the blindness of people who let themselves be led astray by the devil, who uses false masters, and so become involved in sorcery and idolatry at the cost of body and soul.

Unfortunately, curiosity is so great, the devil so cunning, the words so false, and people so naive that it cannot happen in any other way. So my son, listen carefully to what I will tell you in this chapter!

Here are some more important things; you need to follow them exactly. Do not let the devil, people, arts, or other things hinder you. Even if you should fail once, stay on the right path.

It may all seem too simple—the path is straight and easy. Ignore all other fantasies and associated tricks, especially the books that claim to contain wisdom. The only exceptions are the Holy Scripture and the Talmud. I have seen countless books bought for frighteningly large sums, but as Adonai lives, none were worth a cent. All were full of lies and devil's dealings, full of arts of which not one in a thousand were true.

So blind are people that they neither want to see nor understand what amazing rings, circles, pictures, signs and words all strange, and rare idioms, prayers, and disgusting oaths have been written down. How many lies, like a patched-together beggar's cloak, are put together out of the collected beliefs and habits of different people.

What is the pentagram, the hexagram, the seal, and character? The poor people do not know, and the devil does not tell them—he gives them to understand that these were the inventions of wise King Solomon that were revealed to him by Adonai. Oh, God have mercy, did you ever reveal to Solomon—your son—lies as truth, stupidity as wisdom? No, Solomon was no fool like the people. Here we can see the slyness of the demons, as they falsify and darken the Wisdom. With the rings and circles in previous times, the Kabbalah was suggested. Pentagrams and heptagrams are related to the blended Kabbalah which is discussed elsewhere.

Parts of the curious characters are old words and scripts in foreign languages that have been lost or are unknown. The devil brings these with honeyed words onto the path of people so that they lose sight of their goal. Mixed with the true Kabbalah, today's wisdom will become unrecognizable.

The devil mixes lies with the truth so that one cannot tell them apart. Only those who are enlightened by God and his holy angels can tell them apart. The worst is that the devil grants the small wishes of poor people so as to keep them in blindness. I gave examples of this in Book One.

Therefore, my son, turn your ears from all such atrocious books and masters. To give you a general rule to recognize such books: As soon as you see that a master or a book is careless and teaches damaging things—telling of things that are more bad than good—then you see the devil's art without any sacred wisdom.

I experienced this myself when I did Abramelin's work; all other sorcerer's magic disappeared and hid. At Abramelin's place, when I worked the things I studied with Rabbi Moses, I had no success. This was because the cheating devil was ashamed and hid from the sacred wisdom.

Thirdly, noting the days is condemned and forbidden except for special days mentioned by God. So ignore the calendar and all indications of heaven except for those in which the Kabbalah is clearly involved—this is because evil and cheating lies hidden within.

God's wisdom works every day, his grace is available every day, He helps every day, not only on the days that humanity have created. God has special days which need to be honored, as we shall hear in the following chapter.

Chapter Five

No special days for the sacred magic.

The sacred magic requires no special regards for times and dates except for those that have been revealed from the divine secrets by the good spirits.

In our true magic it is easy to find the right days. God mentioned them himself in his law. One day is not better than the other, but the Creator is pleased if we honor his days and do not choose them from our own will or from the advice of the devil.

We have from our forefathers all the Sabbaths, Passover, the feast of the Tabernacles—one on the 15th of the first month, the other on the 15th of the seventh month of the Jewish calendar. The other holidays are in the Tora, especially the third book, the twenty-third chapter.

Nowadays our misery and bondage is great; our enemies obstruct us from doing all the right duties to God. Even so, God in his mercy watches us and reveals through his holy spirits. This is told about in the third vision by his angel.

Everyone can hold the holidays of Adonai—whether circumcised or not, whether Jewish, pagan, or Muslim—because Adonai grants all of them his mercy. If the holidays are not held, this is known by God and the spirits who will punish rather than give wisdom.

All pious people know how to behave in ways that are correct for their place. If Jewish, Christian, pagan, or Muslim do not know what is correct, they can ask our scholars or rabbis—they give advice and people must follow whether or not it is their religious belief. God gave the explicit order to Moses and subsequent scholars and rabbis—through his holy Angel.

Sacrifices or elaborate ceremonies are unnecessary; all that God asks for is a humble and pious life.

It is not necessary to begin on the day after Passover, but there are many reasons why it is the most convenient time. This is because the end of the work periods will occur on the first day of the ceremonies of the Tabernacles, this is why our forefathers considered it as the best time. It is better to follow my advice than to stubbornly make one's own time, which could be the dates of the pagans.

We will not give respect to the elements or the stars, but will consider solely the needs of the person who is doing the work, his relationship with God. This is more important than the dates, the elements, or the stars. This is an important point, read it with care.

It is true that elements and stars have power—they make days different. These differences do not appear in spiritual and supernatural things but only in earthly and natural occurrences. This error causes me to write a special chapter to demonstrate these faults and how to avoid them.

Chapter Six

The planetary hours and how most astrologers are in error.

Astrologers are right, the effect of the stars causes different things to happen at different times. But this is true only for earthly, practical matters, because there are natural powers in the elements.

That the stars—and natural creatures—can rule over kings and supernatural matters cannot happen, and will not happen, because the spirits reign through the organization and disposition of God and the heavens.

Why do you want to question the stars, the sun, and the moon, when you can talk with Angels and the good spirits? That is like asking wild game for permission to hunt.

Oh, blind fools who select with great difficulty the wrong days, and then break them down further into hours and minutes! Yes, the fools say that the planets have hours—what sort of animal is that? The fools look at their books, every day is given to another planet—oh, how many planets, oh, what a nice order!

Oh, you fools and idolaters! What is the use of such divisions into hours? The fools answer that they tell of luck and misfortune. This is not true, it is a lie. But, in part, I have to admit that they can change the weather.

Please tell me how to divide the planetary hours.

I begin the first hour of the day with the planet that rules that day: [for example,] on Sunday, the sun, on Monday, the moon. Then, I divide the length of the day into twelve even parts—these are the hours. And I give each hour a planet in the right order. I do the same for the night. There are long and short days. For example, on a Sunday the sun rises at 7 and sets at 5 o'clock. I divide these 10 hours into the 12, so I get 50 minutes for each planetary hour of the day.

Following the same the rule, the first "hour" of 50 minutes is the Sun; the second, Venus; the third, Mercury; the fourth, the Moon; the fifth, Saturn; the sixth, Jupiter; the seventh, Mars; the eighth, the Sun; the ninth, Venus; the tenth, Mercury; the eleventh, the Moon; the twelfth, Saturn—and so the day ends. Now the night is 14 hours long, each planetary hour is 70 minutes and the planetary hours continue as before. The first, Jupiter; the second, Mars—until the Moon, which brings us to the first hour of Monday.

Now tell me, does the Moon rise every Monday morning and then set together with the Sun? Why does the Christian second day of the week, or the Jewish third day, belong to the Moon? Is it just because of the day's name? It is the only answer. What power has the word, "Moon"? I don't know, you fool, so keep quiet! That is what all the calculations for the planets, hours, and days are like!

Now listen, I will tell you—when has the Moon the most power over the elements? When it is above, or below your horizon? You must admit it is strongest when it is above, because below it doesn't work in your case—then, it works for another.

And, you fool, you very often name a day, a night, or hour after a planet that never even appears above the horizon on that day, that night or that hour.

Abramelin was excellent in understanding natural things. He, as well as Abimelech, taught what I have written.

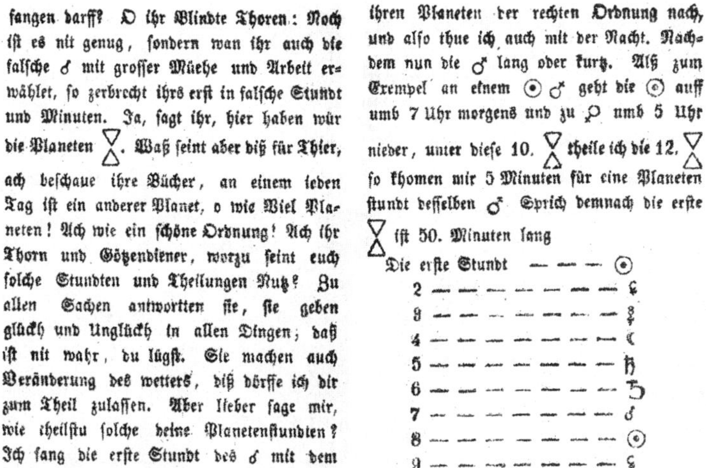
fangen darff? O ihr Blindte Thoren: Noch ist es nit genug, sondern wan ihr auch die falsche ♂ mit grosser Müehe und Arbeit erwählet, so zerbrecht ihrs erst in falsche Stundt und Minuten. Ja, sagt ihr, hier haben wür die Planeten ⧗. Waß seint aber diß für Thier, ach beschaue ihre Bücher, an einem ieden Tag ist ein anderer Planet, o wie Viel Planeten! Ach wie ein schöne Ordnung! Ach ihr Thorn und Götzendiener, worzu seint euch solche Stundten und Theilungen Nutz? Zu allen Sachen antwortten sie, sie geben glückh und Unglückh in allen Dingen; daß ist nit wahr, du lügst. Sie machen auch Veränderung des wetters, diß dörffe ich dir zum Theil zulassen. Aber lieber sage mir, wie theilstu solche deine Planetenstundten? Ich fang die erste Stundt des ♂ mit dem Planeten an, der demselben ♂ vorgesetzt ist, alß dem Sontag die ☉ dem Montag den ☾ und theille desselben Tags Länge in 12 gleiche Theil, die nene ich ⧗en und gib ieglicher ⧗ ihren Planeten der rechten Ordnung nach, und also thue ich auch mit der Nacht. Nachdem nun die ♂ lang oder kurtz. Alß zum Exempel an einem ☉ ♂ geht die ☉ auff umb 7 Uhr morgens und zu ♀ umb 5 Uhr nieder, unter diese 10. ⧗ theile ich die 12. ⧗ so khomen mir 5 Minuten für eine Planeten stundt desselben ♂ Sprich demnach die erste ⧗ ist 50. Minuten lang

Die erste Stundt — — — ☉
2 — — — — — — — ♀
3 — — — — — — — ☿
4 — — — — — — — ☾
5 — — — — — — — ♄
6 — — — — — — — ♃
7 — — — — — — — ♂
8 — — — — — — — ☉
9 — — — — — — — ♀
10 — — — — — — — ☿
11 — — — — — — — ☾
12 — — — — — — — ♄

Und also ist der ♂ geendet.

Fig. 15. Abraham's astrology lesson. From Peter Hammer's edition.

Draw your own stars and see if there is more reason than yours for determining the planetary days and hours when the planets work their power on the Earth.

Chapter Seven

What one should do in the first six months when learning this art.

Now we come to the beginning of the negotiation and the proper arrangement for the meeting. This material is important and dangerous so I want to avoid all possible by-ways and come straight to the point.

On the first morning after Passover, clean your body and put on new clothes. About half an hour before sunrise, go into your prayer room, open the window that faces east, and fall to your knees in front of the altar. Facing the window, pray sincerely in the name of Adonai, thank him for all the mercy that he granted you from your childhood. Humble yourself through confession, ask him to continue to give you his grace and that he will send you his holy Angel, who will protect and guide you so that you do not unconsciously fall into sin.

This was the first morning prayer; continue this for the full half year. But, my son, you will ask me, "Father, why don't you write out for me the form and words of the prayer—how I should say and pray—because I am not smart enough to do it for myself." My son, listen: If you cannot pray, you will have problems, so do not even try to begin this negotiation. Why should God give you Wisdom and Grace if you cannot pray? The prayer should, and must, come from your heart. Do not repeat the prayer without thought, devotion, and understanding, or read it like the godless do. Prayers must come from the whole heart with attention and understanding.

That is why, my son, I have not given you the form of the prayer. This is so you will not try to copy it. You must learn to pray and call to Adonai by yourself. You have all the holy writings full of powerful prayers and praises, from these study and learn to pray, there is no lack of guidance. At first, even if your prayers are simple and weak it does not matter; the important thing is that your heart is directed toward God. God will inflame you with his Holy Spirit who, in time, will advise you and grant you greater skill to ask and pray.

After the prayers, close the window, leave the room, and shut the door so that no one can enter and do not return until sunset. After sunset, repeat your morning prayer. During that day, and in the next days do as I suggest.

The Prayer Room

In the eleventh chapter, I shall give you details about the prayer room. It needs to be cleaned and besmoked and the bed needs to have clean bedding; generally, all beds should be clean and tidy; Adonai has a repugnance for all uncleanliness.

Your bedroom and living room should be near the prayer room. No one should sleep in your bed except your wife. When she has her monthly period, she should not sleep in the bed or enter the prayer room. On the day before the Sabbath, bedding and bed linen should be changed. Besmoke the room and let no child or animal live in it, so that the room will be clean.

Sex and Abstinence

The first year of marriage is especially blessed by Adonai and if you can start in that year it is good and appropriate. If that is not possible, do not concern yourself about your wife. It is only important that she should not interfere with your work because of arguments or uncleanness. You may have sex so as to conceive children, but only in your bed and with the fear of God. You should flee from all sexual indecency and promiscuity, because this is repugnant to Adonai.

Yes, it is best if you can completely avoid all female discussions and companionship. If you should have children, send them away before you start. Do not let them live in the house; the exceptions are the firstborn and the breast-feeding baby.

Managing Daily Life

Now consider your position. Are you are independent? Refrain, as far as possible, from all business, all groups, and all conversations. Were you angry, willful, cheeky, greedy, proud, prickly, sloppy? Let go of all obligations. Live quietly and simply in the fear of God. Remember that this is an important point. This is why Abraham, Jacob, Moses, David, Elijah, Christ, John, Abramelin, and all wise men took themselves to the hermitages and the desert and lived a solitary life until they acquired the wisdom.

Where there are people, there is trouble and sin. This insults the spirits of God, who stay away, and so the doors to wisdom remain closed. So, as far as possible, flee from all company and seek solitude until God has given you his blessings.

A free man who is a servant to a master cannot use every opportunity because he needs to work. Such a man needs to take care that he prays properly and practices sufficient abstinence. He should arrange his circumstances to allow for solitude. He should be loyal, cooperative, and hard-working as if he was responsible to God. Generally, he should avoid the company of people and situations that could cause anger. If curious people ask for information, be kind and brief in your replies. If you need to talk to people on behalf of your master or for your own business, keep the conversation clear and short. A servant or indentured laborer will find it hard to fulfill all these requirements, so it is better to let the matter rest.

In particular, buying and selling—which often cause sin—should be avoided. Rather accept a loss than get yourself involved in complex matters.

Daily, you should set aside two hours—one in the morning and one in the afternoon—in which you study and read Holy Scripture, the Talmud, and related books. In time—and from day to day—you will become more pious, learn to pray better, and to recognize God more readily. Further activities will be set out in the tenth chapter.

Eating, Drinking, and Sleeping

Eat and drink little—avoid farmer's feasts and big, elaborate meals. Eat what God provides alone in your room or with your wife—eat with love and pleasure. Thank Adonai for his kindness. Take care not to sleep during the day, but you can rest after the morning prayer for a short while. It is better to do good works than to be lazy.

Clothing and Servants

Your children should be neat and clean, moderate and honest—as is usual in the place where you live. You, your wife, and family should avoid all arrogance.

Change your clothing on the Sabbath. Have at least two sets of clothes. Wear one one week and the other the next week. Besmoke your clothes before you wear them.

It is better to have few servants in the house. If you have a servant, be careful that he is honest and quiet, that he causes no disturbances, that he wears neat and tidy clothes, and that he is not adulterous. He should not enter your living room. Of course, no one is allowed to enter your prayer room.

These are the things that the student should do. At all times have the books of the law in front of you as the guides to your journey though life—do this as well as you can. Continue this sort of life with respect for the Sabbath until the feast of the Tabernacles. You should celebrate this feast with intense prayers as far as circumstances allow in your community.

All the feast days and traditions that have been given us by our fathers should be celebrated. Your hands should give alms to everyone and you should do good works—as far as God's blessing allows—but don't talk about it.

If God bothers or tests you with sickness during the half year to the extent that you do not have the strength to take yourself into your prayer room, do not let this be a reason to stop the work. Hold to the rules as far as possible, pray in bed, and ask God for health so that you can continue and complete your duty.

If the sickness does not improve for the remainder of the half year or if the sickness occurs in the second or third six-month period, consider this as a sign that it is God's will that you do not learn the sacred wisdom for the time being. Humble yourself and do not try to continue.

Chapter Eight

What should be done in the second half year.

The day after Tabernacles, pray and do as follows:

Before you go to the prayer room for morning and evening prayer wash your hands and face with clean water. Pray with more intensity and devotion—ask like a beggar. Do this and Adonai may order his Angel to lead you on the right path—the path of wisdom and understanding. The more time you spend with Holy Scripture, the more the holy writings will flow into your heart with wisdom and understanding.

Sleeping with your wife is no problem. Wash yourself before the Sabbath. Your wife should do the same. Live as I said before. Lengthen the time for study and prayer as much as possible. Eat, drink, and sleep as I said above.

From the first day before the Sabbath feast of the Tabernacles until Passover, fast as in our tradition. Change your clothes before the feast of the Tabernacles.

Remember that the Sabbath for Jews is Saturday. For Christians, the Sabbath is on Sunday—this has been the practice since the old days.

Chapter Nine

How to behave in the third and final half year.

This begins on the first day after Passover and runs until the end feast of the Tabernacles. Morning, noon, and night, wash your hands, face, and feet before you go to the prayer room. Praise Adonai, make a confession, and then pray to Adonai with great ardor. Ask him to show his mercy, so that he will give you the honor of company with the holy angels. And that they will grant and reveal the hidden wisdom to reign over the unredeemed spirits and all creatures. As the Holy Spirit, gives you inspiration, pray with these and more words.

Do the same before lunch so over the half year you will pray three times a day in front of the altar. Light the incense on the altar, and at the end of the prayer call on the holy angels to carry your smoke and prayers to the face of God and that the holy angels will beg on your behalf and that they will be consistent in their help for all you do.

During this half year, you should act as you did before. The exception remains works of charity.

Spend your time in the words and the law of Adonai so that your eyes will be opened to things that you have not seen, thought, or realized before.

In drink and food you should copy Daniel the prophet, and live on vegetables and water. Also, fast on the eve of the Sabbath. Wash your whole body three times a week—on the second, fourth, and sixth day. Your wife should behave as in the previous half year. Your clothing, change as before . . . add to it a long, snow-white dress—made from wool or linen—for use in the prayer room.

Carry a special incense tray for the burning and cooled coals when you go to and from the prayer room. The incense burner should remain in the prayer room. The coals you remove should—especially in the first half year—be buried in a clean spot in the garden or a similar location.

It is important that, if you are a bonded laborer, you still keep to these rules. So should everyone consider their life's position before they start the work.

Carry these things on until the end of the feast of the Tabernacles.

Chapter Ten

The arts a person can study, practice, and do, which will not hinder the work.

It is best to go to the wilderness and be in solitude until the time is over and the work completed—in the same way that the holy forefathers did. This may be almost impossible; everybody needs to live in the time and with people. If it is not possible to go to the wilderness, then avoid company and business dealings. Because of duty and profession, this is impossible for many people. So I will briefly mention everything that does not hinder the work.

All medicines that can improve the life and health of your neighbor and all arts that stem from this have preference and freedom because they are indispensable. Second, the whole and the blended Kabbala, the sister of Wisdom, helps rather than hinders. Third, all business done for love and charity for your neighbor. It is good to reduce conflict, war, and hatred. To help depressed people. You can do work that is honest and according to the law. Do not leave out the things you must do to further this work. Fourth, you can occasionally practice the so-called liberal arts, but take care not to misuse such arts, particularly astrology.

Especially, flee and avoid all arts that are even close to foreign magic and sorcery—even if they appear justified or holy—because God and Belial should not be mixed together. God wants to be God alone, and have the honor that is due to him—and to no other—forever. All this is allowed only in the first year, and then only in moderation.

In the third half year, you should avoid all worldly things. Spend your time on godly and spiritual things if you want to be involved in the sacred wisdom and spiritual community.

You may walk in a garden for relaxation, but do no work. Between the flowers and fruit you can mediate on the greatness of God. Give up everything except things for your involvement in things of the soul and of God. Let all other things go, be happy and thank God when you find one, two, or three hours to practice the holy law and to learn from the holy books—this will be useful. The less you learn, the smarter and smarter you will become. It is sufficient that you do not fall asleep when praying. It is necessary that you do not fail in the Work through sloppiness or laziness.

Chapter Eleven

How to choose the location to call all the spirits. How to prepare the accessories.

Make the arrangements before Passover so that you can start as soon as it is over. In the wilderness it is easy to find a location. Here, in the middle of a level place, erect an altar. Cover it with a roof of branches and leaves to protect the area from rain. Around the altar there should be an area seven feet wide planted with beautiful and fragrant flowers. The location should be divided into two. First, the altar with its temple and living room and second, the entrance area.

In a town or in houses make note of the following: The prayer room should have at least two windows—one facing the rising sun, the other facing the setting sun, next to a door or an opening, through which the demons can be seen—demons who cannot, or should not, appear in the prayer room. Attached to my prayer room, I had an open arbor that faced the midnight hour. I had two windows built into the prayer room and these together with the door where always open when the demons where called. Through the door and the windows I had a clear view of the arbor and could control the demons.

The prayer room should be square, without additional corners, swept clean, and have a clean wooden floor. Clearly, the room should look like a room for praise and prayer, not like a dog's house or a pig sty.

The place for the spirits should be open, or have many windows. Cover the floor with an even layer of clean sand, two or three fingers deep.

The altar should stand in the middle of the space and the sides should face the four corners of the world. The altar's height and size can be whatever you want—it is best if it is proportionate to your person. It should be built of uncut stones. If made of wood, it should be made of elder or pine. Over it should be a lamp made of gold, silver, or glass, filled with olive oil. This should be lit during the incensing and extinguished afterwards. On the altar, place an attractive metal incense burner made from bronze or silver—if you can afford it—it should remain in place until the work is completed . . . if the altar is in the house. If the altar is outside, these things cannot happen because you will have to move about as occasions require. Everything can be placed inside the wooden altar as in a cupboard.

The two robes—one a long, snow-white shirt or coat, made from pure wool or linen that has not been washed, the second from white, yellow, or rose-colored silk—should not go past the knee, and should have short sleeves. There is no rule about these clothes—the simpler the better. Fasten the robe firmly about you with a neat tie in the same color as the robe.

On your head you should have a hair band of golden-colored silk; fasten onto it the highest names of Adonai cut from thin metal. Similar to the head band of Aaron. At minimum, the letters can be written onto the band with golden letters.

The Preparation of the Oil and Incense

Take one part of the best myrrh, half a part of cinnamon, one part of cassia, one part galanga root, and a quarter of the combined total weight of good, fresh olive oil. Make these into an ointment or oil as is done by the chemists. Keep it in a clean

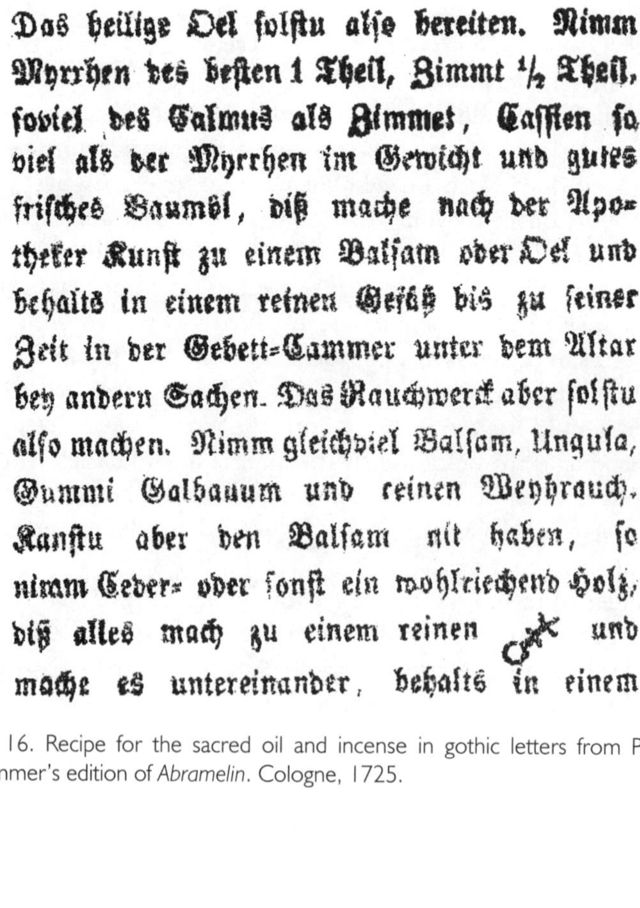
Das heilige Oel solstu also bereiten. Nimm
Myrrhen des besten 1 Theil, Zimmt ½ Theil,
soviel des Calmus als Zimmet, Cassien so
viel als der Myrrhen im Gewicht und gutes
frisches Baumöl, diß mache nach der Apo-
theker Kunst zu einem Balsam oder Oel und
behalts in einem reinen Gefäß bis zu seiner
Zeit in der Gebett-Cammer unter dem Altar
bey andern Sachen. Das Rauchwerck aber solstu
also machen. Nimm gleichviel Balsam, Ungula,
Gummi Galbanum und reinen Weyhrauch.
Kanstu aber den Balsam nit haben, so
nimm Ceder- oder sonst ein wohlriechend Holz,
diß alles mach zu einem reinen und
mache es untereinander, behalts in einem

Fig. 16. Recipe for the sacred oil and incense in gothic letters from Peter Hammer's edition of *Abramelin*. Cologne, 1725.

container until you need it. Put the container together with the other accessories in the cupboard under the altar.

Take equal amounts of balm, gummy galbanum, and pure storax. If you cannot get balm, use cedar or aloe, or other pleasantly-smelling woods. Mix the ingredients together as a powder. Keep it in a clean container. A lot will be needed, so make it every week before the Sabbath. Take it into the prayer room in the evening and put it together with the other accessories under the altar.

You also need a smooth, clean twig, from an almond tree, about a finger thick, reaching from your finger tip to your elbow. Keep it with the other accessories.

Before the start of the feast and the work, take the clean accessories into the prayer room.

Chapter Twelve

How the person or magus should consecrate himself, the prayer room, and its accessories.

The work is divided into sections, times, and pieces. In the same way, there needs to be differences in the consecration we give to the different parts.

In the first two half years you need only do what is described in the seventh and eighth chapters. To this, in the first half year—on every Sabbath—you need to offer incense morning and evening.

In the third half year—the final period—do not get frightened, be diligent, and hardworking. If you have followed my

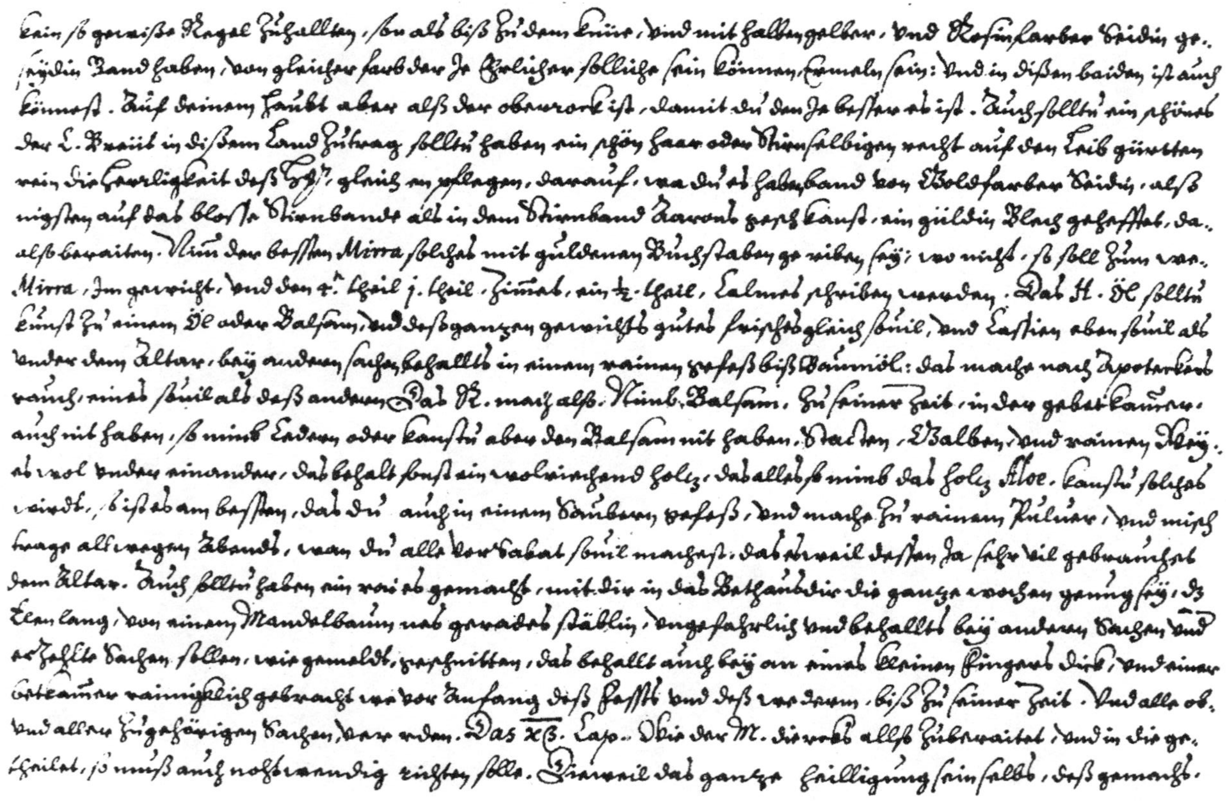

Fig. 17. A page from the encoded MS in the Wolfenbüttel library, containing the recipes for making the sacred oil and incense. This page is a good example of the difficulties created by abbreviations and the script. In the third segment of line twelve is the word Galben (gummy galbanum, or *ferula galbaniflua*). The initial capital in the recipe, a "G", is in German script; it looks like an "H" or a "B." This "G" is used as the abbreviation for God throughout the MS.

teachings, made sincere and ardent prayers to God, then there is no doubt that everything will be easy. Your own intellect and heart will tell you and show you how you should act and behave. Although invisible, your Guardian Angel is around you and leads your heart so that it cannot fail or make mistakes. After the feast of Passover, at the start of the next day, do carefully what is mentioned in the first chapter and also do the following things:

Take off your shoes when you go to the prayer room in the morning. Shut the door after you enter. Walking with bare feet, open the eastern and western windows. Place the burning coals into the incense burner and light the lamp. Then take both robes, the headband, and the little stick. Place all of these onto the altar, take the holy oil in your left hand and throw incense on the coals. Fall to your knees and pray ardently to Adonai.

> *Adonai, Adonai my God, merciful and gracious, patient, faithful, and benevolent. You have proved your grace for a thousand generations, and forgive misdeeds, violations, and sins, and in front of you no one is guilty. You retaliate the misdeeds of forefathers to the third and fourth generations. I recognize my worthlessness. I am not worthy to stand before your holy face, and even less to ask your grace and blessings for the smallest gift. But Adonai, my, Adonai, our alliance is great and the springs of your goodness so overflowing that you give to people who are ashamed of their sins and cannot drink from the spring of your goodness. You loudly invite them to take what you can offer. So Adonai, my God, give me mercy and take from me all my excesses, wash from me all my uncleanliness and sins. Renew my spirit and strengthen it so that it can be strong so that I can understand the secrets of your grace and the treasures of your knowledge.*

> *Consecrate me through this oil of consecration with which you healed all the prophets, clean me and all these accessories with it. Properly cleanse and heal me so that I will be dignified to have the company of the holy angels, the sacred wisdom, and the might that you alone have given your initiated over the good and unredeemed spirits. Amen.*

I used this prayer in my initiation. You do not have to repeat it like a parrot, suffice that I have given you the form and the outline. You have to find the inspiration to pray from your heart, otherwise the work would be useless. So, my son, exercise diligently upon the word of God and the laws of Adonai, so that his spirit lights your heart and awakens it to fervent prayer.

When you have finished this prayer, stand up and spread a little of the oil onto the center of your head. Now dip your finger into the oil, pass your fingers along the four corners of the altar, touch both the robes, the tie, the headband and the stick on both ends.

Go also to both the windows and doors of the prayer room and touch the top sill with the oil on your finger. Return to the altar and write clearly on each of the four sides—with the holy oil on your finger—the clear words:

> *In those places where the memory of my name is grounded, there shall I come to you and bless you.*

In the wilderness, use the sacred oil to touch the four corner posts—whether these hold up the roof of the prayer house or the roof over the altar. The consecration is now complete. Put on the white shirt or robe, put all the other things in the altar. Place yourself on your knees and organize your prayer as

I have described in the first chapter. Do all things as I have suggested in that chapter.

Make note not to carry any of the consecrated accessories out of the prayer room: they must stay there until the completion of the Work. From now on, you also must enter the prayer room—and do God's duty—only in bare feet.

Chapter Thirteen

How the good spirits should be called.

Now it comes to the point. Now you will see if you have sincerely followed my instructions and if you have faithfully completed your duty to Adonai, your God.

After the feast of the Tabernacles at the end of the last half year, get up early in the morning and do not wash yourself, do not dress in the usual robes, but wear a sack or mourning clothes, go barefoot into the prayer room. Go to the incense burner and remove some ashes, sprinkle them on your head. Then light the lamp, incense burner, open the windows, and return to the door. Then fall down onto your knees and bow down and humble yourself before God and his hosts. Cry out with your whole soul that he, Adonai, will hear your pleas and your prayers and grant you the ability to visualize his holy angels. And that the chosen spirits of Adonai will grace you with their companionship. All this you can better accomplish from your own heart than I can describe on these pages.

So you should continue in your prayers until the sun sets. Do not leave the prayer room. Do not let the lamp or incense burner go out. Fast the whole day. Organize things beforehand so that no one needs to talk to you. After sunset and the day of prayers, leave the prayer room. Leave all the windows open and the lamps lit. Break your fast with nothing except bread and water. Then lie down in your sleeping room and face the door. During this time, do not touch your wife; live away from her.

During these days thoroughly and exactly carry out the ceremony—three days for calling the good spirits and then the three days for calling the unredeemed spirits.

Oh, my son, praise and thank the name of God. Do not be hindered by what you may see or hear. Oh, my son, what do you think I mean when I say "see or hear"? I want to make this clear and so will not make fun of the matter. On the first day, before noon—as soon as your ardent prayers fly flaming from your heart and rise through the clouds towards the face of God—you will perceive a supernatural clarity throughout the prayer room and sense a delightful aroma around you. This should give you, in your soul, such refreshment and comfort that you will always continue to praise Adonai for the experience. Do not stop praying, but strengthen your prayers with unquestioning optimism. Continue doing this also on the second day.

On the second morning, you need to be prepared to follow the advice that the Angel gives to you. Go early into the prayer room, place the burning coals and incense into the burner. Relight the lamp if it has gone out. Wear the same clothes as on the previous day. Pray as on the previous morning: in the morning, at noon, and at night for one hour. Eat as I have written before and go to sleep.

On the third day, after you have carefully washed your whole body, go dressed but barefoot into the prayer room. Supernatural clarity will still fill the room. If necessary, relight the incense and lamp. Then, change into your white robe and bow down before the altar and start to thank Adonai, the highest God, for all his good works, especially for giving you the blessing and honor of so precious a gift. Thank the holy angels and the good spirits for shining their light on you even though you are an unclean human and unworthy of the honor.

Finally, turn your prayer from God to your Holy Guardian Angel. Plead and beg that in future—and for the rest of your life—he will not remove his guardianship from you. Ask that he will guide and control you on all the roads and byways of Adonai. Ask him especially to stand by you in this work of sacred wisdom and magic and advise you, so that you can overcome, tame, and urge the unredeemed spirits—for the praise of Adonai and the benefit of all creation.

My son, you will see how well you have done over the eighteen months, when your Guardian Angel—the chosen Angel of Adonai, a delightful, good Angel—appears before you in its radiance and speaks to you in such friendly and sweet words, beyond what any human tongue could express.

The Guardian Angel will remind you what he has done for you and how you have insulted him in the past. He will tell you how you please him in the future. He will also explain to you about what is the true wisdom, where it comes from, if—and how—you fail in your work, what you lack, how you should behave to control the unredeemed spirits, and how to achieve all you desire. You will be overcome with so much friendliness that my guidance will seem like nothing.

My son, I shall now cease with my description of your Guardian Angel—I have passed you onto a teacher who will never let you err. Take care that on this, the third day, you remain in sincere discussion with your Guardian Angel. After sunset, make the evening prayer with the usual incense. Thank God and your Guardian Angel for not leaving you. After this prayer, you will notice that the shining light disappears. Leave the prayer room, lock the door, but leave the windows open and the lamp lit. Go into your living room and relax. Eat what is needed and sleep until the following morning.

Chapter Fourteen

How the unredeemed spirits can be called and overcome.

The following lessons are unnecessary because it is what your Angel has told you. But there are some points I want to tell you about.

After you have rested for the night, stand up before sunlight, wash your whole body, light the charcoal and the lamp. Put on your white robe, over that wear your silk robe, wear the belt and put on your headband. Place the wand on the altar and put incense on the charcoal. Kneel down and pray to Adonai and your Guardian Angel in the usual way. Then, take your wand into your right hand and beg God that he give you the same power that he gave Moses, Aaron, and Elijah.

Move around the altar so that you face the arbor. If you are in the wilderness, under the open sky, face the sunset. Start to call the four spirit kings. The way to do this will have been given to you by your Guardian Angel. It is necessary to speak from the heart, not just to recite from the mouth. Remember that the unredeemed spirits are harder to call than the good. The good appear as soon as they they perceive a good person, while the demons flee. So be fearful of God, and pious.

No spirit can recognize your thoughts before you act them out. So when you call the spirits, call them with an open mind, with all your wisdom and insight. To call spirits by reading out an unfamiliar script will make the spirits regard you as unwise—and so they will be even more stubborn and headstrong.

Do the unredeemed spirits come to every call? Even without calling, there are often many around you but they only show themselves when you are skilled, pious, and courageous.

If they see you as a charlatan they depart quietly or capture you. Words from an unskilled person have no power because no spirit needs to obey the unskilled. The only power the unskilled have is to harm themselves.

The Call on the First Day

Before I go on, have the laws of Adonai and the teachings of your Angel before your eyes. Do not do anything against them, even in the smallest way. The call should be in the common language, or mother tongue. Do not use the high names of God against unredeemed Spirits. It would be the wrong use and a cruelty in the eyes of God.

Your Angel will only let you use these three Holy names—Jehovah, Adonai, Zabaoth. You call the spirits through the respect and obedience that is due to the holy forefathers. You describe to them their situation, their fall before God, and their judgment. You tell them their responsibilities and their duty.

From time to time, the unredeemed spirits have been controlled and overcome by the angels, the holy and the wise—this you can study from the holy books during the eighteen months. Threaten them that you will call down upon them the force of the holy angels and archangels if they are disobedient.

Your Guardian Angel reminds you that your calls should done courageously, not fearfully, not defiantly or arrogantly—but gently. If the spirits do not respond quickly, do not get angry—you will only hurt yourself. Never look for them except when you feel confident and strong. Remind them to follow. Tell them who has your confidence and trust—the everlasting and living God.

Always order them to appear in the form your Guardian Angel suggests. Ask your Guardian Angel this in the evening because he knows your nature and knows which configuration you can withstand—whether or not this can be frightening, dangerous or seductive.

Seals, superstitious conjurations, signs, pentacles, and other godless atrocities are quite unnecessary, for with these the devil's magicians can overcome you. These are the coins with which bothersome Satan can buy you. Your insurance is the arm of the almighty God himself and the guidance of your Angel, so be confident and unworried. If you have followed the suggestions of your Angel, then—in a short time—the spirits will appear in the form suggested on the sand in the arbor.

The spirits on this first day are the four kings. There names are listed in the nineteenth chapter [see p. 119].

The Call on the Second Day

Complete the same prayers and ceremonies as you have done previously. Then repeat the preceding call to the four kings.

Remind the kings that they promised you that they would send you the submissive eight dukes. Then repeat the call again for all twelve. Soon, the eight dukes will appear in the shape that was demanded of each and—as in the following chapter—promise obedience.

The Call on the Third Day

Remind the eight dukes again of what they promised on the previous day. Now ask them to come again with their servants. The dukes will appear in the company of their invisible servants. Call on God for mercy and strength, and call on your Angel for advice and support.

Remember what your Angel has taught you and take the following [advice] with you.

Chapter Fifteen

What one should request from the spirits.

We divide the spirits into three parts and call them on three days. We want to call them to us in the right order so we can talk to them. The calls we make to them are similarly varied.

The Call on the First Day

On the first day, inform the four kings of the might and power with which you call them—from the might of God, who has the kings and all creation under his feet. Then say why they are called—not out of curiosity or because of malice, but to honor God and serve humanity.

At this point, you finally add your request; that when you call, no matter what the time and place, duty or work, whatever sign or word you use, they shall immediately appear and obey your request. And if they cannot appear the kings shall name and send others that are mighty and powerful enough to fulfill your request.

The kings should swear by the strict judgment of God and by the sword, punishment, and chastisement of the holy angels.

Finally, the kings will agree to obey and tell you the names of the dukes who are their replacements. Then the kings should swear to appear, as soon as you call, on the following morning. If they cannot come, they must send you their replacement dukes. For your insurance, go to the door or window of the arbor and with your right hand hold out the twig. Instead of speaking out the oath, each of the kings must touch the twig.

Calls for the Second Day

Repeat to the eight dukes your request. Remind them of their situation as you did for the kings. Also demand from Oriens, Paimon, Ariton and Amaimon that each of them give you the name of—and is responsible for—a servant spirit. You may now ask which spirits you want them to give you. With the guidiance of your Angel, you can select from the list in chapter 19 any or all of the spirits.

Write their names on unused paper and throw it out of the window to the dukes. Then take the oath from them in the same way you did from the kings—tell them that they will come next morning with the servant spirits [whose names] you have written on the paper.

Calls for the Third Day

After the eight dukes have appeared on the third day, call on Astaroth and his henchman to appear in the shape suggested by your Angel. You will see a whole division—or as many as you named on the paper—appear in all their shapes. Repeat the requests you made to the kings. Let them swear to keep the requests you made—as often as you call one of them by name—regardless of whether here or there.

Now, place on the threshold the signs that belong to Astaroth's administration—these are listed in chapter 20. If you do not want to speak to them, let them swear to you that as soon as you pick up one of the signs—or move it to another place—the spirit named within the sign will immediately do what the sign commands and bring you further instructions.

If none is specially named, then all the spirits will be responsible to do the duty. If you make more signs in the future, they will need to follow your requests in the same way. After they have accepted the oath—which the duke can take for them—remove the signs from the door.

Call Magoth, Asmodeus, and lastly, Beelzebub. Call them and treat them as you did Astaroth. Organize all the signs on which they have sworn so you can see where they belong or what their function is. Then call Astaroth and Asmodeus together with their shared spirits. Put out their signs and let them swear on them. Similarly, call Asmodeus and Magoth together with their servants and let them swear on their signs in the same way. Do the same for all those that share the same sign.

Continue in this manner with the other dukes. First, call all four at the same time with their servants, then Amaymon and Ariton together. Finally, call each of them separately—as previously stated. When you have picked up all the signs, demand of each of them your servant spirit. Let them tell you his name, write this down together with the time during which he should serve you.

Then, lay in front of them the signs of the fifth chapter, and let them swear on the signs. Then have them swear that during the six hours of their duty they will be busy and proper in their work and that they shall not lie and be deceptive. If you lend or give a spirit server to another person, the spirit should serve that person as he would serve you; God in his judgment has ordered and decreed this. Do these ceremonies with all the dukes, until all your signs are used. Get all of them—including your four server spirits—to swear.

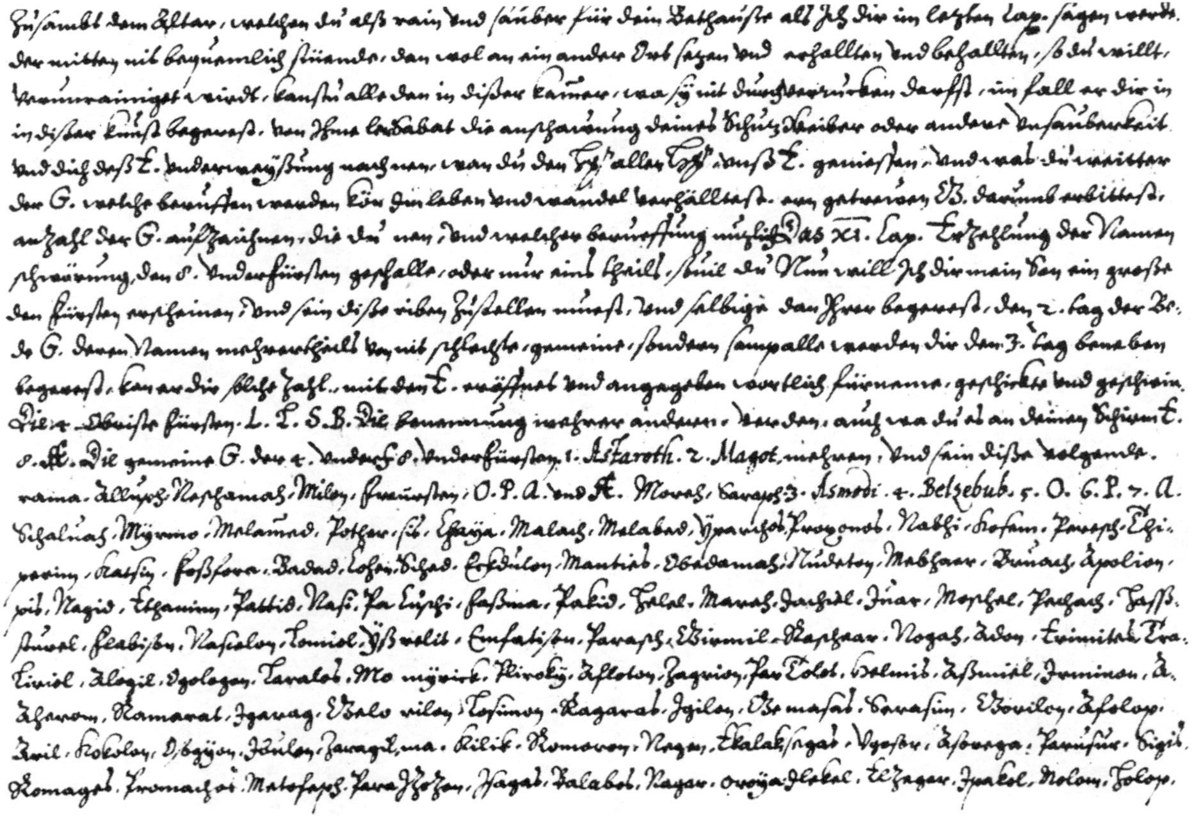

Fig. 18. Another page from the encoded Wolfenbüttel MS. About half way down the list of spirit names commences.

Chapter Sixteen

How to retire the spirits.

To have the spirits retire on the third and following days is easy because they prefer to be away from the presence of a pious man.

When you have finished with the spirits and have accepted their oath, speak to them. Tell them that—for the present—they should return to their realm but they need to remember their oath and if called are to appear immediately or be prepared to be punished.

So, on the third day, retire the dukes and their henchmen. Also, tell your servant spirits to retire but tell them that the one who remains and the others need to be careful to come at their time—the four will retire on their own at the passing of every six hours.

Chapter Seventeen

How to answer questions and how to deal with requests.

The devil will not forget to try to lead you from the way by some method—remain firm and confident. If he should play at being wild, remain firm and confident. If he plays at being humble, do not be rude. Be moderate in your behavior. If he requests or asks you things answer in the way your Angel inspires you.

Realize that the four kings will set upon you and interrogate you, asking who gave you the power to be so cheeky and bold as to call them—because you know how powerful they are and how sinful you are.

They will list for you all your sins. They will particularly try to dispute your belief in God. If you are Jewish, they will say that your belief in God has been cast aside and that you don't follow his law you and that you deal with idols, etc.

If you are a pagan, they will set on you and interrogate you about what you have to do with God and what you have to do with him—as you do not know him.

If you are a Christian, they will ask what you are doing with Jewish ceremonies—why do you not obey the orders and laws of your religion?

Do not let any of this lead you astray. Give brief and clear answers. Question them, ask them why they have not asked if the true God, the creator of heaven and earth, placed them at your feet even if you are a sinner—because he removed your sins. And you—no matter what your religion—recognize him as the only God on Earth and obey him in might, power, and strength—and you acknowledge only God.

With an answer like this, they will change their tune and ask you if they may serve you—and if you could serve them and maybe obey them.

Here you have your Angel's answer: that Adonai created, condemned and punished them to be servants—he did not do this to you.

They will then ask you for another person's soul, body, or organ.

You will then reply to them that none of this is in your control—rather that it is all a matter for God. If there is to be any responsibility for a sacrifice, it is to God and not to them.

Further, they will say that you are not allowed to teach other people about this wisdom, so that nobody else can make similar demands on them. And that you have the duty to teach and praise the wonder of God, instruct your neighbors in, and spread the wisdom of God. At a minimum they will ask you not to hinder or damage their slaves and wizards. You will need to pursue the enemies of God and to suppress their evil and to defend and protect your friends who have been insulted or damaged.

In this, and similar ways, they will pressure you to agree to some form of contract. Even the servant spirits will seek your promise not to lend them or to give them to other people.

Guard against every suggestion of a promise. Answer that every pious man needs to serve other pious people with all his possessions—which includes them.

When they see that there is no hope and that their requests are useless, they will surrender and even plead with you that you should not be too severe or difficult in your demands.

Answer that if they are obedient, friendly, and willing, then your Angel—who will always follow—will, perhaps, be more gentle and merciful.

Chapter Eighteen

Other things one should do regarding the spirits.

In the last four chapters, you heard how to request things from and how to control the unredeemed spirits—also how to send them away and answer them. In the eighteen months you have learned enough so that you do not need to be told anymore—you are their lord, not their servant.

But as you are their lord, not their God, always seem confident—because you are not dealing with people but with unredeemed spirits who know more than they can understand.

If they do not follow your request, consider whether it is their duty and position to help you—spirits have different abilities. Think about this before you attack them. If the lower spirits—and especially the servant spirits—lie to you or are unwilling, then call their superiors, both lower and higher. Remind them of their oath and punishment. When they see your conviction they will admit to their duty. If this does not work, call your Guardian Angel whose punishment they fear. Never become angry or impolite, never be afraid.

If they are insolent, appear in dreadful shapes, are unfriendly or wild, pay no attention. Show them the consecrated wand—knock two or three times on the altar with it—you will quieten and stop all their restlessness.

Be careful, after the spirits have gone, that you carry the incense out of the room into the arbor. Besmoke the area properly, otherwise the spirits can cause bad luck—or they may cause other people damage or unhappiness.

If the word squares in Book Four are sufficient for you, then, on the following day, clean up the sand and put it into running water on which there are no boats. If you want to research more and different things, then leave everything as described in previous chapters.

Keep the prayer room clean and tidy for your use. You may move the altar away from the middle of the room to a more convenient place. Keep this room free from menstruating women or other impurities, so that every Sabbath you can meet your Guardian Angel. If you ask Adonai, our faithful God, to teach you more—and if in your dealings and your life you follow the advice of your Guardian Angel—then you will be taught more by your Guardian Angel.

Chapter Nineteen

The names of spirits you can call and how to call them.

Now, my son, I want to give you an exact list of all the spirits that may be asked for on the second day. These are not bad spirits, but fast, distinguished, and clever. These have been mentioned many times by the angels.

If you ask your Guardian Angel, he can inform you of more.

The Four Kings

1. LUCIFER	2. LEVIATHAN
3. SATAN	4. BELIAL

The Eight Dukes

ASTAROTH	MAGOTH
ASMODI	BEELZEBUB
ORIENS	PAYMON
ARITON	AMAYMON

The servant spirits of Oriens, Paimon, Ariton, Amaymon

MOREH	SARAPH	PROXONOS	NABHI	KOSEM
PERESCH	THIRAMA	ALLUPH	NESCHAMAH	MILON
FRASIS	CHAYA	MALACH	MELABED	YPARCHOS
NUDETON	MEBHAER	BRUACH	APOLION	SCHALUAH
MYRMO	MELAMMED	POTHER	SCHED	ECKDULON
MANTIES	OBEDAMAH	JACHIEL	IUAR	MOSCHEL
PECHACH	HASPERIM	KATSIN	FOSFORA	BADAD
COHEN	CUSCHI	FASMA	PAKID	HELEL
MARA	RASCHEAR	NOGAH	ADON	ERIMITES
TRAPIS	NAGID	ETHANIM	PATTID	NASI
PARELIT	EMFATISON	PARASCH	GIRMIL	TOLET
HELMIS	ASSMIELH	IRMINON	ASTUREL	FLABISON

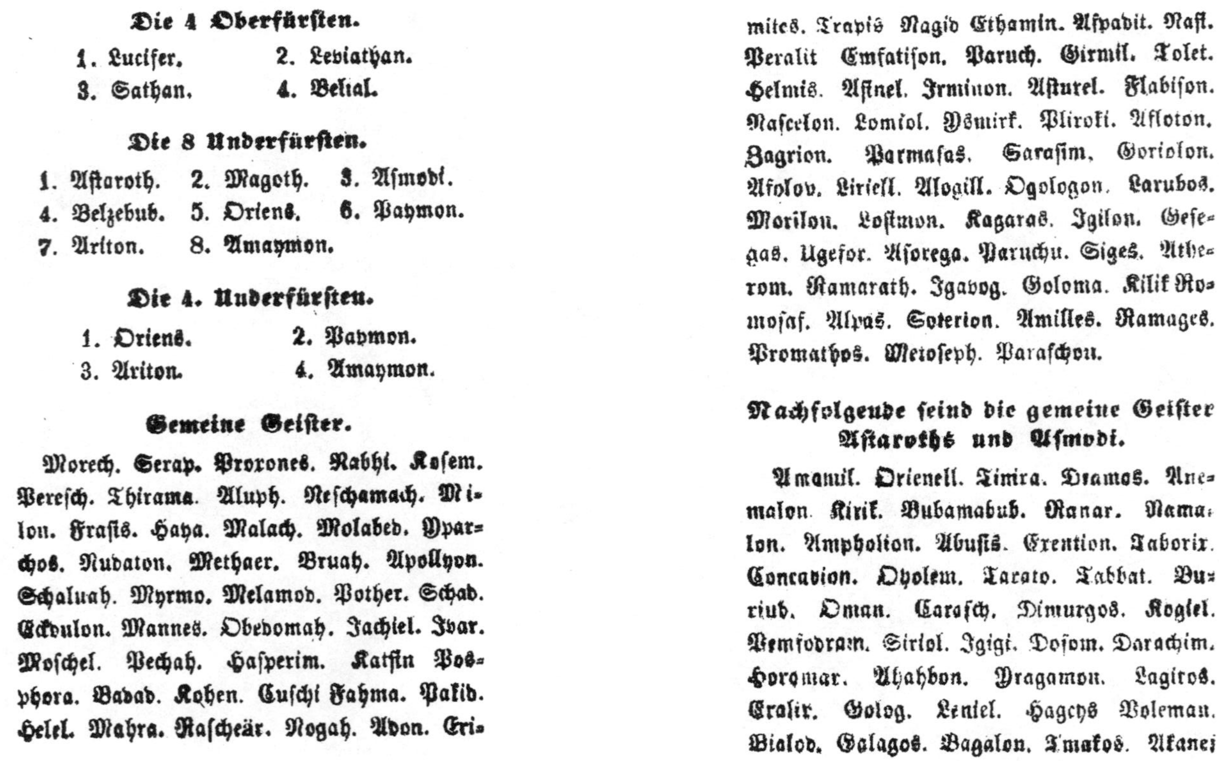

Die 4 Oberfürsten.

1. Lucifer. 2. Leviathan.
3. Sathan. 4. Belial.

Die 8 Underfürsten.

1. Astaroth. 2. Magoth. 3. Asmodi.
4. Belzebub. 5. Oriens. 6. Paymon.
7. Ariton. 8. Amaymon.

Die 4. Underfürsten.

1. Oriens. 2. Paymon.
3. Ariton. 4. Amaymon.

Gemeine Geister.

Morech. Serap. Proxones. Rabbi. Kosem. Peresch. Thirama. Aluph. Neschamach. Milon. Frasis. Haya. Malach. Molabed. Yparchos. Nudaton. Methaer. Bruah. Apollyon. Schaluah. Myrmo. Melamod. Pother. Schad. Eckdulon. Mannes. Obedomah. Jachiel. Ivar. Moschel. Pechah. Hasperim. Katsin Bosphora. Badad. Kohen. Cuschi Fahma. Pakid. Helel. Mahra. Rascheär. Nogah. Adon. Erimites. Trapis Nagid Ethamin. Aspadit. Nast. Peralit Emfatison. Paruch. Girmil. Tolet. Helmis. Asinel. Irminon. Asturel. Flabison. Nascelon. Lomiol. Ysmirk. Pliroki. Afloton. Sagrion. Parmasas. Sarasim. Gorioson. Afolov. Liriell. Alogill. Ogologon. Larubos. Morilon. Lostmon. Kagaras. Igilon. Gesegas. Ugefor. Asorega. Paruchu. Siges. Atherom. Ramarath. Igavog. Goloma. Kilik Romosaf. Alpas. Soterion. Amilles. Ramages. Promathos. Meioseph. Paraschon.

Nachfolgende seind die gemeine Geister Astaroths und Asmodi.

Amanil. Orienell. Timira. Dramos. Anemalon. Kirik. Bubamabub. Ranar. Namalon. Ampholion. Abusis. Exention. Taborix. Concavion. Dyolem. Tarato. Tabbat. Buriub. Oman. Carasch. Dimurgos. Kogiel. Pemfodram. Siriol. Igigi. Dosom. Darachim. Horomar. Ahahbon. Dragamon. Lagiros. Eralir. Golog. Lenlel. Hagcys Boleman. Bialod. Galagos. Bagalon. Tmakos. Akanei

Fig. 19. Spirit names from Peter Hammer's edition. There are differences in the spelling and ordering of the spirit names between the different sources. Franz Bardon copied this list for his book, *The Practice of Magical Evocation*.

NASCELON	LOMIOL	YSMIRIEK	PLIROKY	AFLOTON
HAGRION	PERMASES	SARASIM	GORILON	AFOLOP
LIRIOL	ALOGIL	OGOLOGON	LARALOS	MORILON
LOSIMON	RAGARAS	IGILON	GESEGAS	UGESOR
ASOREGA	PARUSUR	SIGIS	AHEROM	RAMORAS
IGARAG	GELOMA	KILIK	ROMORON	NEGEN
EKALAK	ILEKEL	ELZEGAR	IPAKOL	NOLOM
HOLOP	ARIL	KOKOLON	OSOGYON	IBULON
HARAGIL	IZOZON	ISAGAS	BALABOS	NAGAR
OROYA	LAGASAF	ALPAS	SOTERION	AMILLIS
ROMAGES	PROMACHOS	METOFEPH	PARASCHON	

The servants of Astaroth and Asmodeus

AMAMIL	ORINEL	TINIRA	DRAMAS	ANAMALON
KIRIK	BUBANABUB	RANAR	NAMALON	AMPHOLION
ABUSIS	EXENTERON	LABONIX	CONCAVION	OHOTAM
TARETO	TABBAT	BURIUB	OMAN	CARASCH
DIMURGOS	KOGIEL	PANFOTRON	LIRIOL	IGIGI
DOSOM	DAROCHIM	HORAMAR	AHABHON	YRAGAMON
LAGIROS	ERALYX	GOLOG	LAMAL	HAGEYR
UDAMAN	BIALOD	GALAGOS	BAGALON	TINAKOS
AKANEF	OMAGOS	ARGAX	AFRAY	SAGAREZ
UGALIS	ERMIHALA	HAHYAX	GAGONIX	OPILON
DAGULEZ	PACHAHY	NIMALON		

The servants of Asmodi and Magoth

MAGOG	SOCHEN	DIOPES	LAMARGOS	DISOLEL
SIPHON	KELA	MAGYROS	MEBASCHEL	SARTABACHIM
SOBHE	UNOCHOS			

The servants of Amaimon and Ariton

HAROG	AGEBOL	RIGOLEN	IRASOMIN	ELAFON
TRISACHA	GAGOLCHON	KLORACHA	YEYATRON	PAFESLA

The servants of Astaroth

AMA	TEXAI	KATARON	RAK	SCHELEGON
GIRIAR	ASIANON	BAHAL	BARAK	GOLOG
IROMENIS	KIGIOS	NIMIRIX	HIRIH	OKIRGI
FAGUNI	HIPOLEPOS	ILOSON	CAMONIX	ALAFY
APORMANOS	OMBALAFA	GARSAS	UGIRPON	GOMOGIN
ARGILON	EARAOE	LEPACHA	KALOTES	YCHIGAS
BAFAMAL				

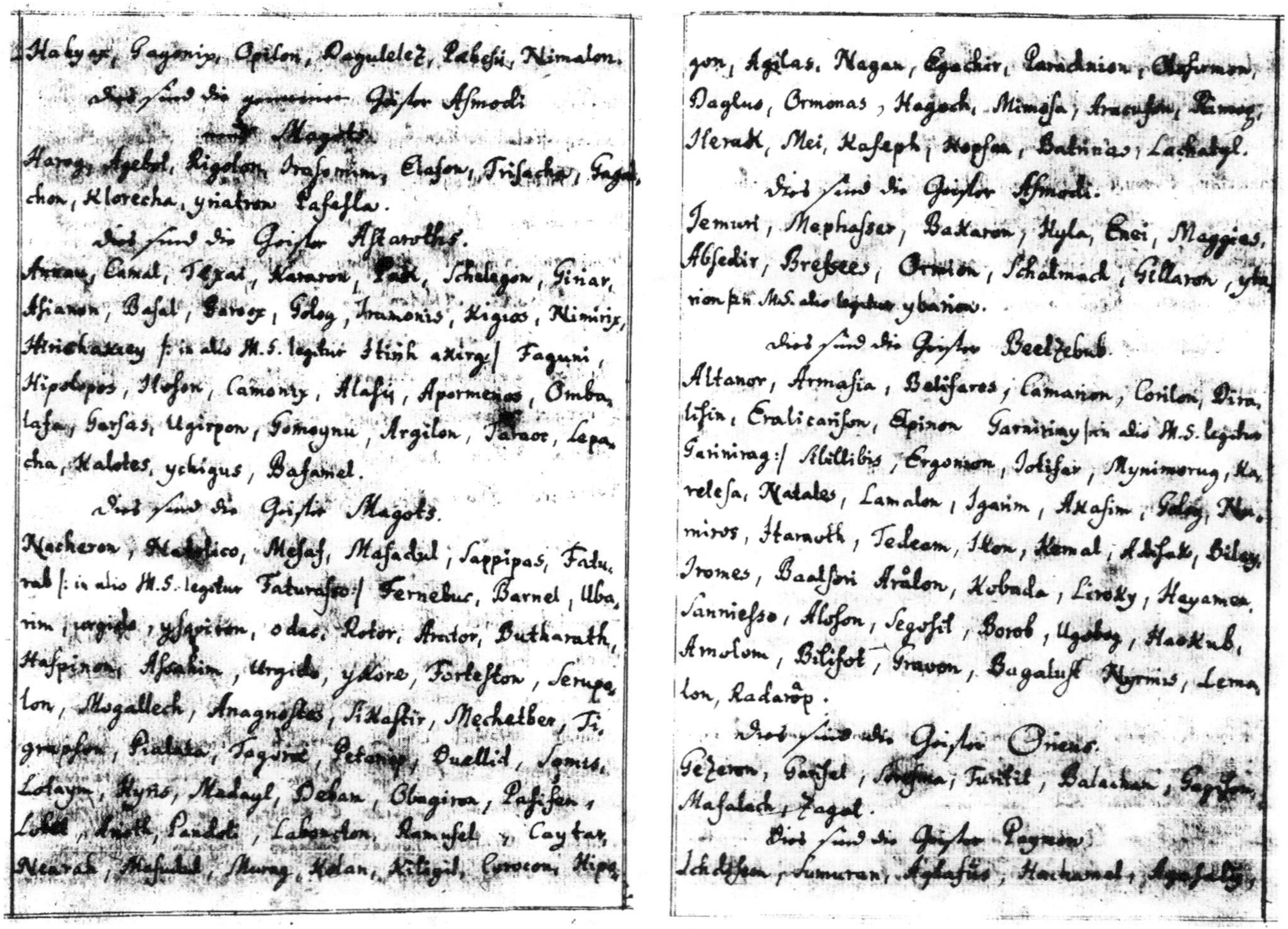
Halyax, Pagonix, Opilon, Daguleléz, Pabesi, Nimalon.
Dies sind die Geister Asmodi
Magots.
Harog, Agebol, Rigolon, Irasomin, Elason, Trisacha, Gagachon, Klorecha, yriatron, Sasasla.
Dies sind die Geister Astaroths.
Aman, Camal, Texat, Kararon, Tack, Schelegon, Giriar, Asianon, Basal, Sarosx, Goloy, Iramonis, Rigios, Nimirix, Hrichaxrey [: in alio M.S. legitur Stirik axirg:] Faguni, Hipolopos, Hoson, Camonix, Alasis, Apormenos, Ombalafa, Garsas, Ugirpon, Gomoynu, Argilon, Taraor, Lepacha, Halotes, yekigus, Basamel.
Dies sind die Geister Magots.
Nacheron, Natolico, Mesas, Masadul, Sappipas, Faturab [: in alio M.S. legitur Faturasso:] Fernebus, Barnel, Ubarim, Pergido, ysspirion, odac, Rotor, Arator, Butharath, Haspinon, Ascahim, Urgido, ylore, Forteston, Serupalon, Mogallech, Anagnostes, Sikastir, Mechelber, Figrapson, Pialata, Tagurie, Petonop, Quellid, Somis, Lolaym, Hyris, Madayl, Deban, Obagiron, Pasisan, Lobel, Luith, Pandoli, Laboralon, Ramusel, Caytar, Nearah, Masalul, Murag, Kelan, Kilegil, Corocon, Hipogon, Agilas, Nagan, Egachir, Paradnion, Chasirnon, Daglus, Ormonas, Hagoch, Mimosa, Aracuson, Pimog, Iterak, Mei, Kaseph, Nopsan, Batinas, Lachabyl.
Dies sind die Geister Asmodi.
Iemuri, Mephasser, Bakaron, Hyla, Enei, Maggias, Absedir, Bressees, Ornion, Schalmach, Gillaron, ybarion [in alio M.S. legitur ybarion].
Dies sind die Geister Beelzebub.
Altanor, Armasia, Belisares, Camarion, Corilon, Diralisin, Eralicarison, Elpinon Garniriny [in alio M.S. legitur Garinirag:] Alillibis, Ergonion, Jolisar, Mynimorug, Karelesa, Natales, Lamalon, Igarim, Akasim, Soloy, Naniros, Harnoth, Tedeam, Ilon, Kemal, Adisak, Bileg, Irones, Baalsori, Arâlon, Kobada, Liroky, Hayamen, Sanniesso, Alofon, Segosel, Borob, Ugobog, Haokub, Amolom, Bilifot, Graron, Bagalust, Kyrmis, Lemalon, Radarôp.
Dies sind die Geister Oriens.
Gezeron, Gaspel, Anagma, Turitel, Balachan, Gagison, Masalach, Zagal.
Dies sind die Geister Paymon.
Ichdison, Sumuran, Aglasius, Hachamel, Agasaly,

Fig. 20. Copy from microfilm of MS 2 in the Dresden library. The spirit names are in Latin script.

The servants of Magoth

NACHERAN	NASOLICO	MESAF	MASADUL	SAPIPAS
FATURAB	FERNEBUS	BARUEL	UBARIM	URGIDO
YSQUIRON	ODAC	ROTOR	ARATOR	BUTHARUTH
MEGALLEH	ANAGNOSTOS	SIKASTIR	MECHEBBER	TIGRAPHON
MATATAM	TAGORA	HARPINON	ARRABIM	KORE
FORTESION	SCRUPULON	PETANOP	DULID	SOMIS
LOTAYM	HYRYS	MADAIL	DEBAM	OBAGIRON
NESISEN	LOBEL	ARIOTH	PANDOLI	LABONETON
KAMUSEL	CAYFAR	NEARACH	MASADUL	MARAG
KOLAN	KILIGIL	COROCON	HIPOGON	AGILAS
NAGAN	EGACHIR	PARACHMON	OLOSIRMON	DAGLUS
ORMONOS	HAGOCH	MIMOSA	ARAKISON	RIMOG
ILARAK	MOKASCHEF	KOBHAN	BATIRMISS	LACHATYL

The servants of Asmodeus

IEMURI	MEBHASSER	BAKARON	HYLA	ENEI
MAGGID	ABHADIR	PRESFEES	ORMION	SCHALUACH
GILLAMON	YBARION			

The Servants of Beelzebub

ALTANOR	ARMASIA	BELIFERES	CAMARION	CORILON
DIRALISIN	ERALICARISON	ELPINON	GARINIRAG	SIPILLIPIS
ERGONION	IOTIFAR	MYNYMARUP	KARELESA	NATALES
CAMALON	YGARIM	AKAHIM	GOLOG	NAMIROS
HARAOTH	TEDEAN	IKON	KEMAL	ADISAK
BILEK	IROMAS	BAALSORI	AROLEN	KOBADA
LIROKI	NOMIMON	IAMAI	AROGOR	IPOKYS
OLASSKY	HAYAMEN	ALOSON	ERGOSIL	BOROB
UGOBOG	HASKUB	AMOLOM	BILIFOT	GRANON
PAGALUST	XIRMYS	LEMALON	RADARAP	

The servants of Oriens

GAZARON	SARISEL	SOROSMA	TURITIL	BALACHEM
GAGISON	MAFALACH	ZAGAL		

The servants of Paymon

ICHDISON	SUMURON	AGLAFYS	HACHAMEL	AGAHALY
KALGOSA	EBARON	ZALOMES	ZUGOLA	LARACH
KAFLES	MEMNOLIK	TAKAROS	ASTOLIT	MARKU

The servants of Ariton

ANADIR	EKOROK	ROSARAN	NAGANI	LIGILOS
SECABIM	CALAMOSI	SIBOLAS	FORFARON	ANDRACHOS
NOTISON	FILAXON	HAROSUL	SARIS	ELONIM
NILION	YLEMLIS	CALACH	SARASON	SEMEOT
MARANTON	CARON	REGERION	MEGALOGIM	IRMENOS
ELAMYR				

The servants of Amaymon

RAMIUSON	SIRGILIS	BARIOL	TARAHIM	BURNAHAS
AKESELY	ERKAYA	BEMEROT	KILIKIM	LABISI
AKOROK	MARAOS	GLYSY	QUISION	EFRIGIS
APILKI	DALEP	DRISOPH	CARGOSIK	NILIMA

Chapter Twenty

How to carry out the Work.

It is not enough to praise and thank Adonai in a thousand tongues, or just to thank your Guardian Angel with much honor; you must make good use of the great treasure that you have found. You have to know how to use such an immense treasure, otherwise it will lead you to harm and damage. It is like a sword in your hand—it can be used for good or evil. You can cut off Adonai and his angels, and you can destroy yourself and lose your life.

The manifestations can be used to overcome your enemy—the devil—and to bring him under your control. This is the purpose of the work. I want to give to you the necessary teachings one more time.

After calling and taking the oaths from the spirits, consider that Sabbath and the following days until the next Sabbath as special days during which you give praise and thanks to Adonai. Do no servant's work, consider the eight days with joy, like the feast of the Tabernacles. Do not call any spirits during this time.

After the eight days, you may start—with humbleness and forethought. The advice which follows will in part show this.

Previously we spoke about Tabernacles, Passover, and other festivals. Now, since your initiation, all days are possible.

1. Do not call and oblige the spirits on the Sabbath for the rest of your life. This is the day of rest and sacrifice for Adonai.

2. Be as fearful, as of the Eternal Fire, to tell any living being what your Guardian Angel has told you—except the person who gave you the knowledge of the art and to whom you are more deeply obliged than to your own father.

3. Do not use the wisdom against—or to harm—your neighbor. The wisdom is to praise Adonai, to benefit and for the use for his creations. Also, I advise you to copy God here—God forgives you—there is no more commendable action on Earth than to forgive.

4. Never start anything without asking. Guard against putting into use anything against the advice of your Guardian Angel.

5. Never use a word that you imperfectly understand, neither for the good angels or against unredeemed spirits. If you do this, angels would regard you as proud and high-handed; and the unredeemed spirits would regard you

as a stupid ass, and none would honor you with their appearance.

6. Guard against all the arts of sorcery, books, and devil's enchantments—no matter what their attraction. These are all inventions of the devil. Without the advice and permission of your Guardian Angel, don't even think about trying any of the arts of sorcery.

7. You will insult your Guardian Angel if you use word squares for accidents or bad luck.

8. Be always clean in body and clothing—particularly in the heart. This is important for the spirits.

9. Think carefully before you use your wisdom to help others with bad and improper things, because in many things a service for another can be a service against oneself.

10. Call your Guardian Angel only in times of desperate need. Understand that the angels are so far above you that it is senseless to compare ourselves with them.

11. Use the servant spirits only for your neighbor's needs. Remember that if you give a servant spirit to another person, the servant can be used against you.

12. Do not involve other spirits in the tasks of the servant spirits—except when they are busy or have been lent to others.

13. Be careful of the servant spirits—with many and big words they can convince you of anything. Keep your relationship with them at a formal level.

14. With the servant spirits, use only verbal commands. The only exception to this are the word squares written down in Book Four, chapter five.

15. Do not attempt too many things on any one day. Do one thing after the other until you are experienced—at the beginning, it is too difficult to do otherwise.

16. Only call the kings or dukes with sufficient reason. It is better to distance yourself from them.

17. It is better that you use as few spirits as possible and that the spirits remain invisible. The important thing is that they do what you request.

18. Everything that was spoken on the third day should not be softly, darkly, or indistinctly mumbled—nor should it be yelled. It should all be said in a natural conversational voice.

19. Every Sabbath the prayer room should be cleaned and swept out. Do this during and after the eighteen months. In the first two half years, do this also after morning prayer. In the third half year do this directly after noon, in the night, and in the next morning.

20. Do not consider any important magical work in the night.

21. After the initiation, you should fast on bread and water every year after Passover and Tabernacles on the day before the Sabbath.

22. For the whole of your life, live and eat in an orderly way—above all, avoid drunkenness.

23. Every year remember, and celebrate, the day of your initiation as if it were the feast of the Tabernacles.

24. During the three days when you are receiving the oaths from the unredeemed spirits, eat only vegetables and water. After that, eat properly.

25. During the eighteen months and for the following three years, avoid losing blood or bleedings except what nature may cause you to lose from the hand or head.

26. During the eighteen months and for the following year do not touch any dead person or animal. Do not kill anything yourself.

27. During the same time, do not eat any blood or meat. Whether raw or cooked—to do so is a cruelty to Adonai and your Angel.

28. Eat no animal that has died in its own blood or has been choked—no matter whether feathered or four-footed.

Follow all the warnings in this chapter—in the whole book and given later—follow carefully, especially in the first years after initiation.

Consider the points below without exception:
Never give a monarch the Craft. Solomon was the first to misuse it. If you were to do this you would both—you and the monarch—lose the mercy. I even gave Kaiser Sigismund the best of my spirits—but never the Work. It should never be given to kaisers, kings or other potentates.

Never sell the Craft. Give it away.

If you do the Work in a town take a house that is out of view. Avoid all curiosity.

Bind, with an oath, the person to whom you are giving the Work. It cannot be given to a known atheist or blasphemer.

Fast for three days before you pass on the Work. The person who receives the Work should similarly fast for three days. During this time he should also give you 10 gold guilders that you will need to distribute among poor people. The poor people should recite the *Psalms Miserere Mei Deus* and *De Profundis*.

It's a good thing, and makes the operation easier, if you repeat all the Psalms of David. They contain great power and virtue. Recite them at least twice the week.

At the same time, you should avoid gambling as you would the plague. It is always an opportunity for blasphemy.

Progress toward Book Four

It is unnecessary to use the word squares. It is sufficient to call the spirit in your natural voice. If people are around you and you cannot speak, you will need to have the word square in your hand—and move it around. If your request is not indicated by a sign, indicate it with two or three words.

Note—with simple words you can speak three languages.

If you have called the spirits in this way, you can then talk to the people who are near you in such a way that the spirits will understand what you request of them. For the master, one or two words are enough.

The spirits cannot read human thoughts. Yet—being cunning and subtle—they are so smart that given the least sign they will know what a person wants.

It is good to spend an hour alone during the night to call the spirits you will require the next day. Do this without ceremony and request everything that you will require the next day. Explain the word square with words or a wave of the hand. This is what Abramelin did in Egypt and Joseph did in Paris.

Now follows the word squares and the results that each spirit can bring. Yet, it is impossible to describe all and everything that spirits can do. If you want to work angelic effects that are not written in Book Four, then request them from your Guardian Angel in the following way:

Fast on the preceding day. Next morning, wash yourself and go into the prayer room. Put the incense burner in its place. Dress yourself with the white robe, light the lamp and the incense.

Then lay a clean, seven-sided gold, silver, or wax tablet—which has been touched with the sacred oil—on the altar next to the incense burner.

Then, on your knees, call to Adonai. Thank him for his mercy, beg him that he sends you his blessing and holy angel, who will explain things to you and help you with your request.

Also, call your Holy Guardian Angel and ask him to honor you with his appearance. Ask him to give you advice so as to enable you to understand and construct the word square for this—or any other—request. Persist in this prayer until you can glimpse the radiance of your Angel in the prayer room.

Then, diligently focus your attention on your Guardian Angel.

Then go to the tablet. On it you will find the name and the word square of the spirit who will fulfill your request. You will find the name of the spirit and his duke like dew or sweat. Do not touch the tablet. Copy the sign, leave the tablet until evening. Then, do the ordinary prayer and give thanks and rewrap the tablet in its silk cloth. The best day to do this is the Sabbath. So as not to make the Sabbath unholy, all preparations can be done on the preceding day.

If neither the Guardian Angel or the sign appear, then you can be certain that the request is not good or allowed by God. It is easier to obtain the word squares for evil things.

~

After besmoking, pray to God and humble yourself to your Guardian Angel. Clothe yourself in the white silk robe, girdle your waist, and wear your headband. Take the wand and stand at the altar facing the arbor, and call the twelve dukes as you did when you took their oaths on the second day—ask them to appear in the same shape.

When the dukes appear, order that they do not leave until they unveil the word square and name of the servant. Soon the duke who is responsible for the request will step out and make appear the word square with the name of the spirit in the sand. The named spirit and his followers will be present but invisible. Make the duke and servant take the same oath as in chapter fifteen. Then dismiss them. Take care to copy the word square because it will be wiped out as the spirits depart. After this, again besmoke the place.

I write this not so you can do or desire what I have described—but only so that you can see the full possibilities of this art. For doing evil things, the unredeemed spirits are quicker, more obedient, and more willing than when asked to do good works.

Write out the word squares wherever and whenever you want. It is sufficient if you know the request that belongs to each word square. You can write all this in an index. The most common—and best—should be written at the beginning of the Work and kept in the altar cupboard.

Beware, after the spirits have taken their oaths on the word squares, take care to keep the word squares safe from the eyes of other people. To see them could be dangerous for people.

The word squares from Book Four below have been given by the Guardian Angel:

Chapters 1, 3, 4, 5, 6, 7, 10, 11, 16, 18, 25, and 28.

The following word squares are given partly by the Guardian Angel and partly by the spirits. Without the permission of the Angel, a pious man is not allowed to use these:

Chapters 2, 8, 12, 13, 14, 15, 17, 19, 20, 24, 26, and 29.

The following—in their totality—were given by the unredeemed spirits:

Chapters 9, 21, 22, 23, 27, and 30.

Here follows the names of the dukes who control the workings of each chapter:

1. Astaroth and Asmodi: Work together for the 6th, 7th, and 16th chapters.

2. Asmodi and Magoth: Work together in the 15th chapter.

3. Astaroth and Ariton: Both in 16th chapter [work] through their servants, but not together—each separately.

4. Oriens, Paymon, Ariton, Amaymon: Work together through their common servants in the 1st, 2nd, 3rd, 4th, 5th, 13th, 17th, 27th, and 29th chapters.

5. Amaymon and Ariton: Together work the 26th chapter.

6. Oriens: Like all the following, Oriens works alone in the 28th chapter.

7. Paymon: 25th chapter.

8. Ariton: 24th chapter

9. Amaymon: 18th chapter

10. Astaroth: 8th and 23rd chapters

11. Magoth: 10th, 11th, 14th, 21st, 30th chapters.

12. Asmodi: 12th chapter.

13. Beelzebub: 9th, 20th, and 22nd chapters.

The workings of the following chapters can also be fulfilled by the servant spirits:

2nd, 4th, 12th, 19th, 20st, 26th in part. The 5th, 6th, 7th, 15th, 18th, 23rd, 24th, 27th, 28th, 30th in total.

If the spirits excuse themselves before they start to fulfill a request, there may be an obstruction. If this happens, use other spirits for the request. Otherwise, they must fulfill your request.

An Explanation of What to Look For, and Care About, in Each of the Chapters in This Book

For Chapters 1, 2, 4, 6, 7, 10, 23, 24, 25, 27, 29, 30

Take the word square in your hand or put it onto your head, under your hood. Then the spirit will speak privately into your ear or will bring you what was requested.

For Chapter Three

Name the spirit and touch the word square that requests the shape in which the spirit will appear.

For Chapter Five

Note that every person can have no more than four servant or familiar spirits. These can do as much as said in point 4 above—they come from the four dukes. The first is effective from sunrise until noon; the second, from noon to sunset; the third, from sunset until midnight; the fourth, from midnight until sunrise the next morning. You can use them as much as you want, as clearly said above. If you have lent them or chased away one or more of them—which you are allowed to do—you cannot use those but must call others to work during their time period. If you want one to depart before the six hours are over, you only need to say this in words—they prefer to do this if they can. If you do not want to talk, knock the sign in which their name appears, and they will go away. You may do the same thing to dismiss all the other spirits. Use similar words or gestures to those mentioned in the sixteenth chapter, so they will know what is in your mind; if you do not like this procedure, use another one. After every six hours, the servant spirit will disappear and the next one will come—unless you have given him away.

For Chapter Eight

Knock on the word square to show the spirit the code it contains. If he should stand at the door you must knock on the bottom.

For Chapter Nine

Let the animals and people look at the word square or touch them with it. To restore them to their former appearance—because they are not really changed, they only appear to be—place the word square on the head or knock on it. At the beginning, name the spirit.

For Chapter Eleven

There are many books on many subjects—particularly in this one—that have been written since the beginning of the world to this day. All the wealth of all the potentates in the world could not pay for them, their value is so great. These books have perished or become lost, in part through Godly advice. God does not want his secrets to be revealed in this way, because through books both the worthy and unworthy can discover many of the secrets of God.

Some books, because of the envy of the spirits, have been destroyed by water, fire, and other destructive elements so that they can no longer fall into the hands of people, and so that the spirits will not be made to obey and serve.

Books on the three subjects mentioned in the chapter 11 have not been destroyed but are partly buried in the earth, partly hidden in walls—and in other places—and partly sunk into the sea. This has happened because the orders of the good spirits and angels who—although they did not want that these books become scattered or destroyed—allowed this to happen. This is because they could not prevent the books falling into the hands of the unworthy. Only the worthy who have done the correct preparation, such as ours, to honor the secrets of God and be of benefit to his neighbor can look for the books. Such a person can use the books and can recognize even things that his mind cannot comprehend.

This type of book can be brought into existence with these word squares. As soon as you give the correct spirit the request the books will appear.

Once I read a book for half a year, it did not disappear—but as soon as I tried to copy or memorize even a single word or a single sign, the book disappeared. Not even from memory was it possible to write one letter.

For Chapter Twelve

Knock the sign and the spirit will bring the report into your ears. Do not repeat anything, no matter how bad it is. Do this for the love of God, who does not want such secrets made known. If you do not do this, you could lose your soul, body, possessions, and blood. When you move the word square name the person whose secrets you are seeking.

For Chapter Thirteen

As said before, humans divide themselves into three parts when they die: body, soul, and spirit. The body gets buried into the ground. The soul travels to God or the Devil. The spirit is given its specific time from the Creator—the holy number of seven years—during this time the spirit cleans itself and travels on earth. Then the spirit devolves itself and travels to where it came from.

The state of the soul is unchangeable. With help from the spirits, we can bring body and spirit into one again. Take care not to misuse the body; the body will do again what it did before when it was body, soul, and spirit, but the person now has no soul. This, one of the highest workings of the art, is a mercy of God that he only grants for good, not bad.

All the high-ranking spirits take part in this work. All it takes is to do the following: as soon as the person dies, lay the word square on him after the fourth part of the day. As soon as he moves, and begins to sit up, dress him in new clothes. Inside the clothes sew a word square like was placed on his body. Whenever new clothes are worn, the word square needs to be placed inside.

It is not possible to extend the time past seven years. At exactly the point that the spirit again becomes one with the body the person will suddenly collapse. I myself saw an example of this when a dead duke—whose name I do not want to mention—who reanimated and was preserved on earth for seven years. Then, the young duke—his son—reached the correct age was able to retain the possession of the kingdom, which without this method would have fallen under the authority of foreign hands.

For Chapter Fourteen

It is easy to make oneself invisible. But it is not allowed that a person can hurt another's body or life in this way. You can do many other evil things while invisible—but this is not fair and proper. God has forbidden this in his holy law, with big penalties, because everyone should take care that this art, as far as possible, should be used for good, not evil or harm. You have here twelve signs from twelve different spirits—all belong to Duke Magoth and all are equally strong. Use the one you want, lay it on your bare head under your hat or hood—this immediately makes you invisible. If you want to become visible, remove the word square.

For Chapter Fifteen

Place whichever word square you want between two bowls or closed containers. Put these near a window, or in a garden, or in a yard, or even a field where there are no people. Within a quarter of an hour you will get what you wanted. With this type of food you cannot sustain people for more than three days. It fills eyes, mouth, and stomach, and satisfies hunger, but gives no strength.

Also know that anything spirits bring never stays for more than 24 hours in front of the eyes. The word squares you have placed in the bowls you will find underneath the bowls—take care that no one sees them. Ask for fresh supplies every day.

For Chapter Sixteen

Call or move one of the main word squares. The spirit will soon show you the treasure or make it appear—whichever. Quickly throw the special word square onto it. If you do this, the treasure will never deteriorate and all the spirits connected with it will flee.

For Chapter Seventeen

Name the place to which you want to travel and put the word square under your hat. Take care that neither falls from your head. Travel during the day in good weather—not at night.

For Chapter Eighteen

Remove the bandage from the injury, clean off the plaster and ointment, lay the word square on the injury and wait about half of a quarter of an hour. Remove the word square and keep it. For internal sickness, place the word square on the bare skin of the patient—it can certainly be seen by other people, but it is better keep it from strange eyes and hands.

For Chapters Nineteen & Twenty

Name the person and move the word square to cause friendship or enmity. If you are doing this for two other people, then you have to name the people. Take out the word square that names the spirit's duty and the kingdom to which the spirit belongs, or touch the person with a general or common word square.

For Chapter Twenty-one

This blending or transformation of oneself happens as follows:

Take the word square in your left hand, run it down your face. If you want to return to your usual self, take the word square in your right hand and run it over the face from bottom to top: with this you can unmask every magician who has disguised himself.

For Chapter Twenty-two

The word squares are buried under stairs, doors, stills, paths, piers, etc. Or the word squares can be laid under beds and stables. People should walk, sit, or lie over the word squares. Or one can take the word squares and touch people or animals with them.

For Chapter Twenty-six

Touch the lock with the script side of the word square. It will soon be opened without any damage so that no suspicion will arise. To close the lock use the other side of the word square. Beware not to misuse this work.

For Chapter Twenty-eight

Put the word square or the coin that you wish to obtain in your purse. Reach in with your right hand—you will find seven pieces inside. Do not spend it for bad things; this would harm you and others. Do not do this more than three times in the day. The coins that you do not use will soon get lost—so take care, that if you need only a little money not to ask for large coins; small or medium coins are of more use.

The Close of the Third Book of Abraham the Jew.

So now—in the name of Adonai the very highest and the highest God—I end this book at this point. He who deals with God and the good spirits is not allowed to exceed the good measure of their will. So, Lamech, my son, when this book comes into your hands, do not be unhappy that compared to my other books—which I have also left behind—this book is not similarly sophisticated or finished in the same high-blown, artistic style

I pass you this weight—as it was granted to me—for you to carry as best you might. I have not put into it delicate language or other fancy cultivated written things. I have, at times, presented things out of order and scattered the material about to force you to turn many pages and to make you read the book many times.

Do not forget my advice and remember my commandments until you lie in your grave. Then, the holy wisdom—in all its splendor and treasure—will become your inherited fortune. On Earth, what bigger inheritance can you have? So follow, my son, him who teaches you out of his own experience. In summary hold these three points:

Three Points

1. God's word, his commands, all of his laws, and especially your Angel's advice and your ancestors' example—never let this out of your heart, your eyes, your mind, or your plans.

2. The unredeemed spirits and their followers, their works, and all their doings—be their unrelenting enemy and try throughout your life to command them and never to serve them.

3. Desire the treasures and gifts of the Godly Wisdom. Try to use and practice them to honor his holy name, to be the joy of the holy angels, and for the use of all God's creations. The opposite, avoid until you are in the grave. So will the blessing and kindness of Adonai never leave you and your children's children forever—the same great Jehovah, the holy Adonai, the God Zabaoth, praise, acclaim, and thanks said for eternity. Amen. Amen.

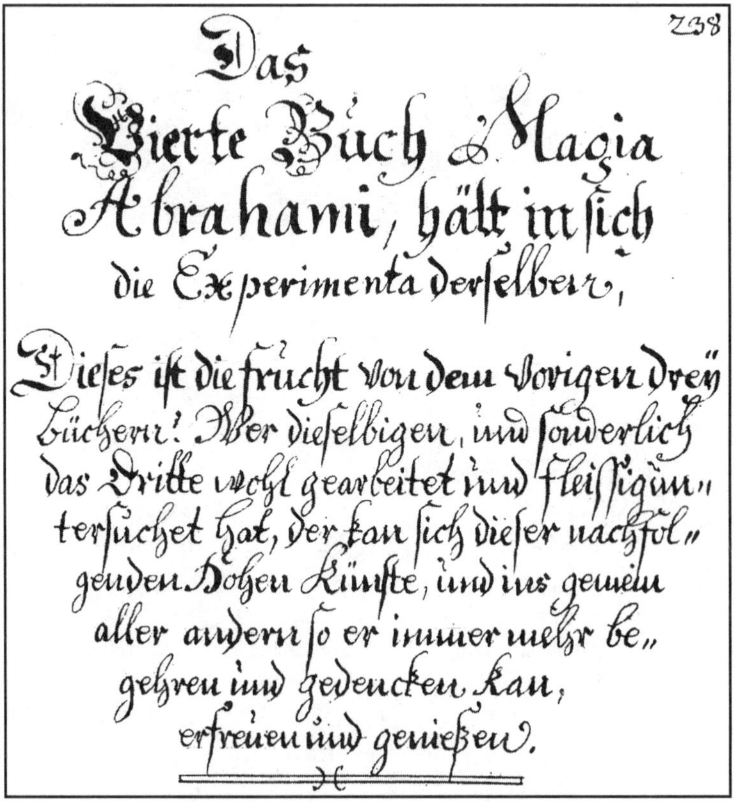

238

Das
Vierte Buch Magia
Abrahami, hält in sich
die Experimenta derselben,

Dieses ist die frucht von dem vorigen dreÿ
büchern! Wer dieselbigen, und sonderlich
das Dritte wohl gearbeitet und fleissig un„
tersuchet hat, der kan sich dieser nachfol„
genden hohen Künste, und ins gemein
aller andern so er immer mehr be„
gehren und gedencken kan,
erfreuen und genießen.

Fig. 21. Title page to Book Four from MS 2 in the Dresden library, in a mixture of German and Latin. Different transcribers added their own headings. A fairly literal translation reads:

The Fourth Book Magia Abrahami
It contains the experiments of the same.
This is the fruit of the preceding three books. The one who investigates the same, particularly the third, and has properly worked and diligently investigated, he can then—from the following high arts and particularly all other arts, if he requests and considers more—find happiness and enjoyment.

Book Four

[Index to Book Three]

The fruit of the preceding three books.

Those who have worked through the previous three books properly—and with diligence—can access and enjoy the following high arts.

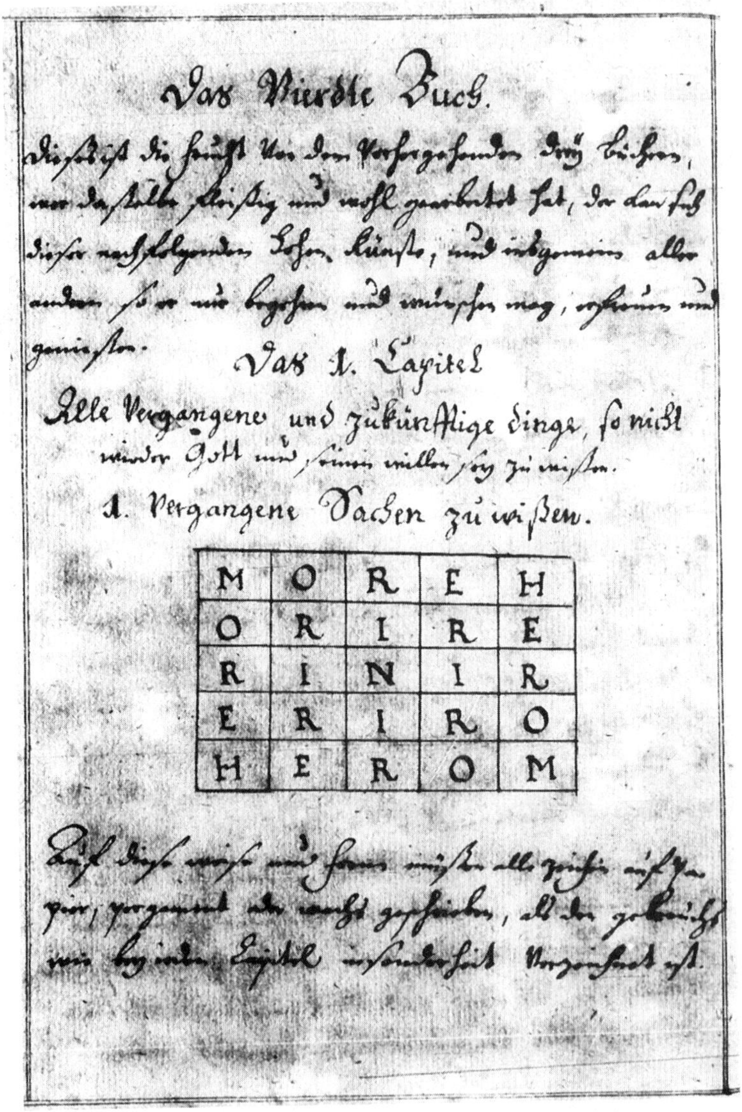

Das Vierdte Buch.

Das 1. Capitel

Alle Vergangene und Zukünftige dinge, so nicht wider Gott und seinen willen sey zu wißen.

1. Vergangene Sachen zu wißen.

M	O	R	E	H
O	R	I	R	E
R	I	N	I	R
E	R	I	R	O
H	E	R	O	M

Fig. 22. Copy from microfilm of Dresden MS 1, of the first square from chapter one. Neither the Wolfenbüttel MS nor Peter Hammer's edition shows the squares constructed.

Chapter One

How you can discover all past and future things—that are not directly against God's will.

1. To know past things
2. Future things
3. Future things
4. To know future things in war
5. Past and forgotten things
6. To foretell coming sorrows
7. Future things
8. Past things
9. To foretell frosts and miracles
10. Future things
11. Future things

1\1

MOREH, ORIRE, RINIR, ERIRO, HEROM

1\2

NABHI, ADAIH, BARAB, HIADA, IHBAN

1\3

THIRAMA, HIGANAM, IGOGANA, RAGIGAR,
ANAGOGI, MANAGIH, AMARIHT

1\4

MILON, IRAGO, LAMAL, OGARI, NOLIM

1\5

MALACH, AMANEC, LANANA, ANANAL, CENAMA,
HCALAM

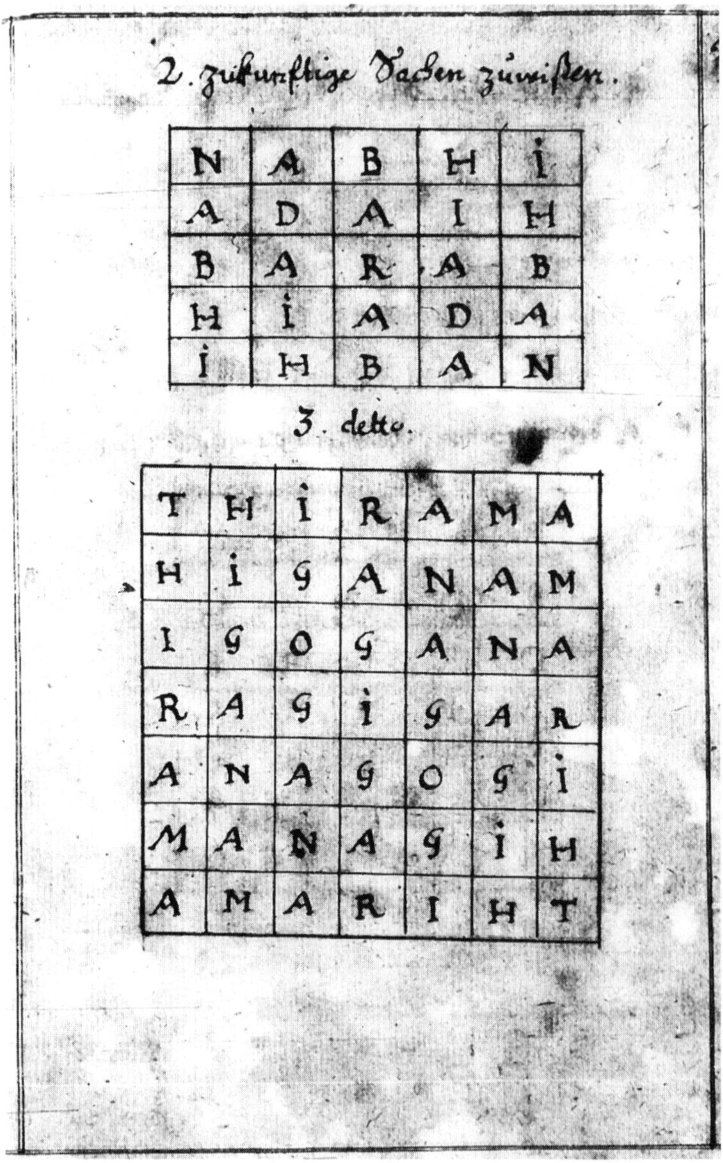

2. zukunfftige Sachen zuwissen.

N	A	B	H	I
A	D	A	I	H
B	A	R	A	B
H	I	A	D	A
I	H	B	A	N

3. detto.

T	H	I	R	A	M	A
H	I	G	A	N	A	M
I	G	O	G	A	N	A
R	A	G	I	G	A	R
A	N	A	G	O	G	I
M	A	N	A	G	I	H
A	M	A	R	I	H	T

Fig. 23. Copy from microfilm of Dresden MS 1. The second and third squares from chapter one.

1\6

NUDETON, USILARO, DIREMAT, ELEMELE, TAMERID, ORALISU, NOTEDUN

1\7

MELAMMED, ERIFOISE, LISILLIM, AFIRELOM, MOLERIFA, MILLISIL, ESIOFIRE, DEMMALEM

1\8

EKDILON, KLISATU, DINANAL, ISAGASI, LANANID, UTASILK, NULIDKE

1\9

SARAPI, ARAIRP, RAKKIA, AIKKAR, PRIARA, IPARAS

1\10

LOSEM, OBODE, SOFOS, EDOBO, MESOL

1\11

ALLUP, LEIRU, LIGIL, URIEL, PULLA

Chapter Two

To have reports about all sorts of doubtful things.

2\1

POTHER, OTHARE, THORAH, HAROHT, ERAHTO, REHTOP

2\2

MELABBED, ELINALSE, LIKAKILB, ANAKAKAB, BAKAKANA, BLIKAKIL, ESLANILE, DEBBALEM

2\3

MEBHAER, ELIAILE, BIKOSIA, HAOROAH, AISOKIB, ELIAILE, REAHBEM

Chapter Three

To make every spirit appear.

1. In the shape of a dragon
2. In human shape
3. In animal shape
4. In bird shape

3\1

MARLIFIM, ITHISIRO, DSEKENIM, ATRARATU, TIRARAIN, MINEKESD, OLARAHLA, SOMFIROS

3\2

SATAN, ADAMA, TABAT, AMADA, NATAS

3\3

LIRBIAC, ESAERMI, RASHEUP, FILEMIR, ISAMANO, REROLIN, IRETISU

3\4

BEMTAUL, EMASDAI, MAKIURO, ESIPPOS, ADAPOSA, MAROMAD, ARORELI

Chapter Four

To create visions.

1. In mirrors, glass, and crystals
2. In caves, vaults, crypts, and grottos underground
3. In the air
4. In jewels and rings
5. In beeswax and through writing
6. Through fire
7. In the moon
8. In water
9. In the hand

4\1

GILIONIM, IRIMIIRI, LIOSASIN, IMSARAIO,
OIARASMI, NITASOIL, IRIIMITI, MINOILIG

4\2

ETHANIM, TIADISI, HARAPIN, ADAMADA,
NIPARAH, ISIDAIT, MINAHTE

4\3

APPARET, PARESTE, PREREOR, AERERЕA, ROERERP,
ETSERAP, TERAPPA

4\4

BEDSEK, ELIELA, DIAPIS, SEPPES, ELIEMI, KATSIN

4\5

NECOL, ARATO, GARAC, IMARE, DIGAN

4\6

NASI, APYS, SIPA, ISAN

4\7

COHEN, ORARE, HASAH, ERARO, NEHOC

4\8

ADMON, DRASO, MAIAM, OSARD, NOMDA

4\9

LELEH, EGADE, LADAL, EDAGE, HELEL

CHAPTER FIVE

To obtain servant spirits—either free or sealed—and how to send them away.

1. In the form of a giant
2. As a page
3. As a soldier
4. In the form of a flower
5. In the appearance of an old man

6. As a rider
7. As a Negro in appearance
8. As an eagle
9. As a snake
10. As a lion
11. As a dog
12. As a monkey

5\1

ANAKIM, NILARI, ALISAK, KASILA, IRALIN, MIKANA

5\2

OIKETIS, IPORASI, KELIRAL, ENIPINE, LARIARK, IDENSAI, SILEKIO

5\3

PARAS, AHARA, RACAR, ARASA, SARAP

5\4

PERACHI, ERIPEIH, RIMENEC, APEREPA, CENEMIR, HIEPIRE, IHCAREP

5\5

RITIR, ISARI, RAKEN, IREPI, RITIR

5\6

RACAB, ARIPA, CILIC, APIRA, BACAR

5\7

CUSIS, VEAHI, SARAS, IHAEN, SISUC

5\8

NESHER, ELEEHE, HEPPEH, SEPPES, EHEELE, REHSEN

5\9

PETHEN, ERAANE, TARCAH, HACRAT, ENAARE, NEHTEP

5\10

KELEF, ERARE, LAMAL, ERARE, KELEF

5\11

KOBHA, ORAIH, BALAH, HIARO, AHBEK

5\12
CEPHIR, ELADI, PARIEH, HEIROP, HIALE, RIPHAE

Chapter Six

For working mines.

1. To do everything so that shafts do not collapse in mines
2. To show the location of gold or silver veins
3. To do all sorts of mining work
4. To do mining with tunnels
5. To take water out of mines and shafts
6. For the spirits to bring wood for smelting
7. To purify the ore
8. To do various mining works

6\1
FELAAH, ERANDA, LAMANA, ANAMAL, HALEF

6\2
ALEABRUHI, LIRMUAPI, ERAIBRIPU, ANIDAMRAR, BUBAUABUB, RARMADINA, UPIRBIARE, HIPAUMRIL, IHURBAELA

6\3
KILOIN, ISERPI, LENIRO, ORINEL, IPRESI, NIOLIK

6\4
NAKAB, ANINA, KIRIK, ANINA, BAKAN

6\5
PELAGIN, ERENOLI, LEREPOG, ALEMELA, GOPEREL, ILONERE, NIGALEP

6\6
KITTIP, IFIADI, TANNAL, FINIT, IDRASI, KITTIK

6\7
MARAK, ALAPA, RANAR, APALA, KARAM

6\8
GADRAR, AIRAPA, DRAMAR, RAMARD, APARIA, RARDAG

Chapter Seven

To have the spirits make alchemy work.

1. To have the spirits bring forth all sorts of metals through the chemical arts
2. To have the spirits do all sorts of chemical work
3. To learn all sorts of alchemical arts from the spirits

7\1
METALO, EZATEH, TARATA, ATARAT, HETAZE, OLATEM

7\2
TABBAT, ARUNCA, BUIRUB, BURIUB, ACNURA, TABBAT

7\3
IPOMANO, PAMERAM, ONALOMI, MELACAH, ARORAMI, NANAMON, OMIHINI

Chapter Eight

To make and prevent storms.

1. To make hail
2. To make a heavy, short shower
3. To make snow and ice
4. To make a thunderstorm

8\1

CANAMAL, AMADAME, NADAHAM, ADAMAHA, MEHADAM, AMAHANA, LOMANAC

8\2

SAGRIR, AFIANI, HIRIAS, RAIRIG, MAISA, RIRGAS

8\3

TAKAT, ATETA, KEREK, ATETA, TAKAT

8\4

HAMAH, ABALA, MAHAM, ALABA, HAMAH

Chapter Nine

To make people into animals—and animals into people.

1. People into donkeys
2. People into deer
3. Animals into people
4. People into wild pigs
5. People into dogs
6. People into wolves
7. Animals into stone

9\1

JEMIMEJ, ERIONTE, MIRTIEM, FOTIFAI, MINTIUM, ETEAURE, JEMIMEJ

9\2

AIACILA, ISIOREL, AICRIRA, CORILON, IRILCIA, LERUIST, ALINAIA

9\3

ISICHADAMION, SERRAREPINTO, IRAASIMELEIS, ORATIBARINP, HARINSTUOTIR, ARABATINTIRA,

DEMASICOANOS, APERUNOILEMI, MILIOTABUEL, NIONTINOLITA, OTISIROMELIS, NOSTRACILARI

9\4

CHADRIS, HARIANI, ARORIAS, DIRALID, SOALIRA, MAIRAH, RISDAHE

9\5

KEKEPH, APIERIP, RELMORE, TEMUNAT, ERONAIL, TIRAILE, ELETRAK

9\6

DISCEBEH, ISARTRIC, SARHIAB, ERBETRE, ETOMMATE, BARIURIS, ERSONITI, HEMANAD

9\7

BEDASEK, EFIRAME, DIRMIAS, AMAFIA, SAIIARD, EMAIRTE, KERADEB

Chapter Ten

To prevent and remove all other magic.

1. To heal magical sicknesses
2. To prevent magical storms
3. When a magician is in the air making a cloud—so that he falls to earth
4. Expose hidden appearances
5. Expose hidden magicians
6. To make a magician's soldiers disappear
7. Hold this word square in your hand to prevent magic from working

10\1

COLI, ODAI, LOCA, IEAR

10\2
SEARAS, ELLOPA, ALATIM, ROTARA, APIRAC, HAMAIS

10\3
NEISIEN, EREAERE, IREPREI, SAPIPAS, IERPERI, EREAERE, NEISIEN

10\4
HORAH, OSOMA, ROTOR, AMOSO, HAROH

10\5
PARACLILU, ARINOCISO, RILARLAIL, ANOTALECU, DORATACAL, ICALAFANA, LIELCARIT, OSICONIRA, NOCILATAM

10\6
MACANES, AROLUSE, CIRACUN, ALAHALA, DERARPE, UNETIRA, LUDASAM

10\7
IKKEBEKKI, KARTUTRAK, KRUTUTURK, ETISATISE, BUTARATUB, ESITASITE, KRUTUTURK, KARTUTRAK, IKKEBEKKI

Chapter Eleven

To obtain lost books, hidden manuscripts, and such.

1. Astronomical books
2. Magical books
3. Pharmacopoeia

11\1
CODSEIM, ORIENTI, HARPINE, AREHPES, BORDERID, INONARO, MIBAHRE

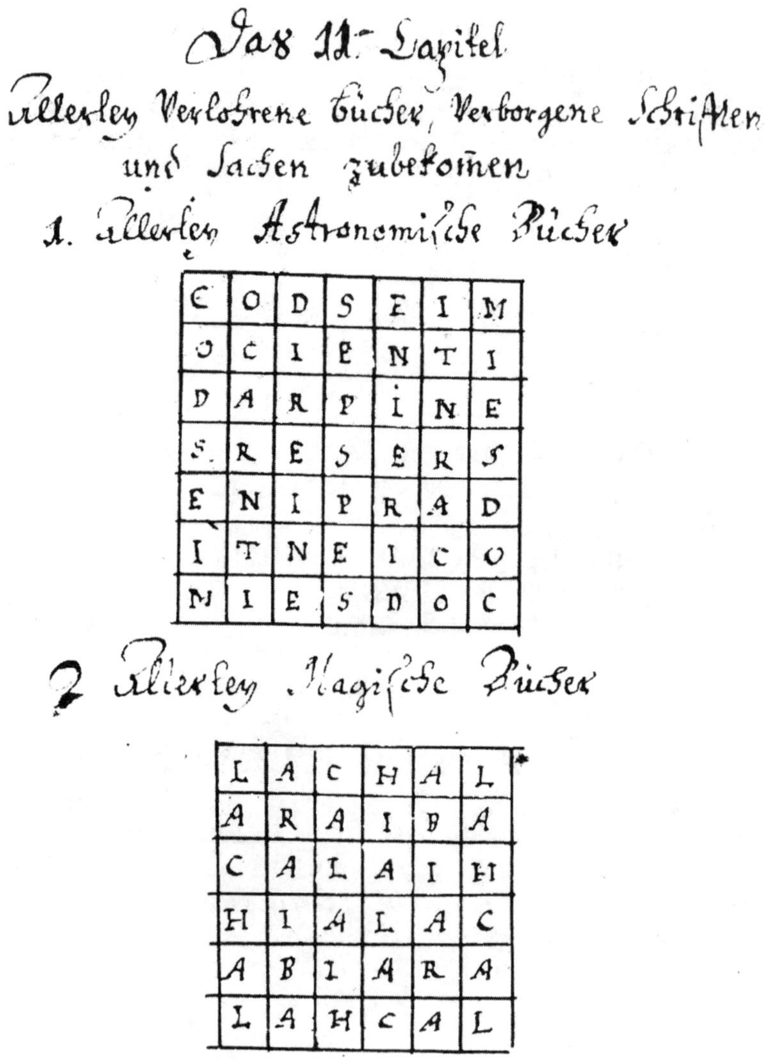

Das 11. Capitel

Allerley Verlohrene bücher, Verborgene Schrifften und Sachen zubekomen

1. Allerley Astronomische Bücher

C	O	D	S	E	I	M
O	C	I	E	N	T	I
D	A	R	P	I	N	E
S	R	E	S	E	R	S
E	N	I	P	R	A	D
I	T	N	E	I	C	O
M	I	E	S	D	O	C

2 Allerley Magische Bücher

L	A	C	H	A	L
A	R	A	I	B	A
C	A	L	A	I	H
H	I	A	L	A	C
A	B	I	A	R	A
L	A	H	C	A	L

Fig. 24. Chapter eleven squares from Dresden MS 2.

11\2
LACHAL, ARAIBA, CALAIH, HIALAC, ABIARA, LAHCAL

11\3
KEHAHEK, ENIFINE, HIRIRIH, AFIRISA, HIRIRIH, ENIFINE, KEHAHEK

Chapter Twelve

To research and hear from people the hidden plans and plots of a person.

1. Secrets from letters or talk
2. Secrets from words
3. Hidden works of a person
4. Secret war plans
5. To discover sexual activity
6. The hidden riches and treasures of a person
7. The hidden arts of a person

12\1
MEGILLA, EPREIAL, HURUNTAL, IENIURS, LITUROG, CAARONO, ALIGEM

12\2
SIMBASI, IRUARIS, MURKARA, BAKAKAB, ARAKRUM, SIRAURI, ISABMIS

12\3
MAABHAD, ADSAISA, ARADRIH, BADAKAB, HIRKORA, ASCADSA, DACHBAM

12\4

MILEHAMAH, IROHIDEIRA, LOPALIDEM, CHAKARIDA, HILAHALIK, ADIRACHHE, MEDILAPOL, ANEDIHORI, HAMAHCLIM

12\5

JEDIDAH, ENITEKA, DERARED, ITAMUNI, DERARED, ALLTINE, HADIDEI

12\6

ASAMIM, SILAPA, ALIGIL, MAGIDE, IPIDRE, MALEEM

12\7

MELACAH, EROBOLA, LORAFIL, ABAHADN, CORALIC, ALIDNE, HABUCEM

Chapter Thirteen

To make a dead person walk for seven years.

1. That he does and talks like a living person from sunrise to noon
2. . . . from noon to sunset
3. . . . from sunset to midnight
4. . . . from midnight to sunrise

13\1

RELBELAC, ERARMINI, BALISAAK, BRILURPI, EINFINAK, LIAREBI, ANAPASUH, HIKIRIBI

13\2

METHIRRAH, ENIASAENA, BIBMAILIR, HOFIBRUAR, TUIBRINSI, ROSAESTAH, RIFNAIAUF, ASACHIRTE, HARRITHEM

13\3
MAPPALAH, ATHRININA, PRINDEIRA, PIREUSON, ANIATKA, LISONPIT, ANIMAESA, HANATHAN

13\4
PEGER, ENIAE, GISIG, EAITE, REGEP

Chapter Fourteen

For invisibility.

14\1
ALAMATA, LISAFIL, AROLORA, MATATAM, ARATORA, LISAFIL, ALAMATA

14\2
ARAPHALI, SIRONIA, ARNTRAH, BETANOP, HIRNERA, ANIORIS, HAHPAST

14\3
CASALI, APODA, SOMIS, ADINA, HASAC

14\4
ALATAH, LISANA, AROGAT, TAGORA, ANASIL, HATALA

14\5
KODER, ORUSE, DULIEL, EFINO, REDAK

14\6
SIMLAH, IRIOSA, CHIRTIL, LITRIM, ASCIRI, HALMIS

14\7
BAHAD, ERIDA, HIRIS, ADILA, HASAC

14\8
ANANANA, NICERON, ACIRDIRA, MEFISEM, AFISUTA, NORECNI, ANANANA

14\9

BEROMIM, EPILISI, RISARDIRP, OLAGIRE, MIRIFAS, ISIRADE, MEMOREB

14\10

ALAMPIS, LONARSI, ANADOAD, MADAILO, PRAEGIAT, ISILANE, SIDOFER

14\11

TAMARE, APAFE, MABED, AFEDE, NEDAK

14\12

TALAL, APOKA, LOBOL, AKORA, LALAT

Chapter Fifteen

That the spirits bring all sorts of things to eat and drink.

1. Bread
2. Meat
3. Wine
4. Fish
5. Cheese

15\1

IAYN, ARNAI, INOKI, IAKLA, NYIAI

15\2

BASAR, ARONO, SOIOS, ANORA, RASAB

15\3

LECHEM, ENRISE, CROBIH, HIBORC, ESIRNE, MEHCEL

15\4

DAGAD, AROKA, GAMAG, AZORA, DAGAD

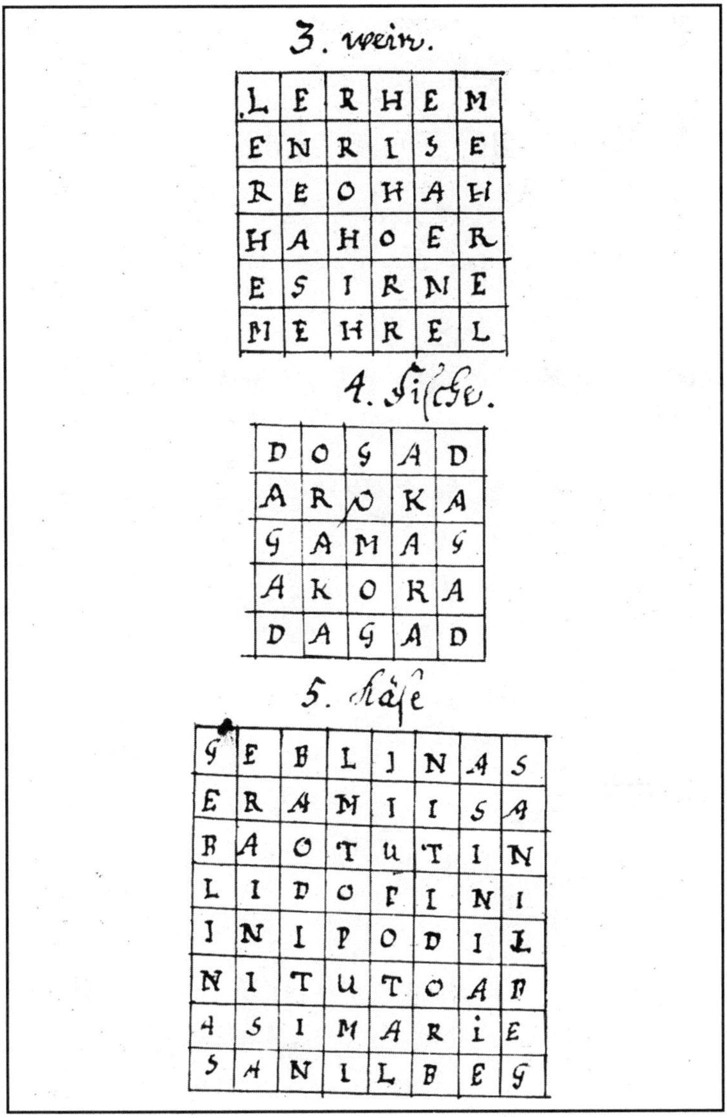

3. wein.

L	E	R	H	E	M
E	N	R	I	S	E
R	E	O	H	A	H
H	A	H	O	E	R
E	S	I	R	N	E
M	E	H	R	E	L

4. Fische.

D	O	G	A	D
A	R	O	K	A
G	A	M	A	G
A	K	O	R	A
D	A	G	A	D

5. Käse

G	E	B	L	I	N	A	S
E	R	A	M	I	I	S	A
B	A	O	T	U	T	I	N
L	I	D	O	P	I	N	I
I	N	I	P	O	D	I	L
N	I	T	U	T	O	A	B
A	S	I	M	A	R	I	E
S	A	N	I	L	B	E	G

Fig. 25. Squares corresponding to chapter fifteen from Dresden MS 2. The squares do not always match the lists in the book. Dresden MS 2 has inaccuracies.

Huius usum vide

Fünffzehntes Capitl.

10. Punkt und 2. Punkt

4. Buchs.

Daß die Geister allerley Sachen, so zu erdenken von Essen und Trinken, bringen.

1. Brodt.

Jayn. Arnai. Inoki. Jakla. Nyai.

2. Fleisch.

Basar. Arono. Soios. Anora. Rasab.

3. Wein.

Lechom. Enrise erobab. Hibeoc. Esirne-Mechal.

4. Fisch.

Dagad. Aroka. Gamag. Azora. Dagad.

5. Käß.

Gebhina. Erainisa. Barbitin. Hidopitini. Insodih. Nidivoab Asinare. Hainhbeg.

Fig. 26. Text for chapter fifteen squares, from Peter Hammer's edition.

15\5

GEBHINA, ERAINISA, BARBITIN, HIDOPIRINI,
INSODIH, NIDIDOAB, ASINARE, HAINHBEG

Chapter Sixteen

To recover treasures.

1. Jewelry
2. Gold
3. Necklaces
4. Jewels
5., 6., 7., 8., and 9. Treasures in general
10. Riches in general
11. Coins
12. and 13. Treasure in general
14. and 15. Especially gold
16. Treasure in general
17. and 18. Money
19. Jewels
20. Necklaces

16\1

TIPHARAH, INRALISA, PRERUSIR, HAROSOBA,
ALUSORAH, RISUREP, AFILARNI, HARAPIT

16\2

CESEP, ELATE, SARIS, ETIKE, PESIE

16\3

AGIS, NILI, ALIG, KANA

16\4

EBEINEKARAH, BALIOLAREIA, BAAALOBBAIR,
NIRPINEALANU, JEIARINIONEK,

ELONIMINOLE, RABEMINALOI, ANALUNARYU, RIGNIOLAABE, ARIROLOEIMB, HARAKEINEBE

16\5

SEGILAH, ERALIPA, GARENIL, ILEMEBI, INIERAG, APILARE, HALIGES

16\6

NECOT, EROTO, CALAC, OTARE, TOCEN

16\7

COSENS, OLAGE, SAPAS, EGALO, NESOE

16\8

OTFAR, TOERA, SEMES, ARCOT, ROISTO

16\9

GENATISIM, EROSIMUTI, MINATARAN, APAMUNARI, TAGITISMI, INOOEROGU, SANAMATIA, HASIOPES, MARANTA

16\10

HAMONOMAH, ARUSOMAGA, MUTIRADAM, OSILAGAMO, NORACARON, OMAGALISO, MADARITUM, AGAMOSURA, HAMONOMAH

16\11

KERMA, ELEIM, REGER, MIELE, AMREK

16\12

MAHAMORAH, ARINEPILA, HITAGEKOR, ANABARIMO, MEGALOGIM, OPOROGENA, RIKIGETOH, ALIPENIRA, HAROMAHAM

16\13

BIKELON, IROLATO, KORAMAK, ELAMATE, LATAROK, NOSEKIB, OTALORI

16\14

NEKASIM, ERARISI, KAIGIOS, ARGENTA, SYNTAK, ISOTATE, MISAKEN

16\15

KONECH, ORIGE, NIMIN, EGIRO, HERAG

16\16

CAHIT, ARIFI, HIRIH, IFIRA, LIHAC

16\17

SEGOR, EROTO, GOLOG, OTORE, ROGES

16\18

BETIFER, ELORAGE, TOTONIS, IROMENI, SANELIT, EGINISI, RESITEB

16\19

TIMINOS, IGALEPO, MAROMEN, ILOSOLI, NEMORAM, OPELAGI, SONIMIT

16\20

RABIHID, AROPATI, BOROMAH, IPOLOPI, HAMOROB, ITAPORA, DIHIBAR

Chapter Seventeen

Traveling in the air.

1. On a ship
2. On a cloak
3. and 4. On a cloud
5. On a stick
6. On a wagon

17\1

BASHEFINA, AGIAMIRON, SILMISARI, HAMOFUSAT, EMIFATISE, SISELARIH, IRASIMLIS, NORIMAGIA, ANIFEHSAB

17\2

NATSA, AROIS, TOLOT, SIORA, ASTAN

17\3

CAPPAIM, AROAMRI, PLIORAK, PARASHA, ASIFIAL, IRAHALA, MIKALAC,

17\4

ANAN, NASA, ASAN, NANA

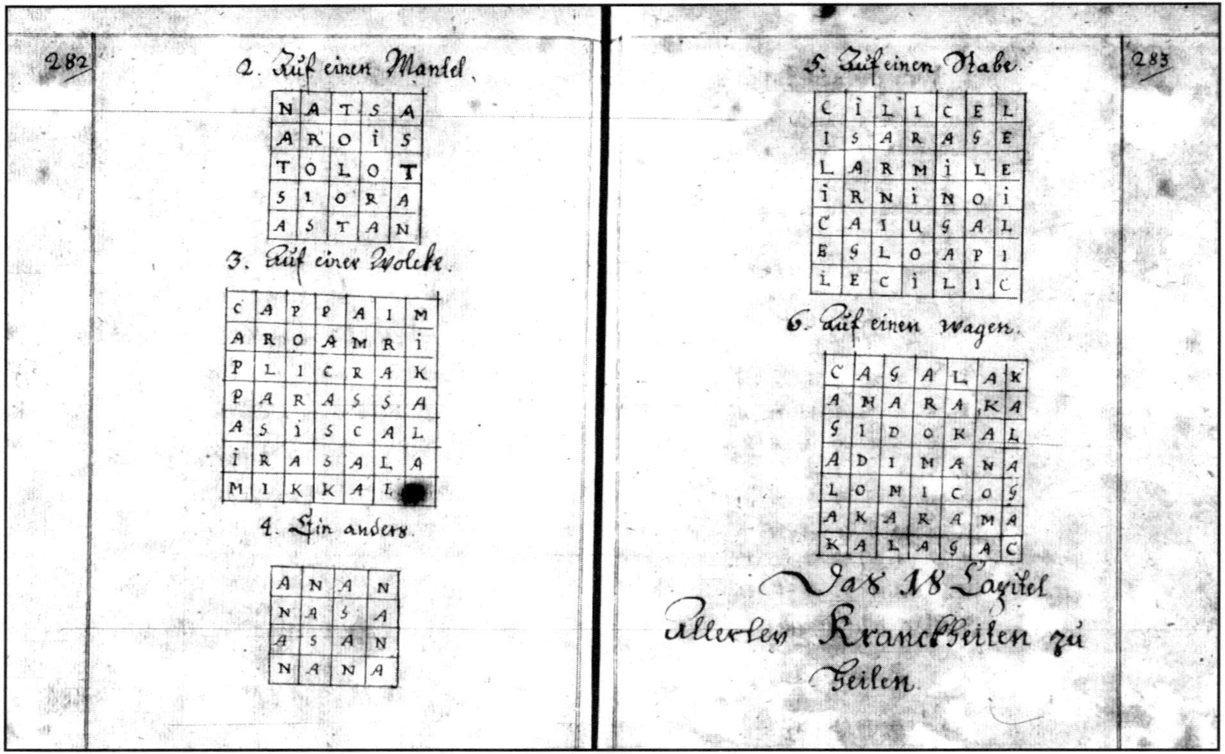

Fig. 27. Squares corresponding to nos. 2–6 in chapter seventeen, from MS 2, Dresden. Square no. 4, for flying on a cloud, contains the word NASA. Rockets fly on clouds . . . no further comment. See also Book Four, chapter ten, square no. 1, to remove magical sicknesses. The word COLI appears. There are other such examples.

Huius usum vide

Siebenzehntes Capitl,

12. und 1. Punkt.

4. Buchs.

In Lüfften fahren.

1. Auff einem Schiff.

Bashesina. Agiamiron. Silmisari. Hamosusat. Emisatise. Siselarih. Irasmilis. Nori. Magia. Anisehsab.

2. Auff einem Mantl.

Nasta. Arois. Tolat. Siora Astan.

3. Auff einer Wolke.

Cappeim. Aroamri. Pliorak. Parasha. Aststal. Irahala. Mikala.

4. Dasselbe.

Anan. Nasa. Asan. Nana.

5. Auff einem Stab.

Cilice.. Isarage Larmile Irminori Caingal Egloapi Tecilu.

Fig. 28. Text for chapter seventeen squares, from Peter Hammer's edition.

17\5
CILICET, ISARAGE, LARMILE, IRMINORI, CAINGAL, EGLOAPI, TECILU

17\6
AGALAK, GIDOKA, ADIMAI, LOMIOL, AKAOMA, KAILAH

Chapter Eighteen

Healing sicknesses.

1. and 2. Leprosy
3. Pimples and ulcers
4. Plague
5. Stroke
6. Fever
7. and 8. Uterine [diseases]
9. Dizziness
10. Intestinal colic
11. Wounds

18\1
TSARAAH, SIRAPLA, ARAMSOH, RAMIUSA, APSUPIH, ALOSITA, HAHAHAH

18\2
METSORAH, ELMINIMA, TARAR, SIRGILI, ONPIAS, RIMLIANT, AGAIARTE, HARSEM

18\3
BUAH, URNA, ANRU, HAUB

18\4
DEBHER, ERAOSE, BARIOH, HOIRAB, ESOARE, REHBED

18\5
SITUK, IRAPE, TARAH, UPALA, KEHAH
18\6
KADAKAD, ARAKADA, DAREMAK, AKESEKA, KAMERAD, ADAKARA, DAKADAK
18\7
RECHEM, ERSASE, EHARAH, HAIAHE, ESAHRE, MEHCER
18\8
BELEM, EMERE, TENER, EREME, MELEB
18\9
ROKEA, OGIRE, KILIK, ERIGO, AEKOR
18\10
ROGAMOS, ORIKAMO, GIBORAM, AKOROKA, MAROBIG, OMAKIRO, SOMAGOR

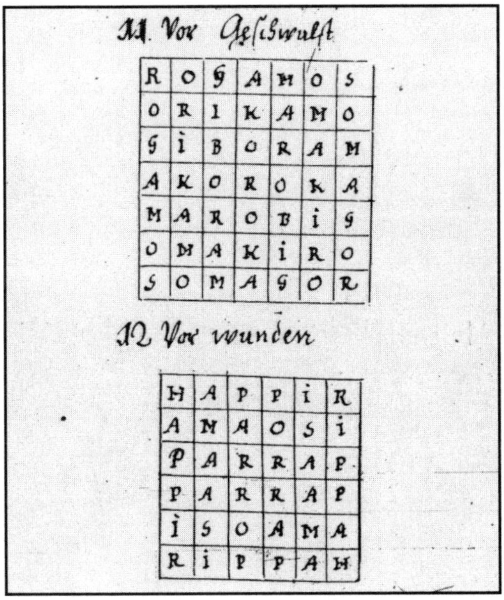

Fig. 29. Squares corresponding to chapter eighteen, Dresden MS 2.

18\11

HAPPIR, AMAOSI, PARAOP, POARAP, ISOAMA, RIPPAH

Chapter Nineteen

To achieve all sorts of friendships.

1. With a bride
2. With a bridegroom
3. Courting
4. From a particular young girl
5. From a particular judge
6. From a widow
7. From a married woman
8. From [an] engaged woman
9. From a particular youth
10. From a particular Prince
11. For peace in general
12. For friendship in general
13. With a famous man
14. With a woman
15. To be loved by a priest
16. For the love of a lord
17. For the love of a particular virgin
18. For a particular bridegroom
19. To be wanted and attractive
20. For adultery in general

19\1

CALLAH, ARIOTA, LOREIL, LAMIEL, AGNIPA, HALLAC

19\2
CATAN, ARISA, TINAK, ASARA, NAKAC
19\3
RAIAH, ARGRA, IGIGI, ARGRA, HAIAR
19\4
DODIM, OBALA, DARAC, ILAPA, MACAR
19\5
SICAFEL, IPERIGE, CEMALIF, ORAMARB, FILAMEC, EGIREPI, IEFOCIS
19\6
ALMANAH, LIAHERA, MAREGEN, AHEBEHA, NIGERAM, AREHAIL, HANAMLA
19\7
SIZIGOS, IPORUSO, ZOLAFEG, IRAGOMI, TURAPEZ, OZETNESR, SAGIZIS
19\8
IALDACH, AGARMAH, LOGARIF, DRISE, AIRDRO, HAFEOM
19\9
ELEM, LARE, ERAL, MELE
19\10
MAGID, AKORI, GOLOG, IROKA, DIGAM
19\11
SALOM, AREPO, LEMEL, OPERA, MOLAS
19\12
AHUB, HAGE, UGIE, BEEZ
19\13
BETULAH, ERIDONA, TIMASOL, UDAMADU, LOSANIT, ANODIRE, HALUTEB
19\14
IEDIDAKT, ERIDONA, DILOGAH, IDOLAIB, DOGAREA, ANACERA, HATIBAT
19\15
SAGAL, APARA, GALAG, ARAPA, LAGAS

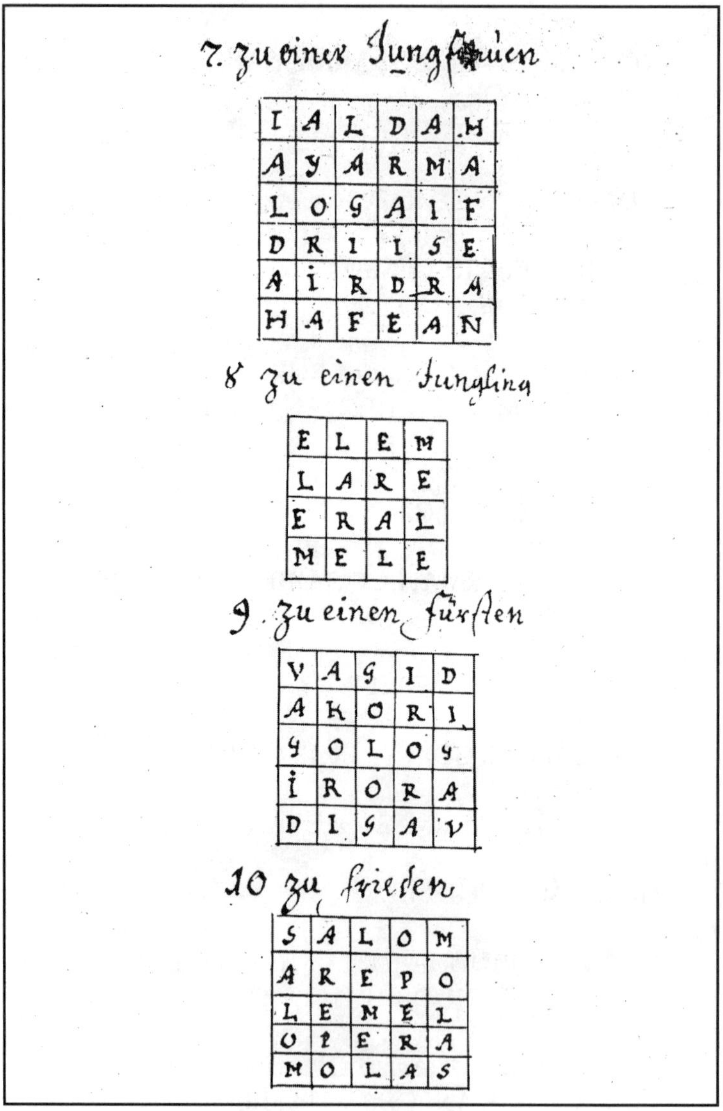

7. zu einer Jungfrauen

I	A	L	D	A	H
A	Y	A	R	M	A
L	O	G	A	I	F
D	R	I	I	S	E
A	I	R	D	R	A
H	A	F	E	A	N

8 zu einen Jungling

E	L	E	M
L	A	R	E
E	R	A	L
M	E	L	E

9. zu einen fürsten

V	A	G	I	D
A	K	O	R	I
G	O	L	O	Y
I	R	O	R	A
D	I	G	A	V

10 zu frieden

S	A	L	O	M
A	R	E	P	O
L	E	M	E	L
O	P	E	R	A
M	O	L	A	S

Fig. 30. Squares from Dresden MS 2. In square number 10, the word SALOM is found. This is almost identical wtih the well-known "Sator" square, slightly changed for other use

19\16
GEBHIR, ERAISA, BAGOLI, HIOLIA, ISLIAH, RAIAHA
19\17
SARAH, AKERA, REMER, AREKA, HARAS
19\18
CATAN, ARIFA, TINAK, ASARE, NAKEL
19\19
TAAFAH, AURETA, ARONIZ, SENACA, ALIORO, THAMEB
19\20
ESEHA, FROIL, CAMAG, THIAMA, ALGAS

Chapter Twenty

For all types of animosity.

1. To start fights and battles
2. To shoot accurately—in general
3. For wrestling in general
4. To commence quarrels in general
5. To quieten the gossip
6., 7., and 8. To make enmity
9. Against gossip
10. To commence war—in general
11. and 12. Make enmity
13. To make fighter unlucky
14. To make differences between man and wife
15. Cause vengeance
16. To make discord and hate between two friends
17. and 18. To make enmity
19. Stir up vengeance
20. To stir up a fight

20\1

RANNA, AGAIN, NATAN, NIAGA, ANNAK

20\2

SELAK, ERAIA, LAMAL, AIARE, KALES

20\3

ATLITIS, TROMALI, LOGOSAT, IMOROMI, TASOGOL, ILAMORT, SITILTA

20\4

ATSAMAH, TIOKAMA, SORAGAM, AKAHAGA, MAGAROS, AMAKOIT, HAMASTA

20\5

ZOGEO, OSONE, GOLOG, ENOFO, OEGOR

20\6

EBIHAH, BERAMA, IRUPAR, HARNAT, AMAOSI, HANTIS

20\7

SIMAB, IRARA, NUMIS, HAMAK, ARIRE, SAREG

20\8

SATAN, AMENA, TEDER, ANEMA, NATAS

20\9

LOSITOS, ORAKIRO, FARAPIT, IKONOKI, FIPORAT, OSIKARO, SOTIFAL

20\10

MILLAMA, IRUENID, LIAMAIS, KEMALOE, ANALAEN, METOERI, ADSERUM

20\11

MIGABAH, ERODISA, GONIMAB, ADISOKA, BIGANOG, SAKOLI, HABAGIM

20\12

GIBOR, ISERE, BELEK, OREAK, REKKI

20\13

MAKIMOS, ADIRATE, KILOTEP, IROMENA, MATETOL, OTENORA, SEPALAH

20\14

GEBHIRA, EKLOAIRA, BUALGAAR, HISOPI, FAGORIAH, RUIFILIB, ASUITAME, HARIBEG

20\15

NEKAMAH, EPARAGA, HASOPIN, AROLANI, MAPOLAS, AGINOSE, HANISEB

20\16

IRAMIDE, NOMINON, HIMARI, SITORIP, ASINIPA

20\17

NAKAM, AROTA, KOBAD, ADARO, MADON

20\18

OHIEB, HIARE, IAMAI, ERACH, BEIHO

20\19

KELIM, EGISA, LIROK, ISOGA, MAKAN

20\20

KERABAH, EMIRUTA, RISOTAB, AROGORA, HOLOSIR, ATURIME, HABAREK

CHAPTER TWENTY-ONE

To take on different appearances.

1. Into an old man
2. Into an old woman
3. Into a youngster
4. Into a young girl
5. Into a boy
6. Into a man with a beard[1]

21\1

ZAKEM, ACOGI, KOLEM, EGARA, MINAS

---

1 This sixth square appears solely in the Wolfenbüttel manuscript.

21\2

DISEKENAH, IPOFIMENA, SORALILEN, ESAMILIME, GILIGILIK, EMILIMASE, NETILAROS, ANEMISOPI, HANEKESIOL

21\3

BACUR, AGOLU, COROL, ULOGA, RUCAB

21\4

IALIDAH, ARIPASA, LIGOZUN, IPOGANU, DOZOLIM, HANUMET

21\5

IONEC, ORALE, NAGAN, ELAIO, KENOI

21\6

DISAKAN, IROGULI, SOLIGUM, AGILASU, KUGAROA, ALUSOAP, NIMIAPA

Chapter Twenty-two

To make sicknesses in people, children, and farm animals.

1. Children
2. Farm animals
3. On the liver
4. On the sex organs
5. On the heart
6. On the neck

22\1

GELADIM, ERALAGI, LAMORUK, OLASULA, DAMORIN, IGULISA, MIKANA

22\2

BEHEMOT, ERARISA, HAIGOEM, ERGOSIA, MIOSACH, OSEIARA, TANAHAL

22\3

CABED, AZOTE, BOROB, ETOZA, DEBAK

22\4

MEBUSIM, ERAGALI, BARONAS, UGOGOGU, SANORAB, ILAGARE, MISUBEM

22\5

LEBHAH, EROASA, BOKOAH, HAOKOB, ASAORE, HAHBEL

22\6

GARAGAR, ARIMASA, RILOPAG, AMOZOMA, GAPOLIR, ASAMIRA, RAGARAG

Chapter Twenty-three

To collapse walls and houses.

1. To collapse a house
2. Walls
3. Lift off roofs
4. Whole buildings

23\1

RAUEH, ARGAR, UGIRP, EARLI, SIPIL

23\2

COMAHON, OSARINO, NAEGRAL, ARGILIT, TIRLAEP, ONAVERI, NOLIPIH

23\3

GAGAG, ASOLA, HOMOG, ALOSA, GAGAG

23\4
BINIAN, NINASI, NUIRAH, IARCAR, AFOATE, NIHCEM

Chapter Twenty-four

For the return of things.

1. Jewels
2. Money
3., 4., 5., and 6. Everything

24\1
KIKALIS, IRINEGI, KINIMEL, ANIDINA, LEMINIK, IGENIRI, SILAKIK

24\2
GENEBAK, ERIKONA, NIROFEH, EKOROKA, BOFORAB, ANAKASA, KALABAR

24\3
MOREH, OLOGE, ROFOR, EGOLO, HEROM

24\4
FONEF, ORATE, NAGAN, ETORO, FENOF

24\5
TALAH, ANIMA, LIGIL, AMINA, HALAT

24\6
GEDESELAN, EROMENISO, DORACUDOM, EMAGAGALA, SECABIHAH, ENUGIRIGA, LIDAHISIM, ASOLAGITO, NOMAHAMON

CHAPTER TWENTY-FIVE

To stay and move around under water for as long as you want.

25\1

MAIAM, ARKOA, IKIKI, AOKRA, MAIAM

25\2

NAHARIAMA, ALOGOMCIM, HOHAMIRCA,
AGALUPIMI, ROMUSUMOR, IMIPULAGA,
ACRIMAFOH, MICMOGOLA, AMAIRAHAN

CHAPTER TWENTY-SIX

To spring open all sorts of closed things and to relock them without a key.

1. Door opening
2. Dissolving chains
3. Opening bolts
4. Opening locks
5. Opening jails

26\1

SAGAR, ADONA, GOROG, ANODA, RAGAS

26\2

KATOK, AGEBO, TELET, OBEGA, KOTAK

26\3

BARIACA, ABARGAC, RASAIMA, IRASOMI, AGIOLIR,
CAMMILA, ACAIRAB

26\4

SEGOR, ELAFO, GASAG, OFALE, ROGES

26\5

SOHARAHOS, ORATITARO, HARUGURAH,
ATULOLUTA, RIGOGOGIR, ATULOLUTA,
HARUGURAH, ORATITARO, SOHARAHOS

Chapter Twenty-seven

To make all kinds of things appear.

1. A beautiful lawn
2. A hunting party
3. A pumpkin
4. A beautiful garden
5. A beautiful palace
6. A rose garden
7. A big lake
8. A snow
9. A grape plant or grapes
10. A vineyard
11. Wild animals
12. Paddocks and fields
13. Farm buildings
14. A castle on a mountain
15. A mountain
16. Flowers
17. Bridges
18. A running spring
19. A village
20. All sorts of trees, also a forest
21. A lion
22. A wild cat
23. Cranes

24. Owls
25. Steers
26. Giants
27. Horses
28. Peacocks
29. Eagles
30. Bears
31. Buffaloes
32. Wild pigs
33. Dragons
34. Unicorn
35. Vultures
36. Foxes
37. Griffins
38. Rabbits
39. Dogs

27\1

HESEB, EGALE, SASAS, ELAGE, BESEH

27\2

KINIGESIA, IRASOGETI, NAGAROSES, ISALITOGE, GORILIROG, EGOTILASI, SESORAGAN, ITEGOSARI, AISEGINIK

27\3

KIKAION, ILAFENO, KALOSAI, AFOKOPA, IESOLOK, ONAPOLI, NOIAKIK

27\4

SELAC, EMIRA, LIRIL, ARIME, CALES

27\5

ATSARAH, TOALISA, SADORIR, ALOGILA, RIROTAS, ASILAOT, HARASTA

27\6

RODONIA, ORAGESI, DALOPEN, OGOLOGO, NEPOLAD, ISEGARO, AINODOR

27\7
AGAMAGA, GULOSEG; ALIRUSA, MORILEM, ASULILA, GESOLUG, AGAMAGA

27\8
SELEG, EPAGE, LARAL, EGAPE, GELES

27\9
OLELAH, LIRODA, ERISUL, LASOME, ADUMAL, HALELO

27\10
SOREK, OBADE, RAGAR, EDALC, KEROS

27\11
CAIOT, AIGRO, IGILI, ORLIA, TOIAC

27\12
JAGEB, AZERE, GESEG, EREZA, BEGAI

27\13
MELUNAH, ESOGALA, LOPODEN, UGOSORU, NADOPOL, ALEROGE, HANULEM

27\14
AKROPOLIS, KOISANILI, RIPORATIL, OSOSUMANO, PARUSURAP, ONAMUSOSO, LITAROPIR, ILINASIOK, SILOPORKA

27\15
KEKASIM, ELISONI, CINOMIS, ASOREGA, SOMERAG, INIGASE, MISAGER

27\16
RERAC, EGASA, RAMAR, ASAGE, CAREP

27\17
DOBERAH, ORAKINA, BALASIR, EKALAKE, RISALAB, ANIKARO, HAREBOD

27\18
MAKOR, ARIDO, KILIK, ODIRA, ROKAM

27\19
MIGIRAS, IROPENA, GADAMIR, IPAKOLI, RIMODAG, ANELORI, SARIGIM

27\20
ESAHEL, SURODE, ARILOH, HOLIRA, EDORUS, LEHASE

27\21
ARIEH, RABUE, IBOLI, EULIR, HEIRA

27\22
LINIROS, IPOSALO, NOCAMAR, ISAGASI, RAMACAN, OLASAPI, SORINIL

27\23
SASAS, ARIKA, SIGIS, AKIRA, SASAS

27\24
KIKIMIS, ILOGETI, KORASEM, IGARAGI, MESAROK, ITEGOLI, SIMIKIK

27\25
PARAH, AZOFA, ROMOR, AFOZA, HARAP

27\26
ANAKIM, NIPOGI, APOKOK, KOKOPA, IGOPIN, MIKANA

27\27
RAMAC, AGORA, MOLOM, AROGA, CAMAR

27\28
MIDIKON, ISOLOZO, DOPETOK, ILOKELI, KOSTOPOD, OZOLOFI, NOKIDIM

27\29
NESIKER, ERAGOZE, SAMATOR, IGARAGI, KOLAMAS, EZOGARE, REKISEM

27\30
DOBIH, OPADI, BALAB, IDAPO, HIBAD

27\31
FUFALOF, ULAHESO, FAROMAL, AHOROMA, LEMORIF, OSAMIGU, FOLAFUF

27\32
CADASIN, ATILATI, DIMONAS, ELOMEGE, SANEMUD, IAGUA, RISEDAR

27\33
TANIN, ASEPIN, NEGEN, IPESA, NINAL
27\34
REEM, ELZE, EILE, MEER
27\35
AIIAH, IUZEA, IZOZI, GEZUI, RAIAH
27\36
SUHAL, UGOMA, HOLOH, AMOGU, LAHUS
27\37
GIRIPES, IPAGOKE, RAZOTAP, IGOSOGI, PALACAR, ELOGAPI, SEPIRIG
27\38
ARNEB, RIAME, NAGAN, EMAIR, BENRA
27\39
KELEF, EMAGE, LAGAL, EGAME, FELEK

Chapter Twenty-eight

In times of trouble, to have as many coins as you need.

1. Gold coins
2. Medium coins
3. Ordinary silver
4. Small coins

28\1
SEGOR, EGAMO, GAZAG, OMAGE, ROGES
28\2
CESEP, EGONE, SOROS, ENOGE, PESEC
28\3
MATHA, AINAB, TURIT, BANIA, ATHAM

28\4
[MISSING TEXT]

Chapter Twenty-nine

To make all sorts of people and armor appear.

1. To make a whole army corps appear
2. To have all kinds of soldiers standing, ready to fight
3. To make a siege appear in front of a town

29\1
MACANEH, ARAMOSE, CARISON, AMILIMA, NOSIRAC, ESOMARA, HENACAM

29\2
MAHARACAH, AFISOLEMA, HIREMUSAC, ASEGAPOLA, ROMAGISIR, ALUPILEGA, CESOSEMEH, AMALIGEPA, HACARAHAM

29\3
METISURAH, ERAGONISA, TAROTISIR, IGOMEDINU, SOTERETOS, UNIDEMOGI, RISITORAT, ASINOGARE, HARUSITEN

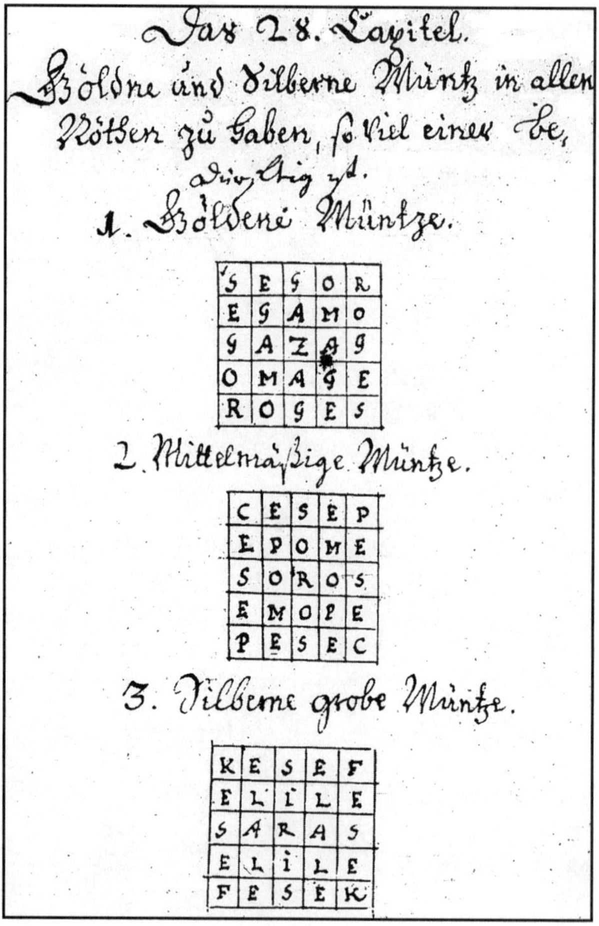

Das 28. Capitel.
Göldne und Silberne Müntz in allen Nöthen zu haben, so viel einer bedürftig ist.

1. Göldene Müntze.

S	E	G	O	R
E	G	A	M	O
G	A	Z	A	G
O	M	A	G	E
R	O	G	E	S

2. Mittelmäßige Müntze.

C	E	S	E	P
E	P	O	M	E
S	O	R	O	S
E	M	O	P	E
P	E	S	E	C

3. Silberne grobe Müntze.

K	E	S	E	F
E	L	I	L	E
S	A	R	A	S
E	L	I	L	E
F	E	S	E	K

Fig. 31. From Dresden MS 2. In square number 2, to get as many "medium" coins as you need, the word SOROS makes up the cross in the middle. Remember George Soros, the speculator who collapsed the English pound and, on another occasion, the nikkei in the 1980s through his manipulation of the stock market?

CHAPTER THIRTY

To have the Spirits perform all kinds of music, singing, and juggling.

1. Music and songs
2. That the spirits appear as monkeys and perform all sorts of strange dances
3. For all sorts of music from stringed instruments
4. That the spirits—appearing as monkeys—perform all sorts of strange acrobatics and juggling

30\1

MEGINAH, ELINALA, GELAGON, HARAKI,
NOGALEG, ATAMILE, HANIGEM

30\2

MEKOLAH, ERLAMOA, KAFISOL, ONIMINO,
LOSISAK, ANOMATE, HALOKEM

30\3

NIGIGIN, IROSORI, GOMIMOG, ISIRISI, GOMIMOG,
IROSORI, NIGIGIN

30\4

MERASEF, EPARUSE, CALAPOS, ARAKISA, SUPINIC,
ESOSIME, FESAREM

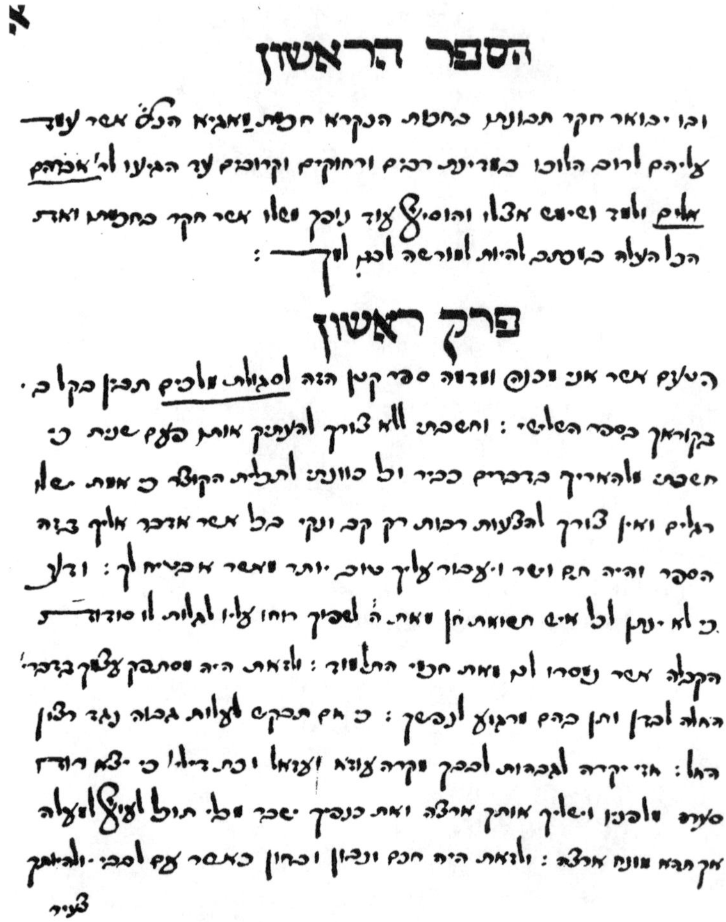

א

הספר הראשון

פרק ראשון

Fig. 32. Hebrew manuscript from the Oxford University Library. This is the only Hebrew rendering of Abraham's work. It is written in an old Hebrew script and contains only Book One in its 38 pages. Judging from the paper used, the MS dates from about 1720.

Appendices

The Editor's Quest.

Though you may find my presentation something like a Gnostic myth, do not be deterred. We find ourselves here in those areas of psychology in which gnosis has its roots.—C. G. Jung, *Collected Works* vol. 12, ¶ 28

I

June 2nd, 1976. Berlin, Motz Strasse, the house where Rudolf Steiner lived in his day. This is the address of Richard Schikowski, a member of the Logen occult scene since the end of World War II, who runs a bookshop and publishing house there. I have never seen such a collection on the subject. I spend half the day there and discover an author from my city, a certain Abraham from Worms. I've found *The Sacred Magic of Abramelin*. My interest in magic is new. Until now, I've been interested in reincarnation, mystic thought, philosophy, and symbols. For a few years I've been meditating regularly.

I unearth Novalis and find him to be a guide into the realms of the soul. C. G. Jung captures my attention. I begin to discover other works on magic. Bardon seems rather inconsistent to me. A convincing practice, but its presentation is far too theatrical—even his signature repels me.

The pivotal event is the moment when I encounter the English translation of *Abramelin*—hidden in a corner, where it has no business being—at the 1980 Frankfurt Book Fair; the sight of it strikes me suddenly and deeply. In the library in the city of Worms I had found an old, extremely comprehensive edition of this Abraham from Worms and had transcribed the text, trying at the same time to bring it into modern High German. I asked myself if I was just playing around, whether my interest was anything more than superficial. The answer was that copy of the American edition of Mathers's *The Book of the Sacred Magic of Abra-Melin the Mage*. Something lay fallow here that was simultaneously relevant to the study of the humanities and deeply connected to me.

The life of Merlin the magician begins to fascinate me. The higher planes start to gain transparency; even the most dissimilar spiritual paths start to seem less contradictory. In the book of Abraham from Worms I notice simple passages such as: "He who never departs never returns home." "Anyone can attain the highest wisdom, no matter whether pagan, Jew, Muslim, or Christian . . ."

II

On the third of March, 1981, I am making my way through the old city of Alexandria. A junk shop catches my attention. I enter the shop, which contains an uncommon assortment of antiquities. There are a few books in a glass case—a handwritten Koran, a wood-block print on centuries-old, buttery parchment in Arabic script, and more. The owner has quite a healthy opinion of how much his goods are worth, and the haggling starts. We come to an agreement, and in the process we start to get to know each other as the hours go by. I am stunned to find out that his name is Dehen. I write my name on a piece of paper and have him read it. He makes the "h" sound into its own syllable, with the result that "Dehn" becomes "Dehen" in his Arabic accent. No less amazed than I, since there are almost no words or names that our two fundamentally different languages have in common, he answers my question of whether he is aware of the origin and meaning of his name by giving me the address of his uncle in Heliopolis.

His uncle, a friendly, older man, is an archaeologist who specializes in predynastic cultures. He invites me to dinner one evening, and tells me of a tribe of Bedouins from Saudi Arabia, the Dohman. They settled in Lebanon, and with the Muslim empire-building efforts they ended up traveling right around the Mediterranean to France. Over a thousand years the name transformed itself into "Dehen." His branch of the family tree returned to Egypt about a hundred years ago. This contact with an extraordinary and well-educated man sends me off on a journey through time, one which would close as yet undreamed-of circuits.

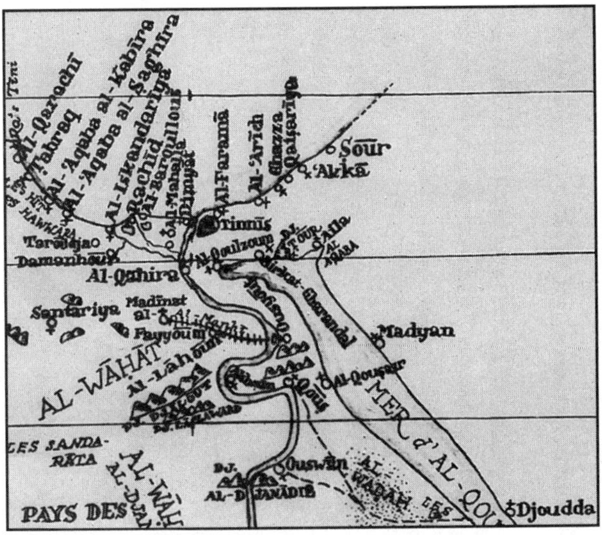

Fig. 33. An old Arabian map from Abou' l-Hasan 'Ali ibn Said, dated 1286. It shows the Nile River from the Delta to Asswan. The map shows locations but the bends in the Nile are wrong. In those days, maps were expressions of ideas, not renderings of geographic facts. "Carte de'l Afrique," Bibliothèque Nationale, Paris. See also p. 194.

His library is extensive, and he very succinctly answers my question as to the odd-seeming mixture of archaeology, Qabalah, and occult literature: Magic is his line of work. "After all, most prehistoric finds," he says, "are associated with rites and rituals." And so my curiosity is aroused.

On another afternoon I am allowed to view his treasures uninterrupted, and I come across Napoleon's reports from his explorations in Egypt. In six large folio volumes, everything had been noted down that could be counted, measured, or observed. Additionally, it contains a register of the name of every village, settlement, and geographical location. One of them is Araki, near to which Abramelin lived in his hermitage.

To make sure, I look for all similar-sounding places and compared them to Abraham's description—Arakieh, 'l Waraq, al Arish, etc. On a later trip, I inspect Waraq in person, since the map showed no signs of discrepancies. It's simply a peninsula, served by a Nile ferry from Cairo. Flooding must be commonplace, as there is no sign of human settlement.

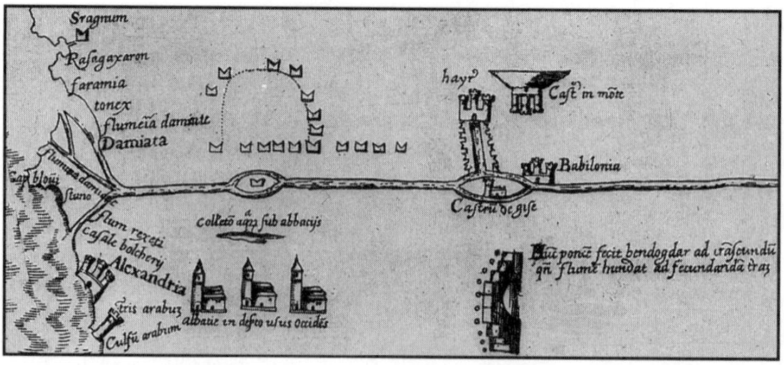

Fig. 34. The Nile Delta. Cairo is called "Babilonia" (Babylon). A detail from Marin de Sanudo's "Karte von Africa." The image comes from a copper etching printed in 1611 in Hanau (a town near Frankfurt, Germany). Even in the 1600s, old maps were still the best sources of information available—in spite of their obvious inaccuracies. Bibliothèque Nationale, Paris.

A Western European could never have found Araki in his wildest dreams. On my later trips, I check every atlas I can get my hands on, be it in Cairo, Jerusalem, or Paris. I now have a complete survey of the cartography of Africa and specifically Egypt from 1350 to 1800. Araki is nowhere to be found, with two exceptions: the atlas volume of the records from that Napoleonic Egyptian expedition of 1803–1804, and the administrative map of the Nile regulation from 1860. These materials are in the French Insitute of Cairo and the Egyptian National Library, respectively.

Abraham did not obtain all his knowledge from books, unlike modern authors and editors, for whom books are a standard tool of the trade. This fact alone about him makes his travel journals, even his very existence, believable.

III

In October 1985, a certain antiquarian bookseller, unknown until then, decided to enter the auction business and sent me his first catalog. It has no specific collections or specialties that might waken my interest, yet I thumb through it, open it at random to glimpse the occasional title, and flip through it again. On one page the phrase, "great revelations" catches my eye. I look back to find the page again and to my great excitement, I discover that this is an auction for *The Book of Abramelin*. It is the Cologne, 1725 Peter Hammer (publisher) edition. The minimum bid is laughably low and reveals the ignorance of the "expert" who had set it. The market sees few rarer books—I'd have thought it completely realistic if the price had had a few extra zeroes. In hopes that there would only be a few bids, I eagerly follow the auction, scrape together the few hundred marks I can spare, and hitch-hike to Pforzheim.

And indeed, there are only four closed bids, but no other potential buyers present. I just barely outbid the rest and find that I have brought, including auction charges, taxes, and a cup of coffee, the right amount of money to the very penny. Broke, but happy, I thumb a ride back to Worms.

Meanwhile, I had been working on Mathers's translation, the volume that had been brought all unawares to the Frankfurt Book Fair. I made a synopsis to reconstruct the original text and hitch-hiked to Paris, because of Mathers, to look in the Bibliothèque de l'Arsenal for his master copy and check the translation.

The conceit with which Crowley and Mathers followed each other is well-known. I imagined that Mathers hadn't worked very scientifically, and the "commentary on the squares" reinforced my assumption. But nothing could have been further from the truth. He remained completely true to the manuscript which, judging from the particulars of the script itself and on the paper, originated in the early 18th century. Unfortunately, one can find it only on microfiche these days.

Nonetheless, it becomes clear to me, after my trip to Paris, that the current German editions and Mathers's are essentially the same text, which I attribute to "Anonymous." It and the Hammer edition of 1725 remain the most reliable basis from which to work.

But there are differences to point out: Hammer contains four books, Anonymous three. Hammer's Book One, Three, and Four correspond to Anonymous's One, Two, and Three.

Hammer's Book Two is a collection of sympathetic magic formulas, which appear in various versions of *The Sixth and Seventh Book of Moses*. Scheible was the first to use the title as an umbrella for several works, which are today well-known in this peculiar combination. He also reprinted the Hammer edition of *Abramelin* in the 1850s. *The Sixth and Seventh Book of Moses* was often newly compiled, containing between two and seven texts—the place of printing is given as "Philadelphia" et al. (Philadelphia is common pseudonym for anonymous mystical editions in middle Europe from the 17th to the 19th century.) In that work, Book Two of *Abramelin* (as I have placed it here) bears the name, "The Secret School of the Arts for Miraculous Magical Powers or the Book of the True Practice of the Ancient Divine Magic, as was transmitted through the holy Kabbalah and through Elohym." The formulas were identical to those in the Hülsemann (Leipzig) edition from the turn of 1900. The edition done by Schikowski Verlag (Berlin) is a reprint of this work. (Karin Kramer Verlag in Berlin has produced a very informative and meticulously edited version. However, in that edition "The Secret School of the Arts for Miraculous Magical Powers, or the Book of the True Practice" does not appear in the title.) I think that the part of Hammer's title ". . . containing within itself the newly-discovered secret books of Moses" is what inspired the title *The Sixth and Seventh Book of Moses*.

There is also an interesting addendum in the "Philadelphia" edition of *The Sixth and Seventh Book of Moses*: "Translated from the Arabic." That confirms my suspicion that this was an addendum obtained by Abraham from Worms himself. Before this clue regarding the Arabic translation came up, I had had a dream about a part of *The Book of Abramelin* in Arabic script and also knew (in the dream) that it had been written one or two centuries before Abraham from Worms.

The next day I visit the Book Fair, and the very first book I notice is a new edition of Maimonides (1135–1204, Saladin's personal physician), who lived in Egypt as a doctor, philosopher, and rabbi. His Arabic name was Musa ibn Maimun. He had written a few of his works, particularly his medical works, in Arabic.

IV

As if by a divine hand, this old printing of Abraham from Worms comes to me. I then begin to experiment with it in my own way.

Specifically it is Werner Larsen, the proprietor of an occult bookshop in Hamburg, who brings me to it. During a visit he

Sechstes u. siebentes

Buch Mosis

oder der

magisch-sympathische Hausschatz,

das ist Mosis magische Geisterkunst,
das Geheimniß aller Geheimnisse.

Wortgetreu nach einer alten Handschrift,
mit staunenerregenden Abbildungen.

Geheime Kunst-Schule

magischer

Wunder-Kräfte,

oder

das Buch der wahren Praktik in der uralten göttlichen Magie, wie sie durch die heilige Cabbala und durch Elohym mitgetheilt worden ist, und als göttliches Geheimniß Cabbala genannt wird, und eine Schwester der göttlichen Weisheit, der sogenannten Magia ist.

Aus dem Arabischen übersetzt.

Fig. 35. Title page of *The Sixth and Seventh Books of Moses*. This is a collection of MS material that includes the recipes from Abraham's Book Two. There are many different editions with the same title. All are compendiums which contained slightly different material. Published in "Philadelphia," a printer's pseudonym of the Middle Ages.

tells me terrible stories about the impact of the Great Egyptian Revelations. He not only knows of the paranoid descriptions of Dion Fortune and C. H. Petersen's suicide following an Abramelin-inspired ritual. He also had his own experiences.

Since the 1970s, I have intensively studied the mindset of the sort of person who assumes no personal responsibility, learns nothing of the origins of materialistic thought patterns and, having just learned by rote the basics of a full-fledged superstition, consciously or unconsciously harbors great and wonderful expectations. This is the same sort of person who (still) believes in a master, despite the fact that he neither has sought nor really wants to find the master within himself. This is the sort of person who wants to seize onto the spiritual world using tangible proofs, and at the same time cannot admit to himself that superstitious is exactly what he is.

It ought to be common knowledge by now that the appearance of an evil spirit reflects a side of our inner selves we cannot accept. I know people to whom the lords of the underworld have appeared, who barely escaped with their sanity. I had to conceal from these people the fact that I often carried around with me the perilous book itself while I was working on the text. One man told me that, while in prison, he had performed the rituals to bring down walls and destroy locks. The Horned One appeared before him, and he nearly had a nervous breakdown.

But that is exactly the purpose of these "evil" formulas and diagrams—they put a person to the test and allow him to grow and develop.

The fourth book, with its magical diagrams, is a two-edged sword. One who is biased, prejudiced, forcible in nature, materialistic, a doubter—such a person can receive some "instant karma" and a bit of hands-on experience with the dark side of his soul. He doesn't need to wait for the problems of daily life to challenge him; he can come face-to-face with himself directly, and even has a guidebook to the various rulers of the underworld he might grapple with over the fate of his soul. It only remains, then, to reinterpret these lords and spirits as psychic dead ends.

Spiritually dedicated souls, on the other hand—seekers, freed minds, humble, patient, and vital individuals—will experience the contents of the fourth book as food for the soul. For them, the book contains not the compulsions of hell but the very glyphs of heaven, and can help them toward a fulfilled existence. The occult is by its nature oriented to self-discovery and needs no instructions or interpretations. It reveals itself effortlessly to someone who has reached this point.

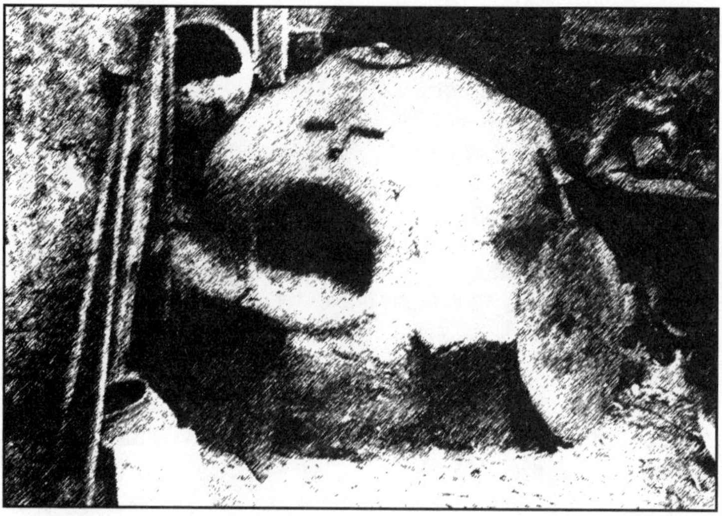

Fig. 36. Oven used for baking holy bread in a Coptic monastery near Araki. Editor's photograph, 1989.

V

At the youth hostel in Cairo, I find the gentleman in the room next door easy to talk to. He claims to be a pharaoh, explaining that he comes from a 3,000-year-old village, which makes him one of the original Egyptians.

I travel to the Red Sea. The Paulus monastery is the remotest of them all. I promise myself that I will spend some time alone in the desert.

Just as I arrive, a monk from a Catholic monastery is being shown around. He is from France, where he lives with two families in a commune. He invites me to join them. Our host introduces himself in excellent English. He takes us on a trip around the monastery that, along with his narration, transports us into the past. Vividly, the monk's life appears before us. The man walks before us as a living transmission from the time of the Pharaohs, a seamless transition from the Pharaonic to the Christian. The Islamic period seems like a short intermezzo. Coptic culture flowed into the established culture without being forced, unlike in Central Europe, where Christianity was spread by fire and the sword. There was a large variety of influences and a number of churches and sects that held sway one after another. Coptic life, at least where it originally existed, embodies the spirit of early Christianity.

We see the workshop of the icon makers and scribes, the tools used for illustration and bookbinding. Fifty years ago they still wrote by hand here, on parchment. All the improvements and extensions of the past few decades were done in the ancient architectural style of the desert fathers. A single generator powers the few carbon filament lightbulbs. The ninth-century mill, the humble rebuilt well, a canoe once used for fishing . . . the ocean is just a few kilometers away.

After the tour we sit down in the refectory. Without a word, Sarab-Amon brings a tub full of hot water. He kneels in front of me. Then he asks me to take off my shoes. He uses a jug to scoop up water, pours it over my feet, soaps them, rinses them. He doesn't notice my speechlessness but performs the task as if it were his duty, without a word. The Frenchman is next. Silent, I feel as if I have been given a precious gift, but the feeling defies all description. I am long since immersed in an experience beyond time, and I drift in a dream over the walls into emptiness.

Once he has cleared everything away, he returns with a round, flat loaf of bread. There are little Coptic crosses like bas-reliefs in the yellow crust. He breaks the bread with the French monk, then with me. We eat a few bites together and the rest is put away. Once it has gotten dark, the full moon throws the shadows of domes and masonry onto the gritty pavement of the monastery's courtyard.

I take trips into the desert for a few days and make a connection to that timeless realm of the dimensions beyond earthly spheres.

Fig. 37. A wadi (valley) in the desert, south of Araki and west of Luxor. Editor's photograph, 1999.

VI

On the next trip, I want to visit Sarab-Amon, but he's no longer there. Meanwhile I've begun looking for Araki; specifically, the hermitage of Abramelin, somewhere between Quena and Nag Hammadi. The old maps show the important places of ancient times that nobody has heard of today, superseded by new ones.

All right, I get information that Sarab-Amon is in the vicinity of Nag Hammadi. Old Gnostic texts and dozens of gospels were found in this place. The Copts say that the province is only 30 percent Muslim.

In the desert I had developed a feeling for the confluence of invisible forces and was back on the level of the first trip: letting myself go without a plan. So I get myself a ticket for the south, ask no more questions, and keep Napoleon's map in my pocket.

Fig. 38. Searching, in 1986, on a rented East German MZ motorcycle, legal to use only in Luxor. To avoid questions I dressed up to look like a local.

In front of the Nag Hammadi train station the next day, I put Sarab-Amon's address in a taxi driver's hand and just have him drive me there. There aren't too many villages on the way, far from highway and railway, on the edge of the Arabian Desert, which is the geographical name of that part of Egypt.

In the first few days he only received guests and accepted invitations. Out of politeness I hold back my own desires until I tell him of my research: my search for Araki, so that I can mount an expedition with Abramelin's hermitage as its goal. Taken aback, he responds that it is just the next village along.

Fig. 39. The two sisters in the shape of Anubis and Horus showing the way. The sisters are the Secret and the Wisdom. Abraham mentions them throughout the third book. Valley of the Kings, editor's photograph, 1989.

VII

On Mount Sinai I meet a man named Christian. We spend a few days in the mountains. It is years before the tourist invasion and personal contact with the fathers of the Katharine monastery is still possible. In addition to the Coptic, I was able to study the Greek Orthodox rite that I knew from Cyprus, but that now took on a new aspect in the realm of the Egyptians.

Christian has obtained the key to a hermitage above the one where Stephanus once occupied, on one of the lateral faces of Moses' mountain, as well as permission to spend a few nights there. He, too, is on a spiritual quest, with a backpack full of books, looking for retreat and a contemplative existence.

But we part ways. He stays in the desert and I return home, looking to make progress in my studies in other ways. His suggestion of the university library in Hamburg leads me to another discovery in my attempt to find traces of Abraham of Worms. Before I discovered Araki, I had directed my attentions toward verifying the author's existence, specifically toward finding editions of his work older than that of 1725.

What I find is a book by Johann Peter Arpe, *Feriae Aestivales*. It contains an abridged version of the *Abramelin* in Latin. From the wording I can see that this is, so to speak, a review of the Hammer edition. Arpe published it in 1726. Unfortunately, it gives me only one clue as to the receipt of Abramelin and provides a general picture of the environment with respect to education and sociology, and of the interdisciplinary context and resonance of the subject matter.

I also discover a little bonus in the form of a few letters glued inside the back cover, which the author (whose estate had apparently contained this volume) had received from his readers. Among them was a certain C. D. von Dehn. Once again, my name shows up in connection with my research into Abramelin. This time the clues point toward Braunschweig.

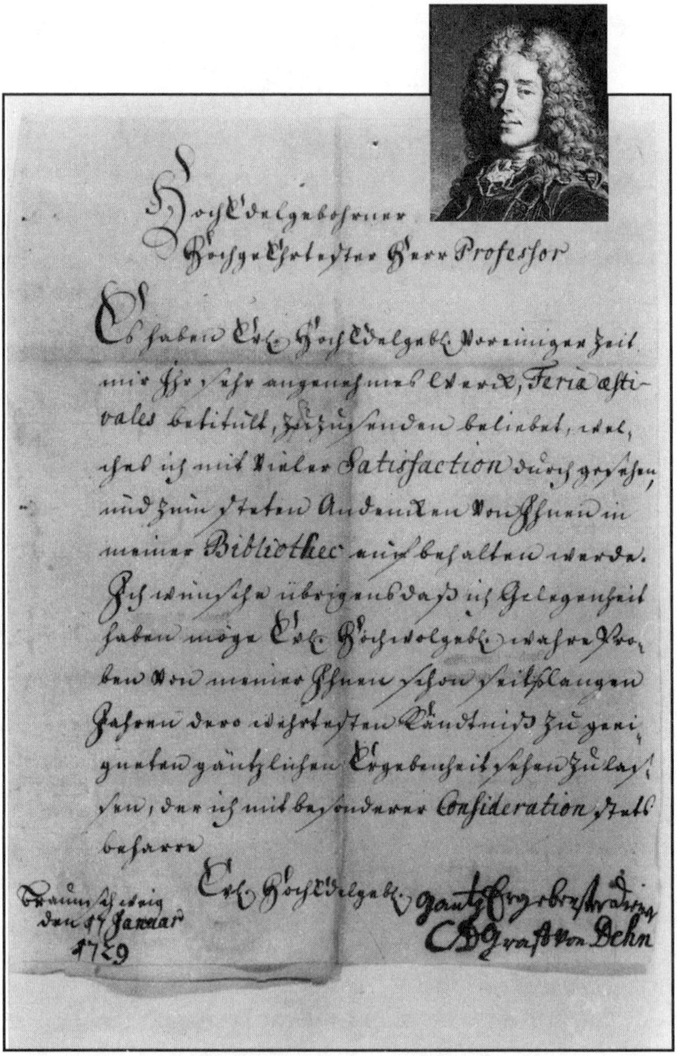

Hochedelgeborner
Hochgeehrtester Herr Professor

Es haben Ew. Hochedelgeb. vor einiger Zeit
mir Ihr sehr angenehmes Werck, Feriae aestivales betitult, zuzusenden beliebet, welches
habe ich mit vieler Satisfaction durchgesehen,
und zum steten Andencken von Ihnen in
meiner Bibliothec aufbehalten werde.
Ich wünsche übrigens daß ich Gelegenheit
haben möge Ew. Hochedelgeb. wahre Pro-
ben von meiner Ihnen schon seit langen
Jahren dero wehrtesten Bekandtniß zu gewi-
dmeten gäntzlichen Ergebenheit sehen zu las-
sen, der ich mit besonderer Consideration stets
beharre

Ew. Hochedelgeb.
gantz ergebenster Diener
C D Graf von Dehn

Braunschweig
den 17 Januar
1729

Fig. 40. Letter found inside a book, *Feriae Aestivales,* which deals with esoteric subjects, including the *Abramelin*. The letter was written by a relative of mine, who was minister of the state and secret minister to the duke of Braunschweig. Conrad Detlev von Dehn lived from 1688 to 1753. His letter thanks the author of the book for his "significant and important work" in polite, formal German. It starts, "Most precious highly-born and most acclaimed Sir Professor . . ." and keeps going that way. The script is perfect, too, as befits a personal secretary.

Die egyptischen

großen Offenbarungen,

in sich begreifend die aufgefundenen

Geheimnißbücher Mosis;

oder

des Juden Abraham von Worms

Buch der wahren Praktik

in der uralten göttlichen Magie und in erstaunlichen Dingen,

wie sie durch die heilige Kabbala und durch Elohym mitgetheilt worden.

Sammt der

Geister- und Wunderherrschaft,

welche Moses in der Wüste ans dem feurigen Busch erlernet, alle Verborgenheiten der Kabbala umfassend.

Aús einer hebräischen Pergament-Handschrift von 1387 im 17ten Jahrhundert **verdeutscht** únd wortgetreu herausgegeben.

Köln am Rhein, bei Peter Hammer. 1725.

Preis, schön gebunden, 4 fl. oder 2 Thlr. 10 Sgr.

Fig. 41. Title page from the first edition of *The Egyptian Great Revelation*, "Containing the discovery of the Secret Books of Moses of The Jew Abraham of Worms Book of the true practice in the ancient sacred magic magic and wondrous things, how they are told through the Sacred Kabbala and Elohym. "Including Power over Spirits and Miraculous works that Moses learned from the fiery bush in the desert, containing all the hidden secrets of the Kabbala. From a Hebrew parchment, from 1387 translated into German in the 17th Century and accurately published. Cologne on the Rhine river, at Peter Hammer's. 1725. Price, nicely bound 4 gilders or 2 taler and 10 silver dimes." Editor's collection.

Count von Dehn was the minister to a descendant of Duke August, who in 1608 was in possession of the Egyptian Revelations, and whose correspondence with the Duke of Anhalt, including this manuscript, is still to be found in Wolfenbüttel.

VIII

I manage to solve a few of the text's conundrums over the course of the years. If Abraham seems to have rejected astrology, then it is the fortune-telling aspect of it that he discards, the deterministic approach, the speculative aspect.

In his work I read again and again how intensely he strove to take responsibility for his own soul, taking nothing for granted. I recognize a Gnostic's attitude: walking the thin line between the rational pursuit of cognition and an intuitive faith in God.

I ask myself, how can I put spiritual principles into practice in the modern world? I discontinue my insurance. Because I am self-employed, I can cancel my health insurance. I had already gotten rid of all my bonds when I dropped out in the 1970s. I grow healthier and healthier. My mental state seems to have direct physical consequences.

As my faith grows, I become more spontaneous. Reading a book on Chartres, I travel there a few days later. Finding a stand-in at my bookshop works out as if prearranged, and I hitchhike there faster than it would have taken by train or my own car.

That summer I also hear about a Hebrew manuscript in Oxford, a version of the Abramelin text. As it turns out, it is vacation time at the Bodleian Library. There is just one man in the Hebrew section who can help me, and he's taking time off. Because I have miraculously been given free access without providing the obligatory German university references, library card, or passport photo, I decide I'd like to at least look at the catalog to see what it has to offer.

In the reading room I ask after the Hebrew specialist again. The librarian says that she happens to have just seen him, although officially he's off until next week. A moment later she reappears with him. He tells me that he is only here to take care of something, that he needs to leave again in ten minutes, but that I can take a look at the manuscript while he's there. For a single moment the fabric of time has torn. What has happened in the worlds beyond to allow this impossible situation to occur?

It is one of the texts that may only be viewed in the presence of the staff. A manuscript on parchment, octavo. Estimating its age is difficult; it must be from sometime before the 1750s. I order a copy on microfilm, and as I'm leaving, the friendly gentleman congratulates me on my good timing.

Fig. 42. Canopen figures, guardians standing atop a funeral urn used to preserve human body organs. Such mummified remains can survive for many thousands of years. Cairo museum, editor's photograph.

IX

Alex Sanders is another stop on this England trip. I had met him at a large convention of witches and enjoyed his hospitality, since after reading my first Abramelin publications he had displayed an interest in meeting me. He recounted in great detail his experiences with the magic of Abramelin. On this occasion I would like to refer to his biography, which tallies for the most part with his stories. To me the "King of Witches" is important, because he was able to demonstrate the intimate connections of "my" magic to the principles of his Celtic and nature-magic roots. The way of life of the Abramelin practice was for him a noble, ethical ideal. His geniality and warmth contradicted all those dark rumors that his dazzling personality had brought about over the years.

X

These stories of mine all take place before the publication of my first edition of *The Book of Abramelin.* A few years still remain before I manage to find the time to complete it. Meanwhile, much has happened. I've found the manuscripts in Wolfenbüttel that recommend a reworking of the text, and that were obviously the source of the French manuscript in the Bibliothèque de l'Arsenal at Paris. I've waded through and carefully compared the Dresden manuscripts. The first edition is sold out, and there are already backorders. I decide to leave Worms after growing to know and love Leipzig. A city of books, in which Goethe was inspired by Auerbach's cellar, and which was a center of spirituality in Germany before the second world war, Leipzig is returning to the cultural brilliance of its old days, and the cosmopolitan atmosphere has asserted itself and is bringing about new dynamics. It will be much easier here to dedicate myself to writing. Among other significant events, Napoleon met his defeat here, while the ruins of Worms, like an echo of the tragedy of the Nibelungs, lay heavily on the soul of the onetime metropolis on the Rhine River, often making this beautiful city seem a dark pit. Also, Jewish life has disappeared from the city. The grave of the MaHaRil remains undamaged, but also in this I find noteworthy assistance only in Leipzig.

Salomon Siegl, head rabbi of Saxony, is the first to be able to read the Oxford manuscript. We translate the text together over a six-month period, and in the process I gain insight into the context of Jewish life. Salomon Siegl devotes time to the work on a regular basis and helps me in my research, until suddenly I begin to grow restless: I want to investigate the last stop in the travels of Abraham from Worms. Until I have at least attempted this, all further effort seems pointless.

Fig. 43. The two sisters. In the middle stands the magician, the one who rules in his spheres, at one side stands the Wisdom and on the other stands the Secret. Cairo Museum, editor's photograph, 1989.

XI

Abramelin Expedition, February/March, 1999. The hermitage of Abramelin, according to Book One, chapter four, is one and a half days away from Araki. Ever since the terrorist attacks on tourists, traveling there is no longer allowed. All intersections are patrolled by police and the military. But I have no time to waste on interminable permit applications. My flight is scheduled under an exact Venus-Jupiter conjunction, and this is the best permit I could ever have. Upon arrival, I have to find a company with the right sort of vehicle. I have the good fortune to meet an Arab in the hotel I'm staying in at Luxor who provides me with a contact at an agency whose specialty is archaeological expeditions. One week after arriving in Egypt I have secured an off-road vehicle with two indigenous drivers—true sons of the desert, having grown up riding horses, and bored stiff by the daily "adventure tours" to Mt. Sinai.

Fig. 44. Luxor, the Mosque in the foreground is located in the couryard of the Luxor town temple. Theben West is across the Nile. In the background are the south-facing wadis that lead to the Valley of the Kings and the Valley of the Queens. Editor's photograph, 1989.

Their first task, namely getting us safely past the police patrols, is a real trial by fire. Our point of departure is south of Luxor—they know a shortcut. We travel on narrow roads, barely wider than a donkey cart, along the Nile canal and over a rocky slope, all the way to the desert road that leads to the Dakhla oasis. Then we turn off onto a side road after about 20 kilometers, which eventually becomes a paved road to Nag Hammadi; a picturesque trip through gorges and wadis, often at a walking pace to circumnavigate boulders and large rocks. Drifts of sand make the trip even more difficult.

At last, after perhaps 70 kilometers, we are through the mountains and once again see the Nile flats before us. Since ancient times, caravans have used similar routes to shorten the trip to Luxor by a day or more. Araki lies in the haze west of Nag Hammadi. A Russian military map shows me exactly where we are, and the GPS pinpoints me to within 50 meters. We turn east before we are seen from the first main road. I estimate that we are a three-hour walk from Araki. Curving tightly, the first wadi leads back into the mountains. We can camp here in a spot where the campfire won't be seen from the Nile. This flat, sandy place is perfect for a sleeping bag. The drivers are overjoyed at all the space in the vehicle, but under a sky like this, wild horses couldn't drag me into a tent or car to sleep. The noise and vibration of the vehicle have probably driven off any snakes or scorpions; at least, there are no signs of any.

I take another walk, during which the full moon rises. The night is bright, and I am accompanied by stark shadows until the wadi ends, blocked by a large boulder. So, we won't be getting any farther on this track—that's why I'm exploring the territory—and I reach a high place shaped like a saddle, filled with quicksand. It's surrounded by rows of boulders, and in the background is the rock desert of the tablelands. I see fox tracks and follow them. The line they form curves outward, then points straight at a square rock as tall as a man, far out in front of me. The tracks split up a few meters in front of the rock. The two foxes each made an identically wide berth around it, met each other again, and then their tracks become lost in the wadi's acclivity. But the rock, cubic and time-scarred, stands there like an envoy from another universe. No one has set foot in this area since the Middle Ages. The last caravans came a hundred years ago, perhaps in the next wadi along. I've shot all of my film. The GPS is comforting—I'll find this place again. We spend about a week in this region. I manage to locate signs of two ancient dwellings, pottery shards and all, both at about the right distance from Araki, both with the characteristic vegetation that indicates possible cultivation and settlement. Visible in the distance is the rock riddled with holes, and a "gateway" on the hill indicates the nearby valley. The rocks at the dried-up stream, where most of the shards lay, look like a collapsed cave. The gateway, though, is a mysterious emblem that has become for me a promising symbol for this trip.

Fig. 45. Collapsed cave. Perhaps Abramelin lived here? In front of the cave is a little well. The cave is cool and hidden in shadow. The main caravan route from Farshout to Luxor passed about two miles from the isolated cave.

Fig. 46. Marker stones above the cave shown in fig. 45. These look like the remnants of a neolithic monument. The cave was just under the hill, about 80 yards away. The stones can be seen from four or five miles away and indicate the Wadi al Hawl that opens just to the south.

XII

December 14, 2000. The flight to Australia to translate Abramelin into English. Steven Guth, with whom I am undertaking this endeavor, had called on Donald Weiser at the Frankfurt Book Fair with me. During Steven's stay in Germany it became apparent to me that I could find no one more knowledgeable of the material. He had delved into various occult schools of thought, knew a lot about magic, was half Jewish, all Buddhist, a full-fledged citizen of the world, and he found this wise teaching of the equivalence of all religions "easy to swallow." In addition, he grew up speaking German and knew the language better than a formally-educated translator.

But our history goes back a bit farther. My father had met him on a trip and was favorably impressed by him. When he eventually came to visit, the lunar node was precisely in its current position, with me visiting him for the first time. It had taken 38 years for the reason behind our connection to be revealed to us. In the past, Steven had helped me to a better understanding of my father, whom in my youth I had reviled more than he could ever imagine. Now, he was assisting in my reconciliation with the man I'd had to make such a great effort to learn to know and love, giving me confirmation of our karmic linkage.

We get the text translated in record time—fifteen weeks—and deliver it to its destination in America. Our intense discussions lead me to a number of answers to questions that had been unanswered since the first German edition.

XIII

I have been living in Leipzig since 1998, a place that provides me with the energy and motivation to dedicate myself to my project. The second edition should exceed the first in its precision; there are new sources that need to be worked in. As is always the case when I involve myself with Abramelin, news and gifts come to me from the spiritual world. And so, after my return from Australia, I discover in the Leipzig university library a collection of portraits in which I run across plates depicting Conrad Detlev A. von Dehn. Though there was no proof to be found in Hamburg that we were related, one of these pictures contains it in the form of my family crest. In addition, a few days before the second edition went to press, I discover a 19th-century account of the then well-known music theoretician Siegfried Wilhelm Dehn. He was originally from Hamburg, studied in Leipzig, and lived in Berlin. The monograph emphasizes that he "brought to light" an old composition of the seven psalms of penance. These psalms, long since forgotten, were offered by Abramelin in prayer. (Ps. 6, 32, 38, 51, 102, 130, 143.)

XIV

April 1st, 2003. Rob Brautigam, a Dutch reader of my *Abramelin* and researcher of Kaiser Sigismund, wrote to me about the *Regesten* he had found. These are official documents of the Middle Ages and they are collected in huge volumes, which are treasures and the source of much historical research. On August 31st, in the year 1426, Kaiser Sigismund had made a Jew, Abraham, living in Leipzig, who had helped him and the Duke Frederic of Saxony so many times, his personal Jew and servant, and bestowed upon him escort and protection throughout the whole Reich—for himself and his family. Rob ends his letter, "It sounds to me that

Sigmund 1426. Ungar. 40. Röm. 16. Böhm. 7. 49

1426			
Aug. 21	Ofen	desgl. mit dem Kg. [Johann II.] v. Castilien u. Leon. — [KU. w. v.] — Not. ib. 127r.	6717
»	»	desgl. mit dem Kg. [Johann I.] v. Portugal. — W. v.	6718
» 23	»	beauftragt den B. Johann v. Vesprim zwischen Hrz. Filippo Maria v. Mailand u. den Florentinern Frieden zu vermitteln. — Rex. Mich. — RR. H 125. (d. 23. aug.)	6722
» 31	»	erklärt Konrad v. Aufsess, weil er das von Kg. Wenzel zur Sicherung der Strasse niedergebrochene Schloss Spies, dessen Wiederaufbau verboten war, wieder erbaut u. befestigt habe, auch auf dreimalige Vorladung nicht zur Verantwortung erschienen sei, in die Reichsacht. — [KU? — R? — Or.?; RR. H 132r mit KU: Rex. Mich.] — Reg. Boic. 13, 78; vgl. auch Chronik. d. dtsch. Städte 1, 427. (sa. vor Egidi).	6723
[» ?]	»	nimmt den Juden Abraham, wohnhaft zu Leipzig, der ihm u. Hrz. Friedrich v. Sachsen viele Dienste erwiesen, zu seinem „sunderlichen Juden und camerknechte" an u. erteilt ihm Geleit u. Reichsschutz für sich u. seine Familie. — KU? — RR. H 128v. (s. d.)	6726
Sept. 1	»	schenkt dem Johann v. Srlin den ihm nach Bedřich v. Klokočov heimgefallenen Zins von 2 Schock Prager Gr. — Ad relacionem d. Ulrici de Rozemberg M. prepos. Bolesl. — R — Or. Wittingau. (prima die sept.) *Mareš*.	6727
»	»	fordert alle Reichsunterthanen zu Feindseligkeiten gegen die Venetianer u. zur Unterstützung seines Bundesgenossen u. Reichsfeldherrn Filippo Maria v. Mailand auf. — Rex. Mich. — RR. H 134v u. 135r.	6728

Fig. 47. Official *Regesten* of Sigismund for the year 1426, listing the documents issued by day. For the last day of August the line translates as: "Sigismund, in appreciation of his former services to himself and the Duke Frederic of Saxony, places Abrahman the Jew, habitant of the city of Leipzig into the position of his 'special Jew and private servant' and grants him escort and protection in the whole empire for himself and his family."

this is likely to be 'our' Abraham. Anyway, I just wanted to let you know." With that, he closes the ring of questions about Abraham's biography. The Worms documents only tell us that Abraham returned shortly before his death in 1427 and nobody knew where he stayed in the years before.

XV

Geo, your quest to find Abramelin's hermitage has always fascinated me. By now we know within about 10 square miles where it must have been. And that's enough to give us some indication of the probable roots of Abramelin's wisdom.

Monasteries, hermits, and Egyptian tombs from the days of the Pharaohs all seem to be within walking distance of Abramelin's location. I think it's fairly evident that Abramelin could have—and perhaps did—exchange self-development ideas with his Gnostic neighbors.

As for the "calling" of spirits. Again, I think geography provides clues . . . the huge nearby pet cemetery and the adjacent Valley of the Kings and the Valley of the Queens in which were buried innumerable dead.

Here is one of my little essays; it gives an insight into the possible source of spirit names. It also suggests why they can be so dangerous to invoke.

Regards,
Steven Guth
Canberra, Australia
April 26, 2002

Yesterday, the day after Anzac Day (Australia's soldiers' national memorial day), the meditation group—seven of us—met behind the War Memorial at the foothill of Mt. Ainslie. Ainslie is a mountain with a kind, loving, and caring energy. Understandably the War Memorial shrine sits at its base and is welded into Canberra and the Australian landscape by roads, ley lines, and tree plantings. The building is being cleared and its nature changed but some war dead can still be sensed, particularly in the shrine chapel, a basilica-like room with service people depicted in stained glass and mosaic under a cupola depicting in Theosophical terms the ascent into heaven, which is finally accessed through a symbolic hole in the roof. The skeleton of an unknown soldier rests in a central grave. The soldier came from the fallen of WWI, and is a link to the battlefield from which his body was recovered.

The meditation group sat in a rough circle on a carpet of leaves under the gum trees at midday on a perfect autumn day. I quickly went into a light meditation, Kathrine, my wife, siting five meters to my right, coughed and there appeared in front of my meditative eyes a person in a WWI soldier's helmet. The face was unclear but it seemed to have been called to the scene by Kathrine's barking cough. Was it there to give healing? What was it anyway? I projected my consciousness into it and to my great surprise suddenly found myself in the Australian camp that was near the Great Pyramid in Egypt—a holding camp for troops before they were allocated to kill and be killed on behalf of the British Empire. I've seen spectacular pictures of the camp with the Great Pyramid towering in the background. This time, I had an aerial view.

Immediately after that came a view of the passageways inside the pyramid that were filled with spirit shapes and energies. It quickly came to me that the pyramids were built to draw in and keep in a convenient location some of the ghosts that were attached to tombs throughout Egypt. The War Memorial with its shrine chamber has a similar, but perhaps more limited, function for the Australian nation.

Then came the realization that the Egyptians had a system going to turn the dead into their servants. They buried their dead in such a way that they remain within the frequency range of the living and so accessible to us—in our physical bodies—to perceive and use.

In one part of my life, I was in daily contact with Aboriginal families. I was continually exasperated to see the low level of care that went into the raising of children who were obviously deeply loved and much wanted. As my friendships grew the explanation became clear; dead children were not lost, but remained with the family in their soul state. So a loved dead child is never lost, just transformed. Chinese ancestor worship is based on similar relationships between the living and the dead, deals being struck with the living by sending down prayers of release, and the dead, in turn, manipulating events to help their living descendants.

It also became apparent to me that the rituals and techniques the ancient Egyptians used gave many of the Egyptian ghosts an extraordinarily long existence, spanning thousands of years. It began to seem that I had in front of me a cat or a dog spirit that had attached itself to the body of an Australian soldier who had syphilis. The ghost's technique for continuing its existence was to attach itself to and use the energy of living, susceptible people. By now this long-dead pet had developed an almost human personality.

I felt that there must be hundreds upon thousands of these beings floating around Egypt. From pet spirits to servants, from priests to kings.

So this is why the occultists of the preceding two centuries were so keen to get to Egypt. Abraham visited Abramelin in the Egyptian desert near Luxor and the Valley of the Kings in the Middle Ages. That may well be where his Guardian Angel, the four servants of the day, and the names of spirits (who fulfill specific tasks) came from. Undoubtly, unless redeemed, they are still around us today—spreading to the four corners of the globe.

Steven Guth

The MaHaRIL and Abraham from Worms— A Historical Analysis.

The MaHaRIL's tombstone in the Worms Holy Sands cemetery is shown in figure 48 (see also fig. 49, p. 222). This is also the grave of Abraham. The stones and paper slips on top of the gravestone are left by people seeking blessings, the granting of a wish, or a bit of magic.

Fig. 48. The MaHaRIL's gravestone in the Worms Holy Sands cemetery. The gravestone is unique; it faces east toward Jerusalem, instead of north as do all the others in this cemetery. The MaHaRIL requested in his will that no other graves be placed within about four feet of his. Jacob ben Jechiel Loans, a well-known 15th-century Kabbalist, is his nearest neighbor.

Although not the oldest grave in the cemetery, it is by far the most visited. It is unique in two ways. It sits in its own quiet little hollow, with surrounding graves set back at least four feet. And it faces toward Jerusalem; all the other graves in the cemetery face the Worms Synagogue. This is because Worms was regarded as the "Little Jerusalem," the second most holy place on Earth. The MaHaRIL requested both these exceptions in his will.

The Holy Sands cemetery is the oldest Jewish

Fig. 49. Jewish Holy Sands cemetery in Worms. The oldest Jewish cemetery in Europe, established around 950. Photograph, Hans Bagehorn, 2004.

graveyard in Europe, with records stretching back to the 10th century. The oldest remaining graves are from the 11th century. The MaHaRIL's grave is in the "Valley of the Rabbis," the oldest part of the cemetery.

The inscription on the grave reads: "The moon eclipsed as he returned home, who by the fulfillment of his inspiration was as a precious fruit." It is difficult to translate this statement. Hidden in the words are double or triple meanings. One finds similar statements made about bodhisattvas in Eastern literature.

There are five lines missing from the gravestone. The remaining lines start with letters that contain the latter portion of the MaHaRIL's wife's name. Her name was Melcha, which comes from the Hebrew word for "Queen." This encoding of hidden words is a Kabbalistic technique known as acrostichon. Similar encoding is found in the word squares in Book Four.

Fig. 50. Washing well, the *Mikwe*, next to the Worms synagogue. The MaHa-RIL, and other Jews, would have used the well for washing before going to the synagogue. The well is still much as it was in the 14th century. The nearby synagogue has been rebuilt since WWII. Editor's photograph, 1990.

Synchronicities between the MaHaRIL's and Abraham's biographies

In considering the known biographies attached to these two names one must bear in mind the following:

1. Attempts may well have been made by the MaHaRIL's transcribers to distance him from the writings of Abraham by allowing confusions. For example, there appears to be a conflict about the place(s) of birth, whether in Worms or Mainz. This can, in part, be explained by the fact that the Worms district included Mainz.

2. The number of Jews in the whole of Germany after the Black Death and subsequent pogroms had dropped to an estimated 10,000, perhaps five percent of the original population. Jews of the Worms district must have numbered, at most, in the hundreds. Traditions were in danger of being lost. This may well have been why both the recipes in Book Two and the traditions collected in the *Sefer MaHaRIL* (first published as the *Minhagim*, Sabionetta, 1556) were compiled.

3. From internal evidence it appears that Books One, Three, and Four where written for Abraham's son Lamech. Book Two, the folk cures, is an addition that makes a useful gift.

Table 1. Biographical Comparison between Abraham and the MaHaRIL.

Dates	Abraham	MaHaRIL
1350's		Considered birth period
1359	Constructed birth date from evidence in Book One, chapters 2 and 3.	
1379, Dec. 24	Death of Moses, Abraham's biological father—from statement in Book One, chapter 3.	
1387, Apr. 27		Date of the death of Moses, MaHaRIL's teacher.
1387	End of studies in Mainz	End of studies in Mainz and initiation as Rabbi
1387, May 10	Beginning of journeys. These lasted for 17 years and covered the Mediterranean world; from evidence presented throughout Book One.	The historical records stop from this period.
1387	Abraham arranges marriage for Emperior Sigismund, as stated in Book One, chapter 8.	MaHaRIL's profession was as a "matchmaker."
1394	Long stay in Constantinople, stated in Book One, chapter 4.	According to Jewish Library records in Berlin, MaHaRIL suffers a stroke.
1400s		Documentation reappears. Evidence from letters indicates he made visits to Vienna, Venice, and upper Italy.
1404	Return via Venice, upper Italy, and the Rhine valley.	
1417	From this time, Abraham was a consultant to Pope Martin V and Pope John XXIII; evidence from Book One, chapter 8.	Travels to Konstance as a member of the Jewish delegation to Congregation with Popes Martin V and John XXIII; evidence from the ample records of the 1417 Congregation.
1422		Pope Martin V issues a papal bull, granting protection for Jewish people.

Table 1. (cont.)

Dates	Abraham	MaHaRIL
1423	Abraham's letter to Byzantine Emperor John II, according to Book One, ch. 8 i., in which he prophecies the ruin of the empire and his own death within a short time.	
1425	Abraham helps Sigismund in a battle.	Abraham "the Jew" mentioned in the register for helping Sigismund in war.
late1420s	Records cease.	Jewish history informs us, that he returned to Worms.
1427		Death, as recorded on the tombstone.
1458	Date noted on manuscript, "Book of Abramelin."	First compilation of the Minhagim by Salman von St. Goarshausen.

Travel Funds

Abraham tells us in Book One that he traveled the Mediterranean world for 17 years. At no point is there any mention of a paid occupation. On the contrary, he tells us of being sick for a year and of giving Abramelin gold guilders to pass on as alms money to the poor people of Araki. How did Abraham finance his travels? Did he take a money belt along? If he had such funds with him, how did he manage to survive without being robbed?

Given this difficulty, one may conjecture that Abraham only traveled in his imagination. No, there is a solution. Medieval Jews had an infrastructure, a system for obtaining funds throughout the known world.

This is well-described by Noah Gordon in his historical novel *The Physician* (Simon & Schuster, 1986). It grew out of the fact that the Jews were a social group that had strict, religiously reinforced ideals about the importance of in-group identity. Signs, gestures, and words—much like the Masons today—were used to ensure religious identity. For some, these ideals were reinforced by the fear that a transgression would harm one's children, and one's children's children "to the hundredth generation."

The system worked on written notes telling of financial obligations—checks, if you will. These could not be stolen because they came with assigns or personal knowledge that identified the note bearer and the truth of the obligation.

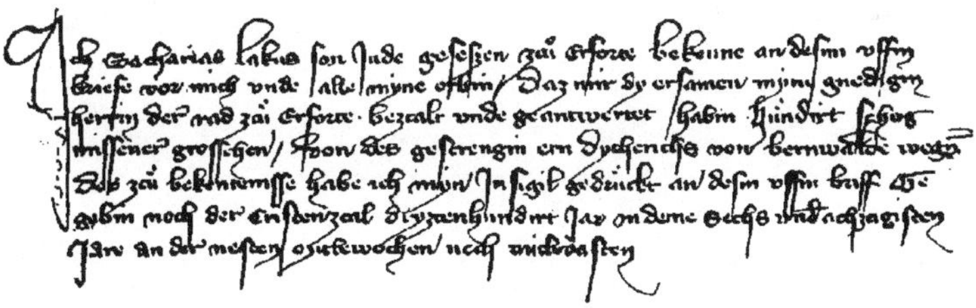

Fig. 51. Traveler's check from the 13th or 14th century. It names the traveler and specifices the amount of money involved. It was used in conjunction with a seal. From *Jeudisches Lexicon,* 1928.

This system also allowed for trading, it made payments possible without the direct need to swap goods for a return journey. Money was only a part of the contractual agreement.

Abraham, as the MaHaRIL, was both a rabbi and an *Ehevermittler* (a matchmaker). He certainly would have been accustomed to operating within this contractual system of family obligations.

Table 2. Abraham's Travels and His Route.

Time	Whom He Met	Place	Duration
1. 1383	Rabbi Moses (1st master)	Mainz	4 years
2. 1387, 13th Tiar	Master Jacob (2nd master)	Straßburg	
3.	Anton (3rd master)	Prague/Bohemia	
4.	different people and the witch—all together the "4th master"	Austria, Linz	
5.		Hungary	
6.	Philip, Philonion	Greece/Epiphus, etc.	
7.			
8.	Simon Moses, Rabbi Abraham	Constantinople	2 years
	Halimeg, Alkoron, Silek, Haliorik, Abimelech	Egypt	3 years
		Palestine	1 year
		Arabia	1 year
		Palestine/Egypt	1 year
	Abramelin	Araki/desert	1 year
		Constantinople	1.5 years
	At brother's home	Venice, Italy	
	Joseph	France/Paris	
		Back to Worms	

Where Was Abramelin's Hermitage?

Let's consider the possibility that Abramelin's system of personal initiation came from Gnostic techniques that were being developed by hermits living in Egypt. Imagine sitting in a cave near the Valley of the Kings, the Valley of the Queens, and the largest dog and cat cemetery known to history. What would you be doing? What would run through your mind, what would be happening in the spiritual space around you? Perhaps something like the path of initiation in Book Three would come out of such a situation.

What is the geographic and historical evidence that such a possibility existed?

In his book, *Christian Egypt,* Otto Meinardus mentions the Monastery of the Angel, "Deir al-Malak." The name does not refer to any particular angel, and this is unique because monasteries are usually dedicated to some holy name. The monastery is about 8 kilometers north-east from Araki, on the eastern side of the Nile (see map, fig. 52). The modern town of Nag Hammadi is nearby. You can see the correspondence with the nameless "Holy Guardian Angel," which Abraham describes in Book Three.

The monastery of Deir al-Malak is occupied by a priest who cares for the village of al-Dâbba. About 300 meters away from the Monastery of the Angel, in a small wadi, are two caves that once hosted history's first Christian hermits. According to Otto Meinardus, the resident priest was the first to hold the famous Gnostic manuscripts discoveries of 1945 in his hands. These were unearthed from a graveyard in the neighboring village of Chenoboskion. Monasteries in this location are the first Christian monasteries; they were established by Pachomius in the 5th century.

There are reports from Abramelin's time related to the location. Take for example the vision of Qummus Murqus, who in the beginning of the 15th century was responsible for the

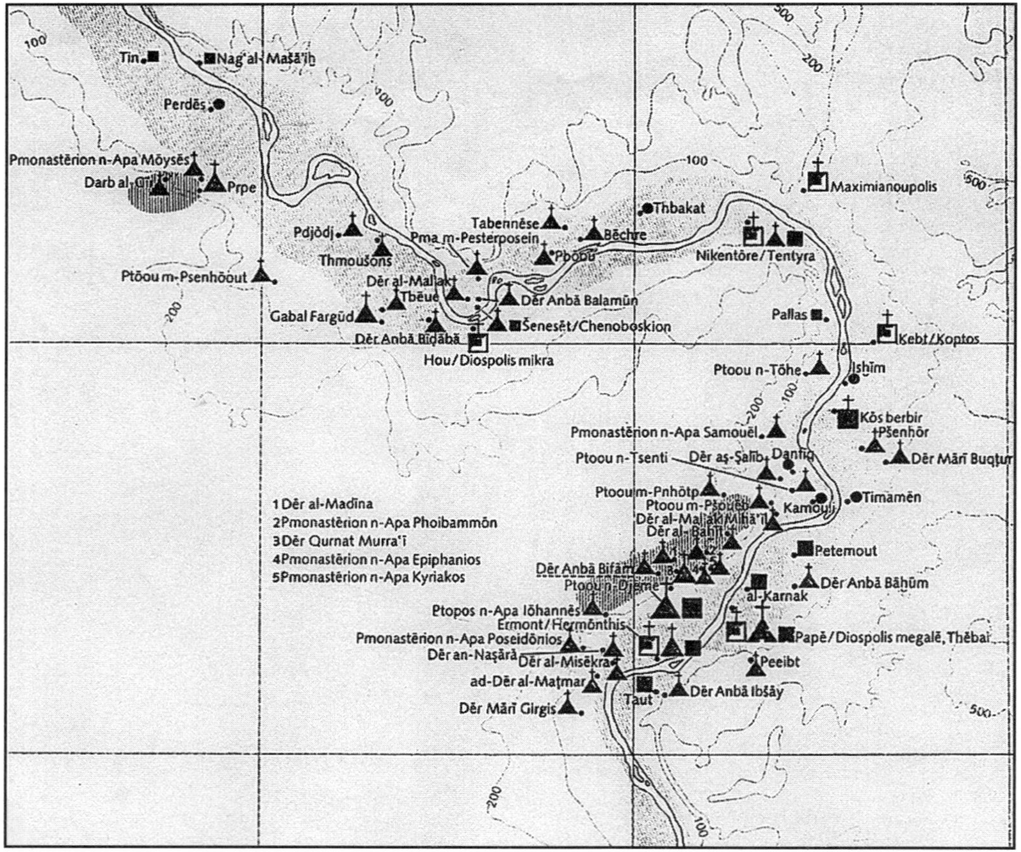

Fig. 52. Monasteries and Pharaonic temples in upper Egypt. The idea for these monastic communities came from desert father Pachomius in the 5th century. University of Leipzig library.

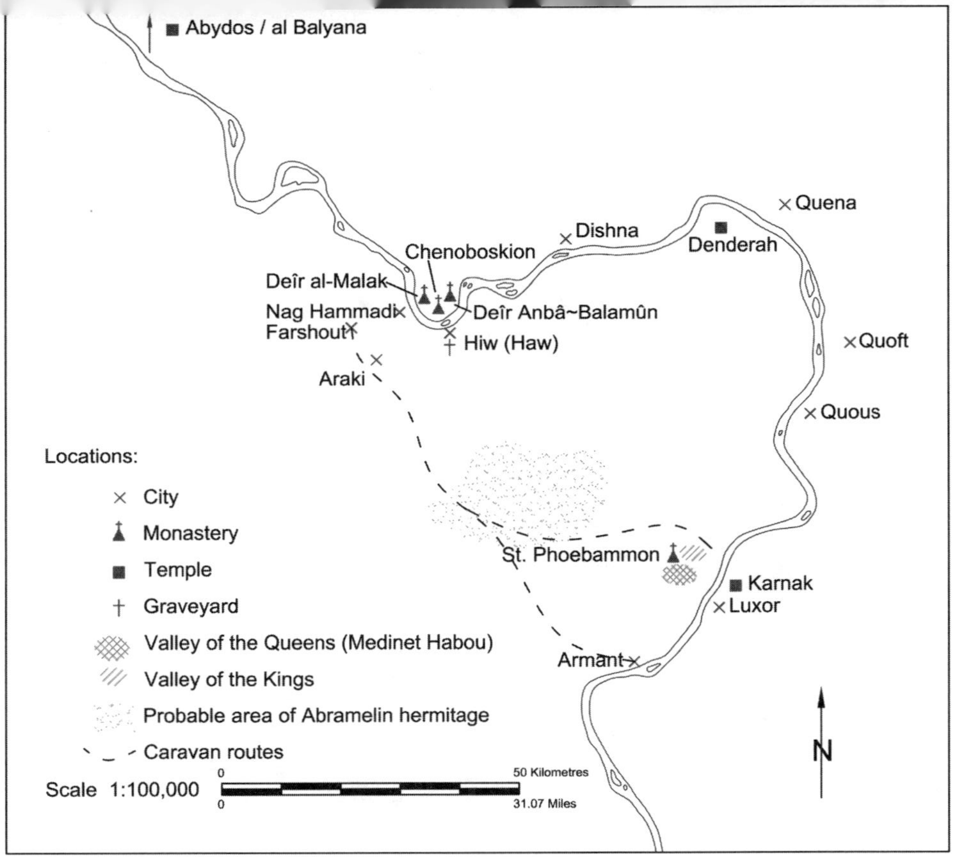

Fig. 53. Map showing the probable location Abramelin's hermatige. The ancient caravan route from Farshout to Luxor and Armant is suggested. This route continued north to Cairo, west to Mecca and south to Aswan. The map shows the locations discussed in the text and includes modern cites. Editor's collection.

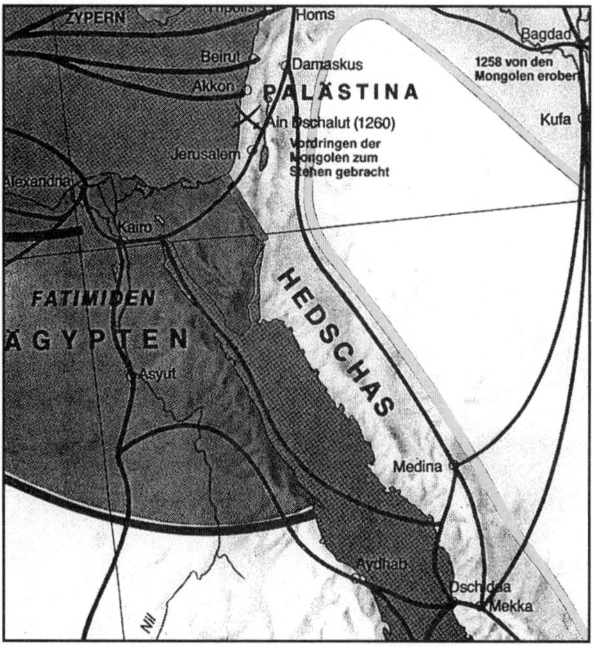

Fig. 54. Rough map of the major international trade route through Egypt, the eastern Mediterranean, and the Red Sea. The route that passed through the probable location of Abramelin's hermitage is clearly indicated. Historical atlas, editor's collection.

Monastery of St. Palemon, "Deir Anbâ Balamun" one kilometer to the west (see maps, figs. 52 and 53 on pp. 230–231).

In the time of the Pharaohs, the area was governed from the town of Hiw (pronounced "how," and known as Diospolis Micra in Roman times—see figure 52). Hiw is well-known for its animal graveyard in which were buried sacred cats and dogs. To the south, on the edges of the desert, is the Monastery of St. Menas "Deir Mârî Mînâ al-Agayebî," which stands on the grave of a Muslim saint. A poor Coptic from Hiw was asked by St. Menas in a vision to build a church on the spot, and he quickly did this. Nowadays Hiw is an insignificant village.

Half an hour's drive to the northwest is the important historical town of Abydos. It was the center of the Osiris worship and the most important of his sites. According to legend, the head of Osiris rested in the temple. The most important temple is the Memnonium Temple of Seti I. Later, Ramses II erected an Osiris temple in the area.

On the northeastern side of the area is the well-known Temple of Denderah. It is considered one of the best-preserved temples in Egypt and is dedicated to Hathor, a goddess who is often depicted with horns on her head. On the roof is a room with a zodiac on the ceiling, the only historical zodiac in Egypt.

In the days of caravans, the paths led from Farshout and Araki to Aswan and Luxor. Tracks led through the wadis, enabling travelers to shorten their travel to the north by cutting across the eastern bend of the Nile. The route came from the direction of the Valley of the Kings and was known as the Farshout route. It seems likely that Abramelin's hermitage was somewhere along or near this route. (See section 11 of "The Editor's Quest.")

Going south, one travels on a flatland into which are cut many wadis flowing to the north. About 15 kilometers away is the Valley of the Kings which is cut into a deep wadi that flows by a curved route southwards into the Nile. The whole area abounds with places of historical interest, of which Luxor is the most famous.

Otto Meinardus mentions the Monastery of St. Phebammon which was unearthed in 1948. It is rich in Coptic paintings and may well have originated in the 5th century. It lies about 8 kilometers to the west of the Valley of the Queens. It is approached through the desert of from the al-Kola al-Hamra. It may well be the closest known site to Abramelin's hermitage.

Lamech —The name of Abraham's son for whom the Books were written— a Kabbalistic investigation.

Who was Lamech? Perhaps a son conceived during Abraham's seventeen years of travel. From the early chapters in Book Three, it appears that Abraham knows his son's horoscope, but not his current situation in life.

Historical records suggest that Lamech was not the name of any known son of the MaHaRIL. So it seems fairly certain that this name is a pseudonym—just as Abraham of Worms and probably the name "Abramelin" are constructs.

Maybe there is a hidden message in the name "Lamech." The easiest solution is to look at the correspondences with his wife's name, "Melcha." All that is needed is to rearrange the letters L and A.

What is the deeper meaning of Lamech? Is the name a key to the personality of a real son?

The Bible's history of Israel names ten consecutive patriarchies, starting with Adam and Seth. The ninth patriarch was Lamech. He was the son of Methuselah and the father of Noah. He lived for 777 years, according to the lineage of the Sethites.

The genealogy of Cain lists a Lamech as another descendant of Adam (according to the table of Cainites). This Lamech is related to the number 7 in the following way: "If Cain is avenged seven times then Lamech seventy-seven times." So this is 3 times seven—777. The Jewish tradition, according to Friedrich Weinreb, relates the following story:

Lamech killed Cain. He was the sixth generation after Cain, already very old, but he still went hunting. His son Tubal-cain, the blacksmith, led him to some animals. He saw a horn behind a bush and pointed it out to Lamech, who could no longer see so well. Nevertheless, he approached and shot. It was Cain, his ancestor, whom he had killed. Tubal-cain thought he saw an animal. Lamech clapped his hands together in agony and despair and killed his own son as well.

The name Lamech, supposedly the name of two different people, yet linked together with the number 7, was chosen by Abraham from Worms.

Abraham may have had two reasons for doing this. The first may be that Lamech was used to denote his son. The second was that Lamech may have been the pseudonym used to hint at the compiler of the manuscript material—Salman von St. Goarshausen. Abraham may have regarded his most important student as a second son. It is interesting that "Salman" is also close to being an anagram for Lamech in German and Hebrew.

First the mystic relationship to the number 7, which is a special number in Kabbalistic studies, and then the obvious duality related to the number two; the double meaning of the names and the idea that the author wished to create a second existence with the pseudonym mirrors the biblical Lamech and his double existence.

Over the years, I have considered how the spirit names and the names in the squares have been used during the centuries. This work leads me to believe that the lines of Cain and Seth really share the same genealogy and the apparent separation only served two different political ideologies.

My exploration of the name Lamech is an example of several approaches to Kabbalistic thinking. It shows how names have inner and hidden meanings. Similar approaches can be used for the recipes in Book Two, the spirit names in Book Three, and for the squares in Book Four.

The Word Squares.

Word squares may well have started in China four or five thousand years ago; the *I Ching* is the Chinese development of the concept. It is also at the core of many Chinese schools of Feng Shui, wherein a nine-division square is said to show the way a house can be harmoniously balanced with the universe.

Arabian astrologers used squares in Abraham's time, both as descriptive tools and as talismans. The squares have a similar relationship to the universe—the worlds below and above—as Pythagorean geometry, which is a way of describing and making a fractal image of the totality.

So a square with the correct names on it makes a gateway between the universe and the person who holds the square. The intention that is put into the situation makes the square work. The squares also help focus intention, so that results can be achieved.

The squares can be mathematical, with letters representing numbers. Or they can be based on the sound of letters, expressed in Hebrew, German, or some other language. They may be directly linked to the names of spirits. All of these systems may have been used in Abraham's squares.

Word Squares as Tools for Self-Development

Abraham's squares can be seen as tools for meditation or ritual and they have been used this way by people for hundreds of years. Some of the word squares in Book Four have symbolical and esoteric meanings that have not been lost by transcription into German script.

For example, in chapter sixteen, "To recover treasures." The first square is for jewelry, and it starts with the word THIPHARA. Tipheret in Kabbalistic wisdom is the "Sphere of Beauty." The treasures refered to are spiritual and inner treasures.

Word square number one in chapter twenty-five, "To walk under water for as long as you want," contains the word MAIAM, the Hebrew and Arab word for "water." Water is the realm of the soul and emotions. One needs to learn how to release emotions and how to communicate directly in the soul realm just like animals, children, or babies. Achieve this level of self-development and you can directly contact angels in the soul realm. With skill, you can stay in the soul/water realm for as long as you like.

Chapter twenty-three, "To collapse walls and houses," can refer to tearing down the barriers within yourself by overcoming your own inner limitations, thereby so liberating your emotional and spiritual aspects.

Chapter three, "To make every spirit appear," can be symbolic for seeing the essence of things at all levels.

Chapter four, "To create visions," can mean learning to see the images and projections that are inside your own personality—learning to see into the visions that are created by your soul.

Other Perspectives

Abraham states toward the end of Book Three that the squares in Book Four are an index to Book Three. In Book Three he sets out pages with, "Explanations of what to look for, and care about, in each of the chapters of Book Four." He then follows with directions on how to use, and what to expect, from the word squares set out in each chapter in Book Four.

Links to other religious structures can be seen in Abraham's divisions and hierarchical organization of spirit names which he set out in Book Three. The major spirits and the forces they represent need to be kept in mind when the word squares are used. Abraham's four kings appear to represent the four elements—earth, fire, water, and air. These are also the key to making esoteric Theraveda Buddhism work as a meditative art.

The eight dukes show an archetypical system clearly expressed in the eight directions of the Native American medicine wheel. Added to the four kings, the dukes give twelve reigning principals, which correspond to the twelve astrological signs.

The four kings can also be seen to relate to the cardinal points in the horoscope: sunrise, noon, sunset, and midnight, and Aries (fire), Capricorn (earth), Libra (air), and Cancer (water), respectively. These are the times—on the equinoxes and soltices—when the elemental forces are at their strongest. The Church understood this when they called their ecclesiastical princes "cardinals." The eight dukes relate to the remaining astrological signs.

The Templar Square

In Book Four, chapter three, Abraham gives word squares "To make every spirit appear." Square number two is "In human shape." This square's rows contain the words, SATAN, ADAMA, TABAT, NATAS. This square is also known as the "Templar Square." Graf von Hardenberg decoded it in 1932, and the following is a paraphrase of his discription.

First, look at the symmetry of the letters. When we construct the square only with the A's and the B in the center, the following figure appears:

.	A	.	A	.
A	.	A	.	A
	A	B	A	.
A	.	A	.	A
.	A	.	A	.

Beginning in the center, by drawing a line from one A to another A, we get the so-called Templar Cross. This may be accidental. But if we now refer to the letters that remained from the first step, we have the following picture:

S	.	T	.	N
.	D	.	M	.
T	.	(B)	.	T
.	M	.	D	.
N	.	T	.	S

What do they mean? It's easy! The Templars called their order *Salomonis Templum Novum Dominorum Militiae Templariorum.* When we look at the initials of that name—S T N D M T—we can see that these are the leftover letters in the square. They group around the "B," the Kabbalistic letter for the logos. In typical Kabbalistic method, it is also written backwards as T M D N T S.

In public, the Templars wore only the cross of the order on their cape. But in secret ceremonies they used the whole square.

Goethe's Magic Square

One of the best-known examples of word squares is in Goethe's classic *Faust.* To return to his youth, Faust makes a deal with Mephistopheles who, in the form of a witch, brings him the poem below.

The Witch's Calculation

This you must ken!
From one make ten,
And two let be,
Make even three,
Then rich you'll be.
Skip o'er the four!
From five and six,
The witch's tricks
Make seven and eight,
'Tis finished straight:
And nine is one,
And ten is none,
That is the witch's one-times-one!

In the 1920s, Dr. Ferdinand Maack discovered that Goethe's poem described a Saturn square that, through the magician's art, could be activated by Venus energy. This, Maack suggests, would have given Faust back the erotic strength of his youth.

The Harmonic Saturn Square

4 9 2
3 5 7
8 1 6

Maack described the encoding as follows:

From one make ten

The magic word square is made from one large square enclosing nine smaller ones, making a total of ten.

And two let be

This number remains unchanged.

Make even three,
Then rich you'll be.

Put three into the number nine and nine into the number three, giving three once again.

Skip o'er the four!

This is where the witch requires that the four is removed. From here she starts to change the correct harmonic Saturn square by replacing the four with zero.

From five and six,
The witch's tricks
Make seven and eight

In the second row, replace the five at the center with the seven from the end. In the third row, swap the positions of the six and eight—the witch's changes continue.

'Tis finished straight:

The four is made zero and through the exchange of five and six with the seven and eight is created the following word square:

The Witch's Square

0	9	2
3	7	5
6	1	8

And nine is one.

The combination of all nine "cells" makes one magic square.

And ten is none.

A magic square with ten squares cannot exist. Later, Goethe has Mephistopheles say:

> The art is old and new, my friend.
> It was the way in all the ages,
> Through Three and One, and One and Three,
> Error instead of truth to scatter. . . .

The witch's magic was able to give Faust temporary sexual ecstasy. With this square, the witch could never have created a faithful and lasting love. This could only have been done with the harmonic Saturn square. Maark goes on to tell us that the harmonic Saturn square is an old magic square and was often used for love and marriage in the Far East.

Spirit Names— Comparison between Sources.

The spirit names are not consistantly recorded by different sources. I have made up a table of showing how the major sources have treated the material. The manuscript sources used in this compilation are discussed in the Introduction, and complete titles are in the Bibliography.

Annotations Used

MSW: Manuscript (encoded), Wolfenbüttel Library, dated 1608

SM: Samuel L. MacGregor Mathers), reprint 1974 New York. Mathers used the anonomous French manuscript from the Bibliothèque de l'Arsenal. He copied it accurately but the French manuscript was flawed.

PH: Peter Hammer's MS, published in Cologne, 1725

MSD2: Manuscript No. 2, Dresden Library, ca. 1720

From source:	MSW	SM	PH	MSD2
Oriens, Paymon, Ariton, Amaimon	1	1	1	1
Astaroth and Asmodeus	2	2	2	2
Asmodeus and Magoth	3	4	-	-
Amaimon and Ariton	4	3	3	3
Astaroth	5	5	4	4
Magot (and Kore in SM)	6	6	5	5
Asmodeus	7	7	6	6
Beelzebub	8	8	7	7
Oriens	9	9	8	8
Paymon	10	10	9	9
Ariton	11	11	10	10
Amaymon	12	12	11	11

Servants of Oriens, Paimon, Ariton, and Amaimon

MSW	SM	PH	MSD2
MOREH	MOREL	MORECH	MOREL
SARAPH	SARAPH	SERAP	SARAP
PROXONOS	PROXOSOS	PROXONES	PROXONES
NABHI	HABHI	NABHI	NABHI
KOSEM	HOSEN	KOSEM	KOSEM
PERESCH	(MELNA)	PERESCH	PERESCH
THIRAMA	TIRANA	THIRAMA	THIRAMA
ALLUPH	ALLUPH	ALLUPH	ALLUPH
NESCHAMAH	NERCAMAY	NESCHAMACH	NESCHAMAH
MILON	NILEN	MILON	
FRASIS	TRACI	FRASIS	
CHAYA	ENAIA	HAYA	
MALACH	MULACH	MALACH	
MELABED	MALUTENS	MOLABED	MOLABETH
YPARCHOS	IPARKAS	YPARCHOS	YPACHOS
NUDETON	NUDITON	NUDATON	NUDATEN
MEBHAER	MELHAER	METHAER	MEBHAER
BRUACH	RUACH	BRUAH	BRUAH
APOLION	APOLHUN	APOLLYON	APOLLION
SCHALUAH	SCHABUACH	SCHALUAH	SCHALVAH
MYRMO	MERMO	MYRMO	MYRMO
MELAMMED	MELAMUD	MELAMOD	MELAMMOD
POTHER	POTER	POTHER	POTHER
SCHED	SCHED	SCHAD	SCHAD
ECKDULON	EKDULON	ECKDULON	ECKDULON
MANTIES	MANTIENS	MANNES	MANTES
OBEDAMAH	OBEDAMA	OBEDOMAH	OBEDEMAH
JACHIEL	SACHIEL	IACHIEL	TACHIEL
IUAR	ACUAR	IVAR	TUAR
MOSCHEL	MOSCHEL	MOSCHEL	MOSCHEL
PECHACH	PEREUCH	PECHAH	PECHAH
HASPERIM	ASPERIM	HASPERIM	HASPERIM
KATSIN	KATINI	KATSIN	KATHIN
FOßFORA	TORFORA	POSPHORA	PHOSPHORA
BADAD	BADAD	BADAD	BUDAD
COHEN	COELEN	KOHEN	KOHEN
CUSCHI	CHUSCHI	CUSCHI	CUSCHI
FAßMA	TASMA	FAYMA	FASMA
PAKID	PACHID	PAKID	PAKID
HELEL	KELEN	HELEL	HELEL
MARA	PAREK	MAHRA	MARAH
RASCHEAR	RACHIAR	RASCHEÄR	RASCESEAR

Servants of Oriens, Paimon, Ariton, and Amaimon (cont.)

MSW	SM	PH	MSD2
NOGAH	NOGAR	NOGAH	NOGAS
ADON	ADON	ADON	ADON
ERIMITES	ERENUTES	ERIMITES	ERIMITES
TRAPIS	TRAPIS	TRAPIS	TRAPIS
NAGID	NAGID	NAGID	NAGID
ETHANIM	ETHANIM	ETHAMIN	ETHAMIM
PATTID	PATID	AFPADIT	ASPATID
NASI	NAJIN	NASI	NASI
PARELIT	PAREHT	PERALIT	PERELIT
EMFATISON	EMPHATISON	EMFATISON	EMPHATISOY
PARASCH	PARASEH	PARUCH	PARASCH
GIRMIL	GEREVIL	GIRMIL	GERMIL
TOLET	TULOT	TOLET	TOLET
HELMIS	ELMIS	HELMIS	HELMIS
AßMIELh	ASMIEL	ASINEL	ASMIEL
IRMINON	IRMINON	IRMINON	IRMINON
ASTUREL	ASTUREL	ASTUREL	ASTUREL
FLABISON	PLATIEN	FLABISON	HABISOY
NASCELON	NUTHON	NASCELON	NASCALON
LOMIOL	LOMIOL	LOMIOL	LOMINOL
YSMIRIEK	IMINK	YSMIRK	YSMIRIK
PLIROKY	PLIROK	PLIROKI	PLIROKI
AFLOTON	ATLOTON	AFLOTON	ASLOTON
HAGRION	TAGNON	ZAGRION	ZAGRION
PERMASES	PARMATUS	PARMASAS	PARMASAS
SARASIM	IARESIN	SARASIM	SARASIM
GORILON	GORILON	GORIOLON	GORILON
AFOLOP	AFARORP	AFOLOV	ASOLOP
LIRIOL	LIRION	LIRIELL	LIRIEL
ALOGIL	PLEGIT	ALOGILL	ALOGIL
OGOLOGON	OGILEN	OGOLOGON	AGOLOGON
LARALOS	TARADOS	LARUBOS	LARALOS
MORILON	MORILEN	MORILON	MORILOY
LOSIMON	LOSIMON	LOSIMON	LOSIMON
RAGARAS	RAGARAS	KAGARAS	RAGARES
IGILON	IGILON	IGILON	IGILON
GESEGAS	GOSEGAS	GESEGAS	GESEGAS
UGESOR		UGEFOR	UGESOR
ASOREGA	ASTREGA	ASOREGA	AFOREGA
PARUSUR	PARUSUR	PARUCHU	PARUSUR
SIGIS	IGIS	SIGES	SIGES
AHEROM	AHEROM	ATHEROM	ASEROM

Servants of Oriens, Paimon, Ariton, and Amaimon (cont.)

MSW	SM	PH	MSD2
RAMORAS	RAMARATZ	RAMARATH	RAMARÄL
IGARAG	IGARAK	IGAVOG	IGARAG
GELOMA	GELOMA	GOLOMA	GOLOMA
KILIK	KILIK	KILIK	KILIK
ROMORON	REMORON	ROMOSAF	ROMOSAF
NEGEN	NOGEN		
EKALAK	EKALIKE		
ILEKEL	ISEKEL		
ELZEGAR	ELZEGAN		
IPAKOL	IPAKOL		
NOLOM			
HOLOP			
ARIL	HARIL		
KOKOLON	KADOLON		
OSOGYON	IOGION		
IBULON	(ALAGAS)		
HARAGIL	ZARAGIL		
IZOZON	IRRORON		
ISAGAS	ILAGAS		
BALABOS	BALALOS		
NAGAR	(MOLIN)		
OROYA	OROIA		
LAGASAF	LAGASUF		
ALPAS	ALPAS	ALPAS	ALPAS
SOTERION	SOTERION	SOTERION	SOTERION
AMILLIS	(DECCAL)	AMILLES	AMILLIS
ROMAGES	ROMAGES	RAMAGES	ROMAGES
PROMACHOS	PROMAKOS	PROMATHOS	PROMATHOS
METOFEPH	METAFEL	METOSEPH	METOSEPH
PARASCHON	DARASCON	PARASCHOU	PARASCHON

Servants of Astaroth and Asmodeus

MSW	SM	PH	MSD2
AMAMIL	AMANIEL	AMAMIL	AMANIEL
ORINEL	ORINEL	ORIENELL	ORIEL
TINIRA	TIMIRA	TIMIRA	TINIRA
DRAMAS	DRAMAS	DRAMOS	DRAMIAS
ANAMALON	AMALIN	ANEMALON	AMMALON
KIRIK	KIRIK	KIRIK	KIRIK
BUBANABUB	BUBANABUK	BUBAMABUB	BIEBANABUB
RANAR	RANER	RANAR	RANAR
NAMALON	SEMLIN	NAMALON	NAMALON
AMPHOLION	AMBOLIN	AMPHOLION	AMPHOLION
ABUSIS	ABUTES	ABUSIS	ABUSIS
EXENTERON	EXTERON	EXENTION	EXERLAOY
LABONIX	LABOUX	TABORIX	TABORIX
CONCAVION	CORCARON	CONCAVION	CONCAVION
OHOTAM	ETHAN	OHOLEM	OSOLEM
TARETO	TARET	TARATO	TARATO
TABBAT	DABLAT	TABBAT	TABBAT
BURIUB	BURIUL	BURIUD	BIERIUB
OMAN	OMAN	OMAN	OMAN
CARASCH	CARASCH	CARASCH	CARASCH
DIMURGOS	DIMURGOS	DIMURGOS	DIMURGOS
KOGIEL	ROGGIOL	KOGIEL	ROGIEL
PANFOTRON		PEMFODRAM	PEMFOTRON
LIRIOL	LORIOL	SIRIOL	LIRIOL
IGIGI	ISIGI	IGIGI	IGIGI
DOSOM	TIORON	DOSOM	DOSOM
DAROCHIM	DAROKIN	DARACHIM	DARACHIM
HORAMAR	HORANAR	HOROMAR	HORAMAR
AHABHON	ABAHIN	AHAHBON	ASABHO
YRAGAMON	GUAGAMON	YRAGAMON	YRAGAMON
LAGIROS	LAGINX	LAGIROS	LAGIROS
ERALYX	ETALIZ	ERALIR	ERALEPP
GOLOG	GOLEG	GOLOG	GOLOG
LAMAL	LEMEL	LENIEL	LENIEL
HAGEYR	AGEI	HAGEYS	HAGEYR
UDAMAN	UDAMAN	VOLEMAN	UDAMAN
BIALOD	BIALOT	BIALOD	BIALOD
GALAGOS	GAGALAS	GALAGOS	GALAGOS
BAGALON	RAGALIM	BAGALON	BUGALON
TINAKOS	FINAXOS	TMAKOS	TINAKOS
AKANEF	AKANEF	AKANEF	AKANEF
OMAGOS	OMAGES	OMAHOS	OMAGOS

Servants of Astaroth and Asmodeus (cont.)

MSW	SM	PH	MSD2
ARGAX	AGRAX	ARGAX	ARGAX
AFRAY	AFRAY	AFREY	AFREY
SAGAREZ	SAGARES	SAGAREZ	SAGAREZ
UGALIS	UGALES	UGALIS	UGALIS
ERMIHALA	HERMIALA	ERIMIHALA	EMIHALA
HAHYAX	HALIGAX	HABÜNZ	HAHYAX
GAGONIX	GUGONIX	GAGONIR	GAGONIX
OPILON	OPILM	OPILON	OPILON
DAGULEZ	DAGULER	PAGULDEZ	RAGULELEZ
PACHAHY	PACHEL	PASCHY	PAHESU
NIMALON	NIMALON	NIMALON	NIMALON

Servants of Asmodi and Magot

MSW	SM
MAGOG	MAGOG
SOCHEN	APOT
DIOPES	DIOPOS
LAMARGOS	TOUN
DISOLEL	DISOLEL
SIPHON	SIFON
KELA	KELE
MAGYROS	MAGIROS
MEBASCHEL	MABAKIEL
SARTABACHIM	SARTABAKIM
SOBHE	SOBE
UNOCHOS	INOKOS
	LUNDO
	BIRIEL
	OPUN

Servants of Amaimon and Ariton

MSW	SM	PH	MSD2
HAROG	HAUGES	HOROG	HAROG
AGEBOL	AGIBOL	ALGEBOL	AGEBOL
RIGOLEN	RIGOLEN	RIGOLON	RIGOLON
IRASOMIN	GRASEMIN	TRASONIM	IRASOMIM
ELAFON	ELAFON	ELASON	ELAFON
TRISACHA	TRISAGA	TRISACHA	TRISACHA
GAGOLCHON	GAGALIN	GAGOLCHON	GAGALCHON
KLORACHA	CLERACA	KLORECHA	KLORECHA
YEYATRON	ELATON	YRIATRON	YRIATRON
PAFESLA	PAFESLA	PAFESSA	PAFESLA

Servants of Astaroth

MSW	SM	PH	MSD2
AMA	AMAN	AMAM	ANNAN
	CAMAL	CAMALAL	CAMAL
TEXAI	TOXAI	TEXAL	TEXAI
KATARON	KATARON	KATARON	KARARON
RAK	RAX	RAH	PAK
SCHELEGON	SCHELAGON	SCHELEGON	SCHELEGON
GIRIAR	GINAR	GIRIAR	GIRAR
ASIANON	ISIAMON	ASIANON	ASIANON
BAHAL	BAHAL	BAHAL	BASAL
BARAK	DAREK	BAROOK	BAROOX
GOLOG	GOLEN	GOLOG	GOLOG
IROMENIS	GROMENIS	IROMONIS	IRAMONIS
KIGIOS	RIGIOS	KIGIOS	KIGIOS
NIMIRIX	NIMERIX	NIMIRIX	NIMIRIX
HIRIH	HERG	HERICH	HIRICH
OKIRGI	OKIRI	AKIRGI	AKREY
FAGUNI	FAGANI	FAGUM	FAGUNI
HIPOLEPOS	HIPOLOS	HIPOLOPOS	HIPOLEPOS
ILOSON	ILESON	ILOSON	ILOSON
CAMONIX	CAMONIX		CAMONIX
ALAFY	ALAN		ALASI
APORMANOS	APORMENOS		APORMENOS
OMBALAFA	OMBALAT		OMBALAFA
GARSAS	QUARTAS	GARSAS	GARSAS
UGIRPON	UGIRPEN	UGIRPON	UGIRPON
GOMOGIN	GONOGIN	GOMOGNU	GOMOYNU
ARGILON	ARGILON	ARGILON	ARGILON
EARAOE	ARAEX	TARGOE	TARAOC
LEPACHA	LEPACA	LEPACHA	LEPACHA
KALOTES	KOLOFE	KALOTES	KALOTES
YCHIGAS	ISCHIGAS	YCHIAGOS	YCHIGUS
BAFAMAL	BAFAMAL	BASAMAL	BAFAMEL

Servants of Magoth

MSW	SM	PH	MSD2
NACHERAN	NACHERAN	NACHERON	NACHERON
NASOLICO	KATOLIN	NATOLICO	NATOLICO
MESAF	LUESAF	MESAF	MESAF
MASADUL	MASAUB	MASADUL	MASADUL
SAPIPAS	SUPIPAS	LAPIPAS	SAPPIPAS
FATURAB	FATURAB	FATURAB	FATURAB
FERNEBUS	FERSEBUS	FERNEBUS	FERNEBUS
BARUEL	BARUEL	BARNEL	BARNEL

Servants of Magoth (cont.)

MSW	SM	PH	MSD2
UBARIM	UBARIN	UBARIM	UBARIM
URGIDO	URIGO	URGIVO	URGIDO
YSQUIRON	ISCHIRON	YSQUIRON	YSQUIRON
ODAC	ODAX	ODAC	ODAC
ROTOR	ROLER	ROTOR	ROTOR
ARATOR	AROTOR	ARATOR	ARATOR
BUTHARUTH	BUTARAB	BUTHARUTH	BUTHARATH
HARPINON	ARPIRON	HARPINON	HASPINON
ARRABIM	ARRABIN	ARRABIM	ASSAHIM
KORE		KORE	YKORE
FORTESION	FORTESON	FORTESLON	FORTESTON
SCRUPULON	SORRIOLENEN	SERUPOLON	SERUPOLON
MEGALLEH	MEGALAK	MAGALECH	MOGALLECH
ANAGNOSTOS	ANAGOTOS	ANAGESTOS	ANAGNOSTOS
SIKASTIR	SIKASTIN	SIKASTIR	SIKASTIR
MECHEBBER	MEKLBOC	MECHEBBER	MECHETBER
TIGRAPHON	TIGRAFON	TIGRAPHON	TIGRAPHON
MATATAM	MANTAN	MALATA	PIALATA
TAGORA	TAGORA	TAGORA	TAGORA
PETANOP	PETUNOF	PETUMOS	PETARIOP
DULID	DULID	DUELLID	DUELLID
SOMIS	HEMIS	SOMIS	SOMIS
LOTAYM	TIRAIM	LOTAGIM	LOTAYM
HYRYS	IRIX	HYRIS	HYRIS
MADAIL	MADAIL	CHADAPL	MADAYL
DEBAM	DEBAM	DEBAM	DEBAN
OBAGIRON	ABAGIRON	OBAGRION	OBAGIRON
NESISEN	NENISEM	PASCHEN	PASIFEN
LOBEL	Cobel Sobel	LOBEL	LOBEL
ARIOTH	ARIOTH	ARIOTH	ARIOTH
PANDOLI	PANDOLI	PANDORI	PANDOLI
LABONETON	LABONETON	LABONETON	LABONETON
KAMUSEL	KAMUSIL	KAMUSEL	RAMUSEL
CAYFAR	KAITAR	COYTAR	CAYTAR
NEARACH	SCHARAK	NEARAH	NEARAH
MASADUL	MAISADUL	MAHADUL	MASUDUL
MARAG	MARAG	CHARAG	MURAG
KOLAN	KOLAM	KOLAN	KOLAN
KILIGIL	KILIGIL	KILIGIL	KILIGIL
COROCON	CORODON	COROCON	COROCON
HIPOGON	HEPOGON	HIPOGON	HIPOGON
AGILAS	AGILAS	AGILAS	AGILAS

Servants of Magoth (cont.)

MSW	SM	PH	MSD2
NAGAN	HAGION	NAGAR	NAGAN
EGACHIR	EGAKIREH	ECHAGIR	EGACHIR
PARACHMON	PARAMOR	PARACHMON	PARACHNION
OLOSIRMON	OLISERMON	OLOSIRMON	OLOSIRMON
DAGLUS	DAGLAS	DAGLOS	DAGLUS
ORMONOS	HORMINOS	ORMONAS	ORMONAS
HAGOCH	HAGOG	HAGOS	HAGOCH
MIMOSA	MIMOSA	MIMOSA	MIMOSA
ARAKISON	AMCHISON	ARAKUSON	ARACUSON
RIMOG	RIMOG	RIMOG	RIMOG
ILARAK	ILARAX	ISERAG	ILERAK
MOKASCHEF	MAKALOS	CHEIKASEPH	MEI, KASEPH
KOBHAN	COLVAM	KOFAN	KOPFAN
BATIRMISS	BATTERNIS	BATIRUMS	BATRINAS
LACHATYL	LOCATER	LOCHATY	LACHATYL

Servants of Asmodeus

MSW	SM	PH	MSD2
IEMURI	ENIURI	IENIURI	JEMURI
MEBHASSER	MEBBESSER	MEBHESSER	MEPHASSER
BAKARON	BACARON	BAKARON	BAKARON
HYLA	HOLBA	HYLA	HYLA
ENEI	ONEI	ENEI	ENEI
MAGGID	MAGGID	MAGGID	MAGGIAS
ABHADIR	ABADIR	ABHACHIR	ABSEDIR
PRESFEES	PRECHES	PRESFEES	BREFSEES
ORMION	ORMION	ORMION	ORMION
SCHALUACH	SCLAVAC	SCHALUACH	SCHALMACH
GILLAMON	GILARION	GILLAMON	GILLARON
YBARION	SBARIONAT	YBARION	YTARION
	UTIFA		
	OMET		
	SARRA		
	HIFARION		

Servants of Beelzebub

MSW	SM	PH	MSD2
ALTANOR	ALCANOR	ALTANOR	ALTANOR
ARMASIA	AMATIA	ARMASIA	ARMASIA
BELIFERES	BILIFARES	BELIFARES	BELIFARES
CAMARION	LAMARION	CAMARION	CAMARION
CORILON	CORILON	CORILON	CORILON

Servants of Beelzebub (cont.)

MSW	SM	PH	MSD2
DIRALISIN	DIRALISEN	DIRALISIN	DIRALISIN
ERALICARISON	LICANEN	ERALICARISON	ERALICARISON
ELPINON	ELPONEN	ELIPINON	ELPINON
GARINIRAG	DIMIRAG	GARINIRAUS	GARNIRIAY
SIPILLIPIS	PELLIPIS	SIPILLIPIS	SIBILLIBIS
ERGONION	ERGAMEN	ERGONION	ERGONION
IOTIFAR.	GOTIFAN	LOTIFAR	IOTIFAR
MYNYMARUP	NIMORUP	CHYMINGMORUG	MYNIMORUG
KARELESA	CARELENA	KARELESA	KARELESA
NATALES	NATALIS	NATALES	NATALES
CAMALON	LAMALON	LAMALON	LAMALON
YGARIM	IGURIM	YGARIM	IGARIM
AKAHIM	AKIUM	AKAHIM	AKASIM
GOLOG		GOLOG	GOLOG
NAMIROS	NAMIROS	NAMIROS	NEMIROS
HARAOTH		ISTAROTH	HARAOTH
TEDEAN	TACHAN	TEDEAM	TEDEAM
IKON	IKONOK	IKON	IKON
KEMAL	KEMAL	KEMAL	KEMAL
ADISAK		ADISAK	ADISAK
BILEK	BILICO	BILEK	BILEY
IROMAS	TROMES	IROMES	IROMES
BAALSORI	BALFORI	BAALHORI	BAALSORI
AROLEN	AROLEN		ARALON
KOBADA	KABADA		KOBADA
LIROKI	LIROCHI		LIROKY
NOMIMON	NOMINON		
IAMAI	IAMAI	IAMAI	
AROGOR	AROGOR	AROGOR	
IPOKYS	KIPOKIS	IPAKYS	
OLAßKY	HOLASTRI	OLASCKY	
HAYAMEN	HACAMULI	HAYAMAN	HAYAMEN
	SAMALO	SAMECHLO	SANNIESSO
ALOSON	PLISON	ALOSON	ALOSON
ERGOSIL	ZAGALO	SEGOSEL	SEGOSIL
BOROB	BOROL	BAROB	BOROB
UGOBOG		UGOBOG	UGOBOG
HASKUB		HAOKUB	HAOKUB
AMOLOM	AMBOLON	AMOLOM	AMOLOM
BILIFOT	BILIFOR	BILIFOT	BILIFOT

Servants of Beelzebub (cont.)

MSW	SM	PH	MSD2
GRANON	GRAMON	GRANON	GRAVON
PAGALUST	MAGALAST	PAGALUST	BAGALUST
XIRMYS		XYRMIS	NYRMIS
LEMALON	LAMOLON	LEMALON	LEMALON
RADARAP	RADERAF	RADUCA	RADAROP
	ORGOSIL		
	SOROSMA		
	ADIRAEL		
	ARCON		
	DORAK		

Servants of Oriens

MSW	SM	PH	MSD2
GAZARON	GASARONS	GEZERON	GEZERON
SARISEL	SARISEL	SARSIEL	GARISEL
SOROSMA	SOROSMA	SORESMA	SORESMA
TURITIL	TURITEL	TURITIL	TURITIL
BALACHEM	BALAKEN	BALACHMAN	BALACHAN
GAGISON	GAGISON	GAGISON	GAGISON
MAFALACH	MAFALAC	MAFALACH	MAFALACH
ZAGAL	AGAB	ZAGOL	ZAGAL

Servants of Paymon

MSW	SM	PH	MSD2
ICHDISON	DISON	ICHDISEM	ICHDISON
SUMURON	SUDORON	SUMURAN	SUMURAN
AGLAFYS	AGLAFOS	AGLAFYS	AGLAFYS
HACHAMEL	ACHANIEL	HACHAMEL	HACHAMEL
AGAHALY	AGAFALI	AGASALY	AGASALY
KALGOSA	KABERSA	KALYOSA	KALGOSA
EBARON	EBARON	EBARON	EBARON
ZALOMES	ZALANES	ZALANES	BULANES
ZUGOLA	UGOLA	ZUGULA	ZUGOLA
LARACH	CAME	CARAHAM	CARAH
KAFLES	ROFFLES	KAFLES	KAFLES
MEMNOLIK	MENOLIK	MEMNOLIK	MEMNOLIK
TAKAROS	TACAROS	TAKAROS	TAKAROS
ASTOLIT	ASTOLIT	ASTOLIT	ASTOLIT
MARKU	RUKUM	MARKY	MARCY

Servants of Ariton

MSW	SM	PH	MSD2
ANADIR	ANADER	ANADIR	ANADIR
EKOROK	EKOROK	EKOROK	EROROK
ROSARAN	ROSARAN	ROSORAN	ROSARAN
NAGANI		NEGANI	NAGANI
LIGILOS		KIGILOS	LIGILOS
SECABIM	SEKABIN	SECADMI	SECABIM
CALAMOSI	CAROMOS	CALAMOSY	CALAMOSY
SIBOLAS	SIBOLAS	SIBOLAS	SIBALAS
FORFARON		FORFASON	FOSFASON
ANDRACHOS	ANDROCOS	ANDRACHOR	ANDRACHOS
NOTISON	NOTISER	NOTISER	NOTIFER
FILAXON	FLAXON	FILAKON	FILAXON
HAROSUL	HAROMBRUB	HORASUL	
SARIS	SARIS	SARIS	
ELONIM		EKORIM	
NILION	MILIOM	NELION	
YLEMLIS	ILEMLIS	YLEMLYS	YLEMLYS
CALACH	GALAK	CALACH	CALACK
SARASON	SAPASON	SAPOSON	SAPASON
SEMEOT	SERMEOT	SEMEOL	SEMEOL
MARANTON	MARANTON	CHARONTON	MARONTHON
CARON	CARON	CARON	CARON
REGERION	REGINON	REGERION	REGORION
MEGALOGIM	MEGALOSIN	MEGALOGIM	MEGALOGIM
IRMENOS	IRMENOS	IRMENOS	IRMENOS
ELAMYR	ELERION	ELAMYR	ELAMYR

Fig. 55. Demons. Modern psychologists would say that the demons of the underworld are expressions of our personal fears and forbidden longings. Woodcut, 15th century.

Servants of Amaymon

MSW	SM	PH	MSD2
RAMIUSON	RAMISON	RAMGISON	RAMYISON
SIRGILIS	SCRILIS	SIRGILIS	SIRGILES
BARIOL	BURIOL	BARIOL	BARIOL
TARAHIM	TARALIM	TARAHIM	TARASIM
BURNAHAS	BURASEN	BUMAHAM	BUMAHAN
AKESELY	AKESOLI	AKEFELY	AKEFELY
ERKAYA	EREKIA	ERKEYA	ERKOYA
BEMEROT	ROMEROC	BEMROT	BEMROT
KILIKIM	ILLIRIKIM	KILIKIM	KILIKIM
LABISI	LABISI	LAPISI	LAPISI
AKOROK	AKOROS	ABAROK	AKOROK
MARAOS	MAMES	EHERAOS	MERAOS
GLYSY	GLESI	GLYSI	GLYFY
QUISION	VISION	OVISION	QUISION
EFRIGIS	EFFRIGIS	EFRIGIS	EFRIGIS
APILKI	APELKI	APILKI	APILKI
DALEP	DALEP	DALEP	DALEP
DRISOPH	DRESOP	DRISOPH	DRISOPH
CARGOSIK	HERGOTIS	CARGOSTE	CARGOSIK
NILIMA	NILIMA	NILIMA	NILIMA

THE SPIRIT NAMES IN THE ORDER LISTED BY SAMUEL MATHERS IN HIS BOOK TWO

ORIENS/PAIMON/ARITON/AMAIMON: HOSEN, SARAPH, PROXOSOS, HABHI, ACUAR, TIRANA, ALLUPH, NERCAMAY, NILEN, MOREL, TRACI, ENAIA, MULACH, MALUTENS, IPARKAS, NUDITON, MELNA, MELHAER, RUACH, APOLHUN, SCHABUACH, MERMO, MELAMUD, POTER, SCHED, EKDULON, MANTIENS, OBEDAMA, SACHIEL, MOSCHEL, PEREUCH, DECCAL, ASPERIM, KATINI, TORFORA, BADAD, COELEN, CHUSCHI, TASMA, PACHID, PAREK, RACHIAR, NOGAR, ADON, TRAPIS, NAGID, ETHANIM, PATID, PAREHT, EMPHASTISON, PARASEH, GEREVIL, ELMIS, ASMIEL, IRMINON, ASRUREL, NUTHON, LOMIOL, IMINK, PLIROK, TAGNON, PARMATUS, IARESIN, GORILON, LIRION, PLEGIT, OGILEN, TARADOS, LOSIMON, RAGARAS, IGILON, GOSEGAS, ASTREGA, PARUSUR, IGIS, AHEROM, IGARAK, GELOMA, KILIK, REMORON, EKALIKE, ISEKEL, ELZEGAN, IPAKOL, HARIL, KADOLON,

IOGION, ZARAGIL, IRRORON, ILAGAS, BALALOS, OROIA, LAGASUF, ALAGAS, ALPAS, SOTERION, ROMAGES, PROMAKOS, METAFEL, DARASCON, KELEN, ERENUTES, NAJIN, TULOT, PLATIEN, ATLOTON, AFARORP, MORILEN, RAMARATZ, NOGEN, MOLIN.

ASTAROTH/ASMODEUS: AMANIEL, ORINEL, TIMIRA, DRAMAS, AMALIN, KIRIK, BUBANA, BUK, RANER, SEMLIN, AMBOLIN, ABUTES, EXTERON, LABOUX, CORCARON, ETHAN, TARET, DABLAT, BURIUL, OMAN, CARASCH, DIMURGOS, ROGGIOL, LORIOL, ISIGI, TIORON, DAROKIN, HORANAR, ABAHIN, GOLEG, GUAGAMON, LAGINX, ETALIZ, AGEL, LEMEL, UDAMAN, BIALOT, GAGALAS, RAGALIM, FINAXOS, AKANEF, OMAGES, AGRAX, SAGARES, AFRAY, UGALES, HERMIALA, HALIGAX, GUGONIX, OPILM, DAGULER, PACHEL, NIMALON.

AMAIMON/ARITON: HAUGES, AGIBOL, RIGOLEN, GRASEMIN, ELAFON, TRISAGA, GAGALIN, CLERACA, ELATON, PAFESLA.

ASMODI/MAGOT: TOUN, MAGOG, DIOPOS, DISOLEL, BIRIEL, SIFON, KELE, MAGIROS, SARTABAKIM, LUNDO, SOBE, INOKOS, MABAKIEL, APOT, OPUN.

ASTAROT: AMAN, CAMAL, TOXAI, KATARON, RAX, GONOGIN, SCHELAGON, GINAR, ISIAMON, BAHAL, DAREK, ISCHIGAS, GOLEN, GROMENIS, RIGIOS, NIMERIX, HERG, ARGILON, OKIRI, FAGANI, HIPOLOS, ILESON, CAMONIX, BAFAMAL, ALAN, APORMENOS, OMBALAT, QUARTAS, UGIRPEN, ARAEX, LEPACA, KOLOFE.

MAGOTH/KORE: NACHERAN, KATOLIN, LUESAF, MASAUB, URIGO, FATURAB, FERSEBUS, BARUEL, UBARIN, BUTARAB, ISCHIRON, ODAX, ROLER, AROTOR, HEMIS, ARPIRON, ARRABIN, SUPIPAS, FORTESON, DULID, SORRIOLENEN, MEGALAK, ANAGOTOS, SIKASTIN, PETUNOF, MANTAN, MEKLBOC, TIGRAFON, TAGORA, DEBAM, TIRAIM, IRIX, MADAIL, ABAGIRON, PANDOLI, NENISEM, COBEL, SOBEL, LABONETON, ARIOTH, MARAG, KAMUSIL, KAITAR, SCHARAK, MAISADUL, AGILAS, KOLAM, KILIGIL, CORODON, HEPOGON, DAGLAS, HAGION, EGAKIREH, PARAMOR, OLISERMON, RIMOG, HORMINOS, HAGOG, MIMOSA, AMCHISON, ILARAX, MAKALOS, LOCATER, COLVAM, BATTERNIS.

ASMODEUS: ONEI, ORMION, PRECHES, MAGGID, SCLAVAC, MEBBESSER, BACARON, HOLBA, HIFARION, GILARION, ENIURI, ABADIR, SBARIONAT, UTIFA, OMET, SARRA.

BEELZEBUB: ALCANOR, AMATIA, BILIFARES, LAMARION, DIRALISEN, LICANEN, DIMIRAG, ELPONEN, ERGAMEN, GOTIFAN, NIMORUP, CARELENA, LAMALON, IGURIM, AKIUM, DORAK, TACHAN, IKONOK, KEMAL, BILICO, TROMES, BALFORI, AROLEN, LIROCHI, NOMINON, IAMAI, AROGOR, HOLASTRI, HACAMULI, SAMALO, PLISON, RADERAF, BOROL, SOROSMA, CORILON, GRAMON, MAGALAST, ZAGALO, PELLIPIS, NATALIS, NAMIROS, ADIRAEL, KABADA, KIPOKIS, ORGOSIL, ARCON, AMBOLON, LAMOLON, BILIFOR.

ORIEN: SARISEL, GASARONS, SOROSMA, TURITEL, BALAKEN, GAGISON, MAFALAC, AGAB.

PAYMON: AGLAFOS, AGAFALI, DISON, ACHANIEL, SUDORON, KABERSA, EBARON, ZALANES, UGOLA, CAME, ROFFLES, MENOLIK, TACAROS, ASTOLIT, RUKUM.

ARITON: ANADER, EKOROK, SIBOLAS, SARIS, SEKABIN, CAROMOS, ROSARAN, SAPASON, NOTISER, FLAXON, HAROMBRUB, MEGALOSIN, MILIOM, ILEMLIS, GALAK, ANDROCOS, MARANTON, CARON, REGINON, ELERION, SERMEOT, IRMENOS.

AMAYMON: ROMEROC, RAMISON, SCRILIS, BURIOL, TARALIM, BURASEN, AKESOLI, EREKIA, ILLIRIKIM, LABISI, AKOROS, MAMES, GLESI, VISION, EFFRIGIS, APELKI, DALEP, DRESOP, HERGOTIS, NILIMA.

How Franz Bardon used the spirit names from the Abramelin

Franz Bardon is well-known in German and American magical circles. In his book, *The Practice of Magical Invocation,* he describes how he met 400 spirits during his ritual work. Curiousity made me investigate where these spirit names came from. Finally, using the Peter Hammer manuscript, I worked out how the long list of spirit names came into being.

Bardon arranges the names in groups of 12—one for each of the signs of the zodaic—and then progresses them through 30 degrees. So he arrives at 30 lines for each of the 12 spirit names: the names of 360 spirits.

If one looks at the Peter Hammer facsimile and counts from the beginning in groups of 12—leaving out the names of the dukes—one arrives at Bardon's complete spirit name list for all 30 degrees. They are even in the same order as presented in Hammer's book. (To allow for comparisons, the table I have prepared below is not in the same order.)

1°: Morech, Serap, Proxones, Nablum, Kosem, Peresch, Thirana, Aluph, Neschamah, Milon, Frasis, Haja,

2°: Malacha, Molabeda; Yparcha, Nudatoni, Methaera, Bruahi, Apollyon, Schaluah, Myrmo, Melamo, Pother, Schad,

3°: Ecdulon, Manmes, Obedomah, Iachil, Ivar, Moschel, Peekah, Hasperim, Kathim, Porphora, Badet, Kohen,

4°: Lurchi, Faluna, Padidi, Helali, Mahra, Rascheä, Nogah, Adae, Erimites, Trapi, Naga, Echami,

5°: Aspadit, Nasi, Peralit, Emfalion, Paruch, Girmil, Tolet, Helmis, Asinel, Ionion, Asturel, Flabison,

6°: Nascela, Conioli, Isnirki, Pliroki, Aslotama, Zagriona, Parmasa, Sarasi, Geriola, Afolono, Liriell, Alagill,

7°: Opollogon, Carubot, Morilon, Losimon, Kagaros, Ygilon, Gesegos, Ugefor, Asoreg, Paruchu, Siges, Atherom,

8°: Ramara, Jajaregi, Golema, Kiliki, Romasara, Alpaso, Soteri, Amillee, Ramage, Pormatho, Metosee, Porascho,

9°: Anamil, Orienell, Timiran, Oramos, Anemalon, Kirek, Batamabub, Ranar, Namalon, Ampholion, Abusis, Egention,

10°: Tabori, Concario, Golemi, Tarato, Tabbata, Buriuh, Omana, Caraschi, Dimurga, Kogid, Panfodra, Siria,

11°: Igigi, Dosom, Darachin, Horomor, Ahahbon, Yraganon, Lagiros, Eralier, Golog, Cemiel, Hagus, Vollman,

12°: Bialode, Galago, Bagoloni, Tmako, Akanejohano, Argaro, Afrei, Sagara, Ugali, Erimihala, Hatuny, Hagomi,

13°: Opilon, Paguldez, Paschy, Nimalon, Horog, Algebol, Rigolon, Trasorim, Elason, Trisacha, Gagolchon, Klorecha,

14°: Irachro, Pafessa, Amami, Camalo, Texai, Karasa, Riqita, Schulego, Giria, Afimo, Bafa, Baroa,

15°: Golog, Iromoni, Pigios, Nimtrix, Herich, Akirgi, Tapum, Hipolopos, Hosun, Garses, Ugirpon, Gomognu,

16°: Argilo, Tardoe, Cepacha, Kalote, Ychniag, Basanola, Nachero, Natolisa, Mesah, Masadu, Capipa, Fermetu,

17°: Barnel, Ubarim, Urgivoh, Ysquiron, Odac, Rotor, Arator, Butharusch, Harkinon, Arabim, Koreh, Forsteton,

18°: Sernpolo, Magelucha, Amagestol, Sikesti, Mechebbera, Tigrapho, Malata, Tagora, Petuno, Amia, Somi, Lotogi,

19°: Hyris, Chadail, Debam, Abagrion, Paschan, Cobel, Arioth, Panari, Caboneton, Kamual, Erytar, Nearah,

20°: Hahadu, Charagi, Kolani, Kibigili, Corocona, Hipogo, Agikus, Nagar, Echagi, Parachmo, Kosirma, Dagio,

21°: Oromonas, Hagos, Mimosah, Arakuson, Rimog, Iserag, Cheikaseph, Kofan, Batirunos, Cochaly, Ienuri, Nephasser,

22°: Bekaro, Hyla, Eneki, Maggio, Abbetira, Breffeo, Ornion, Schaluach, Hillaro, Ybario, Altono, Armefia,

23°: Belifares, Camalo, Corilon, Dirilisin, Eralicarison, Elipinon, Gariniranus, Sipillipis, Ergomion, Lotifar, Chimirgu, Kaerlesa,

24°: Nadele, Baalto, Ygarimi, Akahimo, Golopa, Naniroa, Istaroth, Tedea, Ikon, Kama, Arisaka, Bileka,

25°: Yromus, Camarion, Jamaih, Aragor, Igakis, Olaski, Haiamon, Semechle, Alosom, Segosel, Boreb, Ugolog,

26°: Hadcu, Amalomi, Bilifo, Granona, Pagalusta, Hyrmiua, Canali, Radina, Gezero, Sarsiee, Soesma, Tmiti,

27°: Balachman, Gagison, Mafalach, Zagol, Ichdison, Sumuram, Aglasis, Hachamel, Agasoly, Kiliosa, Ebaron, Zalones,

28°: Jugula, Carahami, Kaflesi, Mennolika, Takarosa, Astolitu, Merki, Anadi, Ekore, Rosora, Negani, Cigila,

29°: Secabmi, Calamos, Sibolas, Forfasan, Andrachor, Notiser, Filakon, Horasul, Saris, Ekorim, Nelion, Ylemis,

30°: Calacha, Sapasani, Seneol, Charonthona, Carona, Regerio, Megalogi, Irmano, Elami, Ramgisa, Sirigilis, Boria.

Belonging to the element of air: Parahim, Apilki, Erkeya, Dalep, Capisi, Drisophi, Glisi Cargoste

Abraham from Worms— Links to Modern Jewish Scholarship.

It is interesting to look at some of the references Jewish scholar Gershom Scholem makes to the Abramelin material.

Scholem is well-known for his discussions on the mystical and Kabbalistic streams in Judaism. Born in Berlin in 1897, he involved himself in Jewish studies and Zionism while still in school. In 1922 Scholem left Germany for Israel and worked in the national library. In 1933, he became a professor at the University of Jerusalem. He died in 1982 and left behind a large collection of works on Jewish mystical and esoteric themes.

I have found only three references to the author "Abraham from Worms" in Scholem's publications. Below are some extracts from his work; there possibly are many more.

> I know of the following hand-written versions [of the *Abramelin*]: Hebrew in Oxford . . . German in Vienna . . . French, one mentioned by Mathers, the other by Papus . . . the book definitely has a Jewish characteristics. The manuscripts go back to the 16th century. There are only a few Christian additions. Both printed versions are compatible. In general the English-French version is better, because the magical words are written as squares. Mather's commentaries and introduction—both very extensive—are not worthless, but need to be used carefully. The English version has a somewhat Christian style, but does not include the German additions regarding Jesus, his disciples, and the Apocalypse that is found on page 104 of the Berlin edition! The historical dates differ in the various editions. Mathers

did not know about the German text. Steinschneider, *Hebräische Übersetzungen*, paragraph 543 believes the book is a forgery by a Christian fraud, who for the 15th (and even the 16th) century—from where it undoubtedly came—clearly had excellent Hebrew.[1]

A special problem is raised by the pseudepigraphic text known in the German editions as *Des Juden Abraham von Worms der wahren Praktik in der uralten göttlichen Magie und in erstaunlichen Dingen, Wie sie durch die heilige Kabbala und durch Elohym mitgetheilt worden* (allegedly Cologne, 1725); the English edition, translated and edited by S. L. MacGregor Mathers from the French manuscripts, is entitled *The Book of the Secret Magic of Abra-Melin the Mage, as delivered by Abraham the Jew unto His Son Lamech* (London, 1898). The evocation of one's guardian angel and related preparatory rituals occupy a central place in this book. It would require a more detailed investigation to determine whether this book was indeed written by a Jewish occultist of the Renaissance period, as it claims (and as is supported by the author's excellent knowledge of Hebrew), or by a non-Jewish German author who tried to project himself into the Jewish mentality. The latter view is supported, not only by the extensive use of Christian symbols, which he might not have known to be Christian, or (which might be interpolations), but especially by the joining of the concepts of Kabbalah and magic as a pair to designate divine knowledge. This combination suggests an author writing under the influence of the Christian Kabbalah of Pico della Mirandola, who introduced this conceptual pair into Renaissance thought. In my article "Alchemie und Kabbala," *Monatsschrift für Geschichte und Wissenschaft des Judentums*, 69 (1925), p. 95, I supported the view that the author was Jewish, as I had not yet realized the influence of Pico. In any event, the entire

---

[1] Gershom Scholem, *Bibliographia Kabbalistica* (1927), p. 2. Published in German, translation of this passage is mine.—tr.

> work, which is extremely interesting, requires a special examination (I might add, of course, that no Jew ever called his son Lamech).[2]
>
> . . . For a long time I considered the well-known work of magic, *Des Juden Abraham von Worms Buch der wahren Praktik in der uralten göttlichen Magie*—translated into both German and English (via French) allegedly from a Hebrew manuscript of 1387 and supposedly published in Cologne in 1725 (more likely in 1800)—to be of Jewish origin; cf. *Monatsschrift für Geschichte und Wissenschaft des Judentums* 69, p. 95, and *Bibliographia Kabbalistica* (1927), p. 2. I changed my mind when I found clear evidence of the writings of Pico della Mirandola and his juxtaposition of Kabbalah and magic not only in the title but in the text of the book itself. The book was in fact written in the 16th century by a non-Jew who possessed a striking knowledge of Hebrew. This author also uses the term *melakhah* for alchemy (IV, 7), but only in the German translation! It is the same book that found wide distribution in occult circles in its English version as *The Book of Secret Magic by Abra-Melin the Mage, as Delivered by Abraham the Jew unto His Son Lamech, A.D. 1458*, trans. S. L. Mathers (London, 1898). Mathers was not aware of the German original—which is preserved in many manuscripts—parts of which date back to the 16th century.[3]

It is clear that Scholem was not aware that "Abraham from Worms" was a pseudonym used by the MaHaRIL, the well-known rabbi whose songs continue to be used in many synagogues. One wonders what he would have written if he had known? How would he have fit the somewhat gnostic material in Abraham's four books into the mainstream of Jewish scholarship?

---

[2] Gershom Scholem, *On the Mystical Shape of the Godhead: Basic Concepts in the Kabbalah* (New York: Schocken, 1991), pp. 314-315, n. 24.

[3] Gershom Scholem, *Alchemy and Kabbalah* (Putnam, CT: Spring Publications, 2006), pp. 28–29, n.40.

Bibliography

A. Primary Sources. Manuscripts

Abraham eines Juden von Worms untereinander versteckte zum Theil aus der Kabala und Magia gezogene, zum Theil durch vornehme Rabbiner als Arabern und anderen so wie auch von seinem Vater Simon erhaltene, nachgehend aber meisten Theils selbst erfahrene und probirte, in diese nachfolgende Schrift verfaste und endlich an seinen jüngeren Sohn Lamech hinterlaßene Künste: so geschehen und geschrieben circa Annum 1404. Wolfenbüttel Library, Codex Guelfibus 10.1.

Abraham ben Simon bar Juda ben Simon. *Das Buch der wahren Praktik von der alten Magia.* Anno 1608. Wolfenbüttel Library, Codex Guelfibus 47.13.

Abraham von Worms. *Die egyptischen großen Offenbarungen, in sich begreifend die aufgefundenen Geheimnisbücher Mosis; oder des Juden Abraham von Worms Buch der wahren Praktik in der uralten göttlichen Magie und erstaunlichen Dingen, wie sie durch die heilige Kabbala und durch Elohym mitgetheilt worden. Sammt der Geister- und Wunder-Herrschaft, welche Moses in der Wüste aus dem feurigen Busch erlernet, alle Verborgenheiten der Kabbala umfassend.* Köln, 1725.

Cabala Mystica Aegyptiorum et Patriarchum. Anonymous. Saxon State and University Library, Dresden. MS N 161

Magia Abraham oder Underricht von der Heiligen Cabala. Signatur TS. Saxon State and University Library, Dresden. MS N 111

Mathers, Samuel L. MacGregor, trans. *The Book of the Sacred Magic of Abra-Melin the Mage.* New York: Dover, 1974.

Sefer Segullot Melachim. Anonymous. Oxford Universtiy, Bodleian Library. MS.OPP.594.

B. Secondary Literature

Abraham von Worms. *Die heilige Magie des Abra-Melin.* Berlin: Hrg. Beecken, 1957.
———. *Die egyptischen großen Offenbarungen...* synoptic reconstruction by Georg Dehn. Osnabrück, 1984.
———. *Das Buch der wahren Praktik in der göttlichen Magie.* München: Hrg. Jürg von Ins, 1988.
———. *Buch Abramelin das ist Die egyptischen großen Offenbarungen oder des Abraham von Worms Buch der wahren Praktik in der uralten göttlichen Magie.* Leipzig: Hrg. Georg Dehn, 2001.
Alcalay Reuben. *The Complete English-Hebrew Dictionary in Four Volumes.* Tel-Aviv, Jerusalem, 1959.
———. *The Complete Hebrew-English Dictionary in Four Volumes.* Tel-Aviv, Jerusalem 1963.
Arpe, Peter Friedrich. *Feriae aestivales,* vol. 4.
Bardon, Franz. *Die Praxis der magischen Evokation.* Freiburg im Breisgau, 1956.
Barry, Kieren. *The Greek Qabalah.* York Beach, ME: Samuel Weiser, 1999.
Barth, Friedrich. *Die Cabbala des Heinrich Cornelius Agrippa von Nettesheim.* Stuttgart, 1855.
Berliner, Adolf. *Aus dem Leben der deutschen Juden im Mittelalter.* Berlin, 1900.
Boos, Heinrich. *Geschichte der rheinischen Städtekultur von den Anfängen bis zur Gegenwart mit besonderer Berücksichtigung der Stadt Worms.* Berlin 1899.
———. *Urkundenbuch der Stadt Worms.* 3 vols. 1886.
Britannica, the New Encyclopedia. 30 vols. Chicago, e.a. 1973.
Brockhaus Conversationslexikon 13. Aufl. Leipzig, 1885.
Brumlik, Micha. *Die Gnostiker.* Frankfurt am Main, 1992.
Dehn, Georg (G`O). Drachen. In *Mescalito* 9. Worms, 1986.
———. *Abraham von Worms. Die Geschichte ABRAMELIN.* In *Mescalito* 8. Worms, 1986.
Endres, Franz Carl. *Mystik und Magie der Zahlen.* Zürich, 1951.
Fortune, Dion. *Psychic Self-Defense.* York Beach, ME: Samuel Weiser, 1979.

Frick, Karl R. H. *Die Erleuchteten.* Graz, 1973.

Golowin, Sergius. *Die Magie der verbotenen Märchen.* Hamburg, 1975.

———. *Hexen, Hippies, Rosenkreuzer. 500 Jahre magische Morgenlandfahrt.* Hamburg, 1977.

Gray, William G. *Western Inner Workings.* York Beach, ME: Samuel Weiser, 1983.

Grimm, Jacob und Wilhelm. *Deutsches Wörterbuch.* 16 vols. Leipzig, 1860-1954.

Habiger-Tuczay, Christa. *Magie und Magier im Mittelalter.* Munich, 1992.

Huysmans, Joris Karl. *Tief unten* (Là-Bas). Potsdam, 1921.

Jüdisches Lexikon. Ein enzyklopädisches Handbuch des jüdischen Wissens in vier Bänden. Berlin, 1927. Frankfurt, 1987.

Jones, June. *Der König der Hexen.* Worms, 1984.

Jung, Carl Gustav. *Psychologie und Alchemie.* Olten, 1987.

———. *Der Mensch und seine Symbole.* Olten, 1968.

Kehrein, Joseph. *Fremdwörterbuch mit etymologischen Erklärungen und zahlreichen Belegen aus deutschen Schriftstellern.* Stuttgart 1876.

König, Peter-R. *Das OTO-Phänomen. Hundert Jahre Magische Geheimbünde und ihre Protagonisten von 1895 - 1994.* München, 1994.

Lennhoff-Posner. *Internationales Freimaurer-Lexikon.* Wien, 1932.

Lewis, Bernard. *Die Juden in der islamischen Welt.* Munich, 1987.

Meinardus, Otto F. A. *Christian Egypt.* Cairo, 1965.

Meyers großes Konversationslexikon. 6. Aufl. Leipzig, Wien, 1906.

Nettesheim, Agrippa von. *Die magischen Werke.* Wiesbaden, n.d.

Ouspensky, Piotr D.: *Ein neues Modell des Universums.* Weilheim/ Obb, 1970.

Pauli, Reinhold. *Geschichte von England.* vol. 5. Gotha, 1858.

Poliakov, Leon. *Geschichte des Antisemitismus.* 6 vols. Worms, 1977–1986.

Regardie, Israel. *Das magische System des Golden Dawn.* Freiburg, 1987.

Schick, Hans. *Das ältere Rosenkreuzertum. Ein Beitrag zur Entstehungsgeschichte der Freimaurerei.* Struckum, n.d.

Schlosser, Friedrich Christoph. *Weltgeschichte für das deutsche Volk.* Zweite Ausgabe. 19 vols. Oberhausen und Leipzig, 1870.

Schmidt, Heinrich. *Philosophisches Wörterbuch.* Stuttgart, 1978.

Scholem, Gerhard. *Bibliographia Kabbalistica.* Leipzig, 1927.

Scholem, Gershom. *Alchemy and Kabbalah.* Putnam, CT: Spring Publications, 2006.

———. *Kabbalah: A Definitive History of the Evolution, Ideas, Leading Figures and Extraordinary Influence of Jewish Mysticism* (New York: Meridian, 1978), p. 186.

———. *On the Mystical Shape of the Godhead: Basic Concepts in the Kabbalah.* New York: Schocken, 1991.

Sechstes und Siebentes Buch Mosis oder der magisch-sympathetische Hausschatz, das ist Mosis magische Geisterkunst, das Geheimnis aller Geheimnisse. Leipzig, n.d.

Steiner, Rudolf. *Wie erlangt man Erkenntnisse der höheren Welten.* Dornach, 1972.

Vehlow, Johannes. *Lehrkursus der wissenschaftlichen Geburtsastrologie.* Bd.VIII. Berlin, 1955.

Vollmar, Klausbernd. *Das Enneagramm.* Munich, 1993.

Walker, Benjamin. *Die Gnosis.* Munich, 1992.

Weinreb, Friedrich. *Schöpfung im Wort.* Weiler im Allgäu, 1994.

Wewers, Gerd A. *Geheimnis und Geheimhaltung im rabbinischen Judentum.* Berlin, New York, 1975.

Windecke, Eberhard. *Das Leben König Sigmunds. Nach Handschriften übersetzt von Dr. von Hagen.* Leipzig, 1899.

Zedler, Johann Heinrich. Großes vollständiges Universal-Lexikon. 64 vols. Graz, 1961.

Ziegler, Leopold. *Überlieferung. Ritus, Mythos, Doxa.* Olten, 1948.

About Georg Dehn and Steven Guth

The Book of Abramelin is the second book Georg Dehn (pictured on the right in the photograph) has published. It took almost twenty years of research until he was ready to print the first German edition. During those years he ran a bookshop in Worms. Georg was a consciencious objector and a house parent in a social work experiment with prisoners. One fateful day, in 1976 he found Schikowski's big old esoteric bookshop in Berlin, which led to the Abramelin work and book, and also gave Georg the impetus to open a bookshop in his hometown.

Georg is a long-time book collector and part of his book business included antiquarian books. He ran an alternative news magazine for a few years and wrote his first novel about his drop-out experiences in the 70s. Georg's first "big thing" happened when he was 16—with two friends he organized the first Open-Air Rock Festival in Germany (*www.open-air-hamm.de*), which continues to this day, perhaps setting a record for the longest-running annual rock 'n' roll event in the world.

Georg helped found the German Green party in 1979 and became their first member on the Worms city council in 1982. During this time, he founded an urban renewal project which has survived to this day—"The Factory"—with artists and New Age people; *www.schauraum-fabrik.de.*

Georg's esoteric studies led him through many subjects, including Buddhism, magic, biblical studies, the theories of C. G. Jung, and finally, astrology. He became a professional astrologer in 1986, working out of a spare room of his bookshop. After selling his business and moving to Leipzig in 1997, Georg became a full-time astrologer.

In 2002 he issued the second edition of the *Abramelin*. It was so well-received that he decided to open a publishing house called "Araki" after the farming village in upper Egypt, near where the wisdom of Abramelin originated (see www.araki.de).

STEVEN GUTH (pictured on the left in the photo) was born to Viennese parents in Sydney, Australia, during WWII. His father was a Jewish clothing manufacturer, his mother was Catholic, and the household only spoke German. Steven's first day at school came as a complete linguistic surprise. Steven met his wife Kathrine at university where Steven's interests led him to social psychology. After graduation the couple ran a graphic design and importing agency for a few years. A job offer from Sydney University's adult education deptartment led the couple to 5 years of work with Aboriginal people in community development roles. It was contact with aboriginal people that lead Steven into an investigation of esoteric concepts and schools of thought, while time spent in Singapore with Katherine's extended family sparked Steven's interest in Buddhism.

Steven has written children's books, school texts (in geography) and many esoteric and spiritual articles. A sampling of recent pieces can be found at *http://www.kheper.net/ecognosis/* Steven is fortunate in having met and spent time with more than a dozen or so significant mentors along the path of his life—Anthroposophists, Theosophists, dowsers, healers, priests, philosophers, pagans, and Buddhist monks. Steven gives occasional lectures on various esoteric topics to the local and Sydney Theosophical and Anthroposophical societies. The couple now lives with their extended family (including 3 grandchildren) at "Bibaringa," a 550-acre horse ranch on Mt. Stromlo ridge, ten minutes from the center of Canberra.

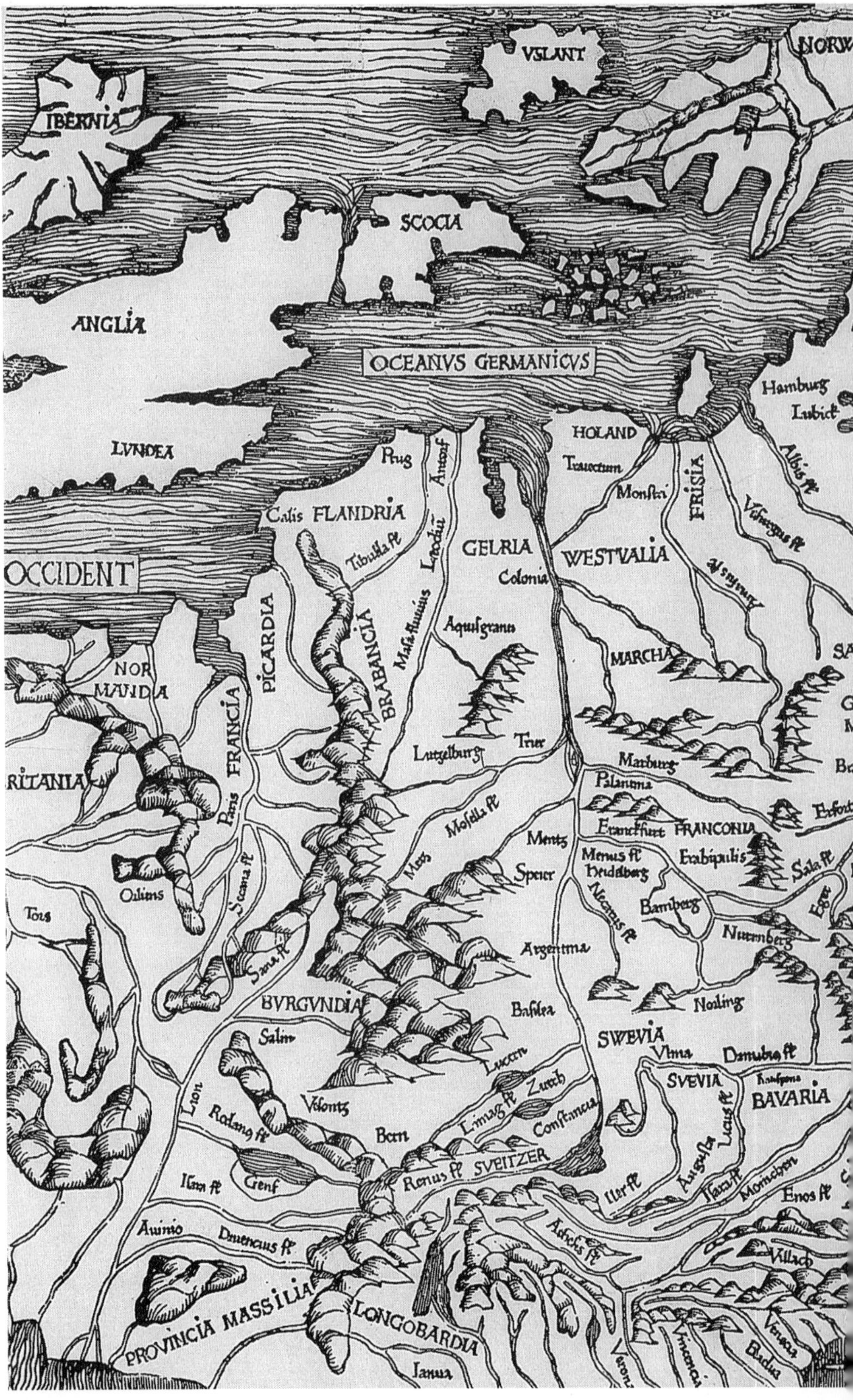

VSLANT
NORWEG
IBERNIA
SCOCIA
ANGLIA
OCEANVS GERMANICVS
Hamburg
Lubick
HOLAND
LVNDEA
Prug
Antorf
Traiectum
Monster
FRISIA
Albis fl
Calis FLANDRIA
Visurgus fl
OCCIDENT
GELRIA
WESTVALIA
Tibulla fl
Leodiu
Colonia
PICARDIA
Mosa fluuius
Aquisgrani
BRABANCIA
MARCHA
NOR
MANDIA
FRANCIA
Lutzelburg
Trier
RITANIA
Marburg
Paris
Palantina
Mosella fl
Erfort
Franckfurt
FRANCONIA
Mentz
Menus fl
Heidelberg
Erabipulis
Sala fl
Metz
Speier
Orliens
Secana fl
Necarus fl
Bamberg
Tors
Nurnberg
Argentina
Sana fl
BVRGVNDIA
Basilea
Noiling
Salin
SWEVIA
Vlma
Danubius fl
Lucern
SVEVIA
BAVARIA
Zurch
Lion
Vesontz
Limag fl
Constancia
Rodang fl
Lucus fl
Bern
Augusta
Renus fl
SVEITZER
Ilara fl
Isara fl
Genf
Iler fl
Monchen
Enos fl
Auinio
Druencus fl
Athesis fl
Villach
PROVINCIA MASSILIA
LONGOBARDIA
Ianua
Verona
Vincencia
Venegia
Padua